"A valuable workbook on how to turn business relationships from win-lose into win-win-win."

> —**William Ury**, coauthor, *Getting to Yes*;
> author, *Getting to Yes with Yourself*

"This timely guide to building a more human and more sustainably high-performing organization is concrete, actionable, and suffused with the passion of its authors to create great workplaces and change the experience of all of us who spend the greater part of our lives at the office!"

> —**Tony Schwartz**, CEO, The Energy Project;
> author, *The Way We're Working Isn't Working*

"The *Conscious Capitalism Field Guide* illuminates the path that businesses can take to become more conscious. It should be essential reading in boardrooms and business schools."

> —**Chade-Meng Tan**, former "Jolly Good Fellow," Google;
> *New York Times* bestselling author, *Joy on Demand* and
> *Search Inside Yourself*; and adjunct professor,
> Lee Kuan Yew School of Public Policy

"This book is a road map for corporate leaders interested in creating cultures that value innovation and social consciousness and building successful organizations that make a positive impact on the world."

> —**Ron Shaich**, founder, Chairman, and CEO, Panera Bread

"This book gives a compelling account of why the successful companies of the future will be those rooted in a deeper sense of purpose, which it combines with a highly practical road map on how to move from aspiration to action."

> —**Paul Polman**, CEO, Unilever

CONSCIOUS CAPITALISM
Field Guide

TOOLS FOR TRANSFORMING YOUR ORGANIZATION

CONSCIOUS CAPITALISM

Field Guide

RAJ SISODIA, TIMOTHY HENRY, AND THOMAS ECKSCHMIDT

WITH JESSICA AGNEESSENS AND HALEY RUSHING

HARVARD BUSINESS REVIEW PRESS

Boston, Massachusetts

HBR Press Quantity Sales Discounts

Harvard Business Review Press titles are available at significant quantity discounts when purchased in bulk for client gifts, sales promotions, and premiums. Special editions, including books with corporate logos, customized covers, and letters from the company or CEO printed in the front matter, as well as excerpts of existing books, can also be created in large quantities for special needs.

For details and discount information for both print and ebook formats, contact booksales@harvardbusiness.org, tel. 800-988-0886, or www.hbr.org/bulksales.

Library of Congress Cataloging-in-Publication Data

Names: Sisodia, Rajendra, author. | Henry, Timothy (Co-author of Conscious capitalism field guide), author. | Eckschmidt, Thomas, author.
Title: Conscious capitalism field guide : tools for transforming your organization / by Raj Sisodia, Timothy Henry, and Thomas Eckschmidt.
Description: Boston, Massachusetts : Harvard Business Review Press, [2018] | Includes bibliographical references.
Identifiers: LCCN 2017051702 | ISBN 9781633691704 (pbk. : alk. paper)
Subjects: LCSH: Social responsibility of business—Handbooks, manuals, etc. | Business ethics—Handbooks, manuals, etc. | Capitalism—Moral and ethical aspects—Handbooks, manuals, etc. | Corporations—Moral and ethical aspects—Handbooks, manuals, etc. | Social values—Handbooks, manuals, etc.
Classification: LCC HD60 .S573 2018 | DDC 658.4/06—dc23 LC record available at https://lccn.loc.gov/2017051702

The paper used in this publication meets the requirements of the American National Standard for Permanence of Paper for Publications and Documents in Libraries and Archives Z39.48-1992.

Contents

Foreword

By John Mackey, Cofounder and CEO,
Whole Foods Market

In the five years since Raj Sisodia and I wrote *Conscious Capitalism: Liberating the Heroic Spirit of Business*, society has seen the remarkable growth of Conscious Capitalism. It is steadily becoming a worldwide movement to change how we think about business and how we conduct it. Many thousands of businesses are now inspired with a higher purpose beyond simply maximizing profits. Indeed, countless young entrepreneurs are starting up businesses, with their highest intention being to make the world a better place and to elevate humanity. Social entrepreneurs are creating many thousands of organizations that seek to solve the challenges we collectively face. Increasingly, the boundaries between business entrepreneurs and social entrepreneurs are beginning to blur as their higher purposes intermingle with one another.

I believe both our book and our nonprofit organization have been major factors in the larger movement toward a Conscious Capitalism world. Our book has now sold over 160,000 copies and has been translated into thirteen languages around the world. Our nonprofit organization, www.consciouscapitalism.org, now has chapters in more than thirty US cities and fourteen other countries.

Several other important organizations are also helping business consciousness to evolve in positive directions. These include the benefit corporation movement (B Corp movement), which has created an alternative corporate organizational form. Benefit corporations require boards of directors to take into account not only the shareholders' interests but also the well-being of other stakeholders and larger social and environmental good in their decision making. This alternative corporate organization form is now legal in thirty-three states and several other countries (see http://benefitcorp.net/). The B Team is an international nonprofit organization dedicated to creating social, environmental, and economic good through business. It is led by a number of well-known business leaders such as Richard Branson, Paul Polman, Mark Benioff, Muhammad Yunus, Ratan Tata, and many other notable leaders (see http://bteam.org). A third organization having a large global impact is Inclusive Capitalism, whose purpose is to make capitalism more equitable, sustainable, and inclusive (see www.inc-cap.com /about-us). All these organizations share a desire for business to place social and environmental values on at least equal footing with shareholder value—what is often referred to as the *triple bottom line.*

The triple bottom line is a wonderful idea and is one of the major inspirations for the Conscious Capitalism movement. However, a more comprehensive framework is necessary for truly meaningful change. Professor Ed Freeman's seminal work on stakeholder theory formed the basis for the second pillar of Conscious Capitalism. It has moved from an interesting academic idea to one that is at the center of how many leaders think about their businesses—consciously creating value for all their major stakeholders. Although the identity of major stakeholders can vary across organizations, in *Conscious Capitalism* we identified six: customers, employees, suppliers, investors, society, and the environment. Whereas the triple bottom line tries to ensure that society and the environment are taken equally into consideration along with profits for investors, stakeholder theory proposes a "sextet" bottom line, which also includes customers, employees, and suppliers. All six of these major stakeholders are important, and the truly conscious business sees the web of interdependencies that exists between all of them and manages the business to simultaneously create value for all of them.

Of course, creating value for all six major stakeholders is not always easy—at least until we change the way we think about stakeholders. The always-present temptation is to make tradeoffs between the stakeholders so that one stakeholder gains at the expense of the others; if we look for tradeoffs, then we will surely find them. What is more difficult to do, but also absolutely necessary, is to shift our consciousness to look for win-win-win strategies—what Raj and I call Win[6]. Once we *see* the various stakeholder interdependencies and give ourselves permission to create strategies in which all are winning, that is what we actually will create.

While I've been greatly encouraged by the overall progress of Conscious Capitalism during the past five years, I've been deeply disturbed by one very powerful countertrend—shareholder activism toward public corporations. This activism is driven by the philosophy of maximizing shareholder value—usually, short-term shareholder value as the activist firms seek to make as much money as quickly as possible. Most shareholder activists don't care about any of the four tenets of Conscious Capitalism or indeed too much about anything besides driving greater profitability and higher stock prices over the short term. Shareholder activists generally take an ownership stake in public corporations from 1 percent to 10 percent and then use their stock position to pressure the board of directors and the CEO to take various actions to increase short-term profitability and the stock price. Usually, the actions entail massive layoffs of employees and other major expense cuts, huge stock buybacks, and dividend payouts. It can also mean putting the company up for sale to the highest bidder. If the board and the CEO do not cooperate with their demands, they often seek to replace directors with their own board candidates and lobby to remove the CEO as well.

Over the last few years, many large corporations have been pressured by shareholder activists. These include Dell, Apple, Microsoft, Procter & Gamble, DuPont, and Panera Bread. In response, Michael Dell took his company private, and Ron Shaich, the founder and CEO of Panera, sold his to JAB, a large international holding company. Both leaders were perhaps primarily motivated by their desire to escape the shareholder activists hounding their companies.

In 2016 and 2017 our company, Whole Foods Market, faced two shareholder activist challenges. The first one, by Neuberger Berman Group, began in the summer of 2016, after it had purchased 3 percent of our stock. The firm began making various demands to the management team: reduce our cost structure, bring in new directors onto our board, hire a new chief financial officer, eliminate our co-CEO structure, and put the company up for sale. We listen carefully to all our stakeholders, including our shareholders, and do the best we can to make them happy. Where Neuberger Berman's suggestions made sense to us to improve the company, we implemented them. Where we believed its suggestions would be harmful to the company, we ignored them.

In April 2017, a second shareholder activist, Jana Partners, announced that it had bought 8.8 percent of the company. When we met in person with Jana representatives two weeks later, they made no constructive suggestions on how we could improve the company. Instead, they told us we were doing a terrible job managing the company, and they made two demands: replace seven of our twelve directors on our board, give Jana veto power over all seven, and put the company up for sale. If we did not agree to their demands within five days, they would escalate their attack against the company. They did not tell us what their escalated attack would involve, but our "activist defense" bankers and attorneys believed it would be a proxy battle to take over our board. If they won such a battle, the new board would fire the existing management team and replace us with new management, which would then put the company up for sale to the highest bidder.

We reacted very quickly to Jana's threats and implemented two tactics that proved to be very effective. First, we had five of our most senior directors, who were judged by our activist defense advisers to be highly vulnerable to losing in a proxy contest with Jana, resign from the board. We replaced them with five very highly regarded new directors who would be very difficult for Jana to beat in a proxy contest. The resignations included several excellent directors whom we hated to lose, but all of them were willing to make this personal sacrifice for the good of the company.

Second, we decided to look for a white knight to acquire the company. We all believed it would be a disaster for Whole Foods Market if we were forced into a sale to another supermarket company, most likely one that didn't share our purpose, values, quality standards, or culture. That was a path that none of the leaders of the company wanted to go down. But we could very likely be forced down that path because of unrelenting pressure from both Neuberger Berman and Jana. Was there another partner that would allow Whole Foods Market to retain its unique and defining qualities, while evolving itself over the next few years and adjusting to new market realities? The more I thought about it, the more I realized that there might just be one company that would be a perfect fit for us, a company that I had greatly admired for the past twenty years: Amazon.

We reached out to the Amazon people to gauge their interest in Whole Foods Market at the end of April. When it turned out they were very interested, we set up a meeting in Seattle just a few days later. A team of four Whole Foods Market executives met with four Amazon executives, including their founder and CEO, Jeff Bezos, on a Sunday afternoon. We were simply blown away by our first conversation with them. The Amazon executives were all brilliant and highly creative people. We spent several hours that day discussing the various possibilities of what we could do together. Our team was very excited and was sold on merging with Amazon after the first meeting. It turned out that the Amazon team felt the same way. The deal happened extremely quickly, with the merger agreement being signed just six weeks after the first meeting.

So Whole Foods Market's experience with shareholder activism appears to be having a very happy ending for all our stakeholders. But what would have happened if Amazon hadn't been interested in buying us? Could any other white knights have fit well with the Whole Foods Market Conscious Capitalism business model? Possibly, but I don't have a clue who they might have been. Could Whole Foods have stayed independent and successfully fought off both Neuberger Berman and Jana and prevented them from forcing the company into an undesirable sale to the highest bidder regardless of the sale's impact on our higher purpose and our Conscious Capitalism business philosophy? Maybe, but it would have been very difficult to do. Competition in the natural- and organic-foods business has increased tremendously over the past five years. Whole Foods needs to cut costs, centralize more of our purchasing to gain greater economies of scale, and lower our prices to close the gap with many of our competitors. Could we do all three of these without harming our sales, profits, and culture, while shareholder activists would be continuously breathing down our necks ready to pounce on the company if anything went wrong with these plans or if the plans didn't yield immediate results? Perhaps, but the odds didn't favor it. It was quite likely that the unique, conscious company that Whole Foods had evolved into would have been destroyed. Now, with Amazon as our partner, we will have the time to evolve the company in the positive ways that it needs to evolve to be more competitive, while gaining access to Amazon's tremendous technology and supply-chain expertise to help us evolve quicker and in unique ways.

Shareholder activism, as currently constituted and practiced, is a clear and present danger to the Conscious Capitalism movement, which hopes to increasingly win over public companies to this very special business model that promises to make our world a better place and to elevate humanity to a higher level. Activist shareholders base their actions on the misguided belief that maximizing shareholder value is the only purpose of business and should be pursued at all costs. This is the virulent parasite that has burrowed very deep into the structure of financial capitalism; it threatens to kill its host and to discredit the institution of capitalism itself.

The Conscious Capitalism movement needs to meet this threat head-on in all ways possible—especially philosophically and legally. The B Corp movement is an excellent starting point; it offers a way to change the legal environment about the purpose of corporations. It offers some protection from shareholder activists who pursue short-term stock-price maximization for investors at the expense of all other stakeholders. However, financial capitalism as we now know it needs a complete makeover if Conscious Capitalism is going to continue to fulfill its mission in the world. This major task still lies in front of us, and it will require brilliant and dedicated financial entrepreneurs to develop new solutions to this massive challenge.

In the meantime, companies throughout the world should remain undeterred on their path to becoming more conscious and creating greater value of many kinds for all their stakeholders. For some businesses, despite the rapid spread of the Conscious Capitalism philosophy, it will remain just that—a philosophy—and its adherents, no matter how well intentioned, might struggle to convert this philosophy into actual practice. But thanks now to Raj Sisodia, Timothy Henry, and Thomas Eckschmidt and the *Conscious Capitalism Field Guide: Tools for Transforming Your Organization*, the transformation is more attainable. Raj, Timothy, and Thomas methodically lay out scores of exercises, tasks, and examples that will help the reader ultimately evolve as a conscious business leader. I am confident that this field guide will prove to be an invaluable resource to leaders looking for a systematic, practical, and proven approach to bringing Conscious Capitalism to life in their organizations. It has been an exhilarating and deeply meaningful forty-year journey for me. I have no doubt that it will prove to be equally exciting and meaningful for you as well—along with all the people whose lives will forever be transformed by your embrace of this way of being in business.

Preface

What This Book Is, and Who It's For

Conscious Capitalism is a philosophy—along with a set of guiding principles and best practices—based on the simple idea that business is about more than making a profit. It is an approach to business built on the fundamental, universal truth that people aspire to more—to meaning and purpose, and to flourishing and fulfillment.

Conscious Capitalism does not hold the notion of profit in contempt—no business could exist without making money. Rather, the philosophy provides an alternative approach to the essential pursuit of profits, one that emphasizes ideas like trust, collaboration, and compassion. It says that business is good, even heroic, because it creates prosperity. And it says that it can do so much more to elevate humanity than most people think possible.

Four core principles of Conscious Capitalism offer the blueprint for practicing this radically different approach to building and leading business. They are higher purpose, stakeholder orientation, conscious leadership, and conscious culture.

The idea of Conscious Capitalism has been around for a couple of decades and was first popularized by John Mackey, cofounder and CEO of Whole Foods Market. Now a global movement, the organization dedicated to the spread of Conscious Capitalism has grown rapidly since its inception in 2008, with chapters in over thirty US cities and a dozen countries around the world. The idea is finding great appeal in diverse cultures and economies because it taps into deep human aspirations about how people want to live and work in the world today. It places the flourishing of human beings at the center of business enterprise.

The foundational book that captures the core ideas and spirit of the movement is *Conscious Capitalism: Liberating the Heroic Spirit of Business*, by John Mackey and Raj Sisodia. Published in 2013, the book builds on the idea that, as we move deeper into the twenty-first century, the main source of competitive advantage will increasingly lie in the human capabilities, the culture, and the operating model of an organization. Conscious Capitalism is basically an issue of bringing out the best in your people for the benefit of all the people whose lives your organization touches. The organizations that enable their people to be at their best will have the best teams and the best performance. This assertion forms the core argument of the book and our movement.

Since the publication of Mackey and Sisodia's book, companies large and small around the world have developed a growing interest in embarking on a journey of Conscious Capitalism. To meet that need, this book, *Conscious Capitalism Field Guide*, is a hands-on guide for businesses—young and old, small and large, private and publicly traded—to implement the core principles of Conscious Capitalism in their own organizations. The book can also be used by nonprofits and the public sector; the principles of operating as a conscious, purpose-driven organization are universal.

Our Promise to You

If you read this book, and more importantly, if you and your leadership team carefully do all the exercises that are provided, you will walk away with a detailed plan for building a more conscious business. This plan will include both near-term (twelve to eighteen months) and longer-term (three to five years) actions. To help you create that plan, the field guide is built on a series of exercises—practical initiatives you can take to design your own unique journey to becoming a more conscious organization. We want to meet you where you are today and help you craft the next steps on your journey.

Here are some specific tasks that you can expect to accomplish:

- Write a purpose statement for your company, and develop a plan for communicating it to your organization.

- Map all your stakeholders, identify their needs, and understand how you can create more value for each of them.

- Understand how to create win-win-win relationships with all your stakeholders.

- Create a culture playbook for your company.

- Create a personal leadership development plan.

- Develop a leadership checklist for your organization.

- Set priorities for the coming year and beyond.

By understanding the principles of Conscious Capitalism and engaging with these exercises, with your teams, and with others in the organization, you will have the tools for creating a more conscious business, as Whole Foods Market, Google, Starbucks, Southwest Airlines, Patagonia, and many other successful companies built on the tenets of Conscious Capitalism have done.

Who the Book Is For

This field guide is designed for leaders and their teams—the group that has the responsibility and authority to shape the future of the organization as a whole or stand-alone units within a larger organization (typically known as strategic business units or corporate functions). The journey we describe is that of the organization, not the individuals. But you cannot have a conscious organization without conscious leaders, and you cannot be a conscious leader without being a conscious human being. To that end, the book also includes guidance on how the senior leaders of the organization can elevate their own consciousness and how they should alter their approach to leadership development in the entire organization.

The field guide is written for companies that are at various levels of consciousness. They could be startups or mature companies, at the very outset of the journey or already on their way. They could be public or private companies, large or small, domestic or global. They could be for-profit companies or nonprofits, consumer-facing or business-to-business. The principles of Conscious Capitalism are universally applicable to all kinds of organizations.

In addition, this book can help companies in the very early stages of a Conscious Capitalism journey or companies that have been pursuing various aspects of Conscious Capitalism for several years. We lay out the entire journey for you, providing options for each tenet of Conscious Capitalism: a beginner's set of options, a middle-level set, and a more advanced set. In this way, we aim to meet you where you are so that the steps are relevant and actionable for you.

Finally, this field guide is also a resource for consultants working with teams and organizations. Sometimes, a third-party facilitator can help keep the team on track and can occasionally push the team to dig a bit deeper on some issues. However, we recommend that if you consider using consultants, make sure they are deeply versed in Conscious Capitalism, either through regular attendance at the annual Conscious Capitalism conferences or by participating in training programs offered by Conscious Capitalism Inc. (see our website at www.ConsciousCapitalism.org for information on our various programs and events).

Note to readers: If you are new to Conscious Capitalism and haven't read the book *Conscious Capitalism: Liberating the Heroic Spirit of Business*, please make sure you read chapter 1 of this field guide to get a grounding in the context, the concept, and the business case for Conscious Capitalism. Otherwise, you can start your journey with chapter 2.

How to Use the Book: From Aspiration to Action

The transformation to Conscious Capitalism is a journey. In a sense, on any journey, you never quite arrive. It's a little like the development of human beings' levels of consciousness; there's no end state per se. But the higher you climb, the broader your vision. In this way, a conscious organization is constantly exploring and developing new ways to operate and be successful.

By the time you finish reading this field guide, you should have a very clear set of priorities for the next twelve to eighteen months. You'll see plainly where you are today and know where you're going so that you can continue your journey and have the highest possible impact on your business. We hope to help you move from aspiration to action.

Throughout the field guide, we also talk about who needs to be onboard with this journey. As you begin to build support in your organization, the support must come from several levels: your leadership team (referred to here as your top team), your public company or advisory board, your middle managers, and then eventually the entire organization. Stakeholder buy-in also requires clarity on *why* you are pursuing Conscious Capitalism and how best to implement this philosophy in your organization. It takes courage to move in a new direction or to take a significant next step on the journey. We hope this book will give you the support you need to feel more confident in moving these inspiring concepts into action in your organization.

How the Book Is Structured

The first four parts of this field guide cover the four tenets of Conscious Capitalism: higher purpose, stakeholder orientation, conscious culture, and conscious leadership. The final part focuses on bringing it all together into an actionable plan. By the time you complete the book, you will have developed an implementation plan and strategy for you and your business to successfully embrace Conscious Capitalism.

Each opening chapter in parts 1 through 4 introduces you to a tenet and shares examples through stories and other comments from interviews with business leaders. Besides introducing the tenets, these chapters provide a glimpse of what other companies on this journey have done.

Subsequent chapters in each part present exercises, assessments, and other tools. We will suggest how you can dive deeper into specific aspects of your business by using tools such as customer and employee surveys that address levels of engagement and trust. The point is to understand the gap between where you aspire to be and where you are today. The stronger your understanding of that gap, the better you can determine the next steps that will have the biggest impact on the business.

We then provide exercises and practical actions that will help you assess the possible next steps for each tenet. In this way, you can begin to create your own action plan for implementing the practices and principles of Conscious Capitalism.

For each of the four tenets (purpose, stakeholder orientation, culture, and leadership), you can address where you are at three levels. At the first level, you examine the building blocks of Conscious Capitalism. For example, do you have a purpose? Does the leadership team know who your stakeholders are? At the second level, you look more broadly at the organization in terms of raising awareness and understanding of the tenets of Conscious Capitalism. For example, do people in the organization know who your stakeholders are? The third level is about bringing the tenets to life in the core DNA and culture of the organization. For example, in conscious leadership development, have you clearly defined the kind of leaders you want involved in developing the organization, and are you supporting them? The exercises take you through these levels systematically.

When you work through each step with your team, be aware that you need to walk before you can run. We help you through this process by offering the basics first and then outlining exercises that go into more depth. When you and your team are starting out on the exercises in this field guide, begin with those that correspond with your level of development.

How to Use the Exercises

The exercises proposed in the book should be done by the business leader and his or her direct reports. For the most impact, we recommend that the leadership team do the exercises as a group and discuss every exercise, outcome, and gap together. Doing so will allow for faster alignment and change for the organization. Nonetheless, leaders would also benefit from working through this book on their own—and then engaging with their team.

Given the importance of bringing your team members along and getting them deeply involved in the transformation to Conscious Capitalism, we recommend a two-step process for involving your team. First, you need to expose your leadership team to the concept of Conscious Capitalism and enlist their support (chapter 19 details how to accomplish this step). Then you must move from this aspirational vision to a concrete and prioritized plan for action.

The second step is to work through the action plan with your team and will require setting aside time when the team can focus on the plan. In our experience, the team needs to take this work in chunks, which are represented by the five sections of the book.

There are two basic models for working through an action plan. Choose the approach that best fits your team and the circumstances.

One approach is to plan for a two- or three-day retreat in which the entire team is taken off-site. In this situation, we recommend working through each of the five parts of the book in sequence, spending three or four hours on each part. For each tenet, focus on the areas that are most pertinent to your own situation. For example, in part 1, "Higher Purpose," your focus would depend on how well formulated your purpose is. If your organization has not yet developed a clear statement of purpose, or if the team feels that the current purpose doesn't fit your current needs and should be updated, then your team should focus on this tenet of Conscious Capitalism. On the other hand, if you already have a well-defined purpose, the next step is to make sure everyone knows that purpose and then, later, to ensure that you are living it.

Another approach is to schedule a series of five sessions, one for each part of the book, for three or four hours each, over not more than five or six weeks. The goal here is to ensure that you have enough time both to do the relevant exercises for your team and to discuss the potential impact on your business and the next concrete steps to move this tenet into action.

How to Use the QR Codes

Throughout this field guide, you will encounter QR codes, the square bar codes that allow you to access additional information from the authors, from our interviewees, and from other sources. To read the codes through your cell phone, you can download one of three apps available for IOS, Android, and Windows:

- Inigma (IOS, Android, Windows, BlackBerry)
- Zapper (IOS, Android, Windows)
- QR Code Reader by Scan (IOS, Android, Windows, Kindle)

If a QR code does not work, visit our website www.ccfieldguide.com, where all videos are posted and referenced by chapter to make it easier to access and link them to the chapter you are reading.

Throughout the book, we have provided spaces for you to record your responses or ideas in the various exercises. The spaces might not be large enough for a full "download" of your ideas and team feedback. You can use sticky notes to gather feedback and collect ideas before entering your responses to each exercise throughout the book.

The Longest Journey Begins with the First Step

This book is meant to be used! Do the exercises, discuss them with your team, decide, and move to action. Our highest hope is that you and your team will launch into a new phase of transforming your business and hence by example begin to change the perception of business in the world. For now, we wish you *bon voyage* on this profoundly transformative journey to Conscious Capitalism. The pathway is not intended to be a personal one (though it includes some personal elements); instead, it is a leadership-team journey to bring about true transformation for your organization. Start now!

How to Maximize the *Conscious Capitalism Field Guide* Experience

By Timothy Henry, Trustee, Conscious Capitalism, Inc.

This quick video presents a recommendation from one of the coauthors on how to make the most out of the book with your team and your business.

URL: https://www.ccfieldguide.com/preface-video

Search Words: Conscious Capitalism Field Guide Timothy Henry Video

Chapter 1

Why Conscious Capitalism?

Before starting the field guide proper, we begin in this chapter with a brief review of the history of Conscious Capitalism for those who are new to the ideas or who would like a refresher. Here, you'll find the background historical and contemporary contexts that gave birth to the idea of Conscious Capitalism; the four tenets that comprise both the intellectual foundation and the blueprint for practicing Conscious Capitalism; and the business case for Conscious Capitalism. The chapter ends with some things to keep in mind as you start—or continue—your journey to Conscious Capitalism.

The Context

Free-Market Capitalism

So-called modern free-market capitalism or industrial capitalism was born from three seminal events that occurred within a quarter century of each other. The first, the beginning of the Industrial Revolution around 1750, was perhaps the greatest single advance in the history of human civilization, elevating our productive capacity and thus material living standards dramatically. The second event, the 1776 publication of *An Inquiry into the Nature and Causes of the Wealth of Nations*, explained the power of free markets. And the US Declaration of Independence, also in 1776, was the first time a country came into existence purely because of a set of ideas, all of which revolved around personal freedom: religious, political, and economic.

This potent combination of events proved to be transformative for humankind: the technological revolution of the Industrial Revolution; the intellectual breakthrough of *The Wealth of Nations*; and the oxygen of freedom that existed first in the United States (though it was restricted to white males). Life for ordinary human beings improved on an almost vertical trajectory. After millennia in which average people saw very little improvement in the duration and quality of their existence, the last two centuries have seen extraordinary gains. Capitalism has lifted far more people out of poverty than has any other idea or institution in history—by orders of magnitude. Since 1800, per-capita incomes worldwide have risen fifteenfold in real terms (adjusted for inflation); the percentage of people living in extreme poverty has dropped from 90 percent to around 9 percent. Life expectancy has more than doubled, our population has risen sevenfold, and literacy has gone from 12 percent to 86 percent worldwide.[1]

At a Crossroads

Despite all that extraordinary progress, we stand today at a perilous crossroads. The institution of capitalism is being threatened by its own excesses and myopic interpretation. Many people today are cynical, discouraged, and divided. Facing a crisis of confidence, business is no longer seen by many as a force for good in society but rather is seen as a core part of the problem. The rising skepticism about business leads to a questioning of the legitimacy of businesses to operate in society when the wealth and other benefits created by businesses seem so strikingly unevenly distributed. This disconnect raises serious questions about the business models that exist today.

To understand this disconnect, we need to go back to capitalism's birth. In *The Wealth of Nations*, Scottish moral philosopher Adam Smith established that individuals' pursuit of self-interest was the foundation for how societies rooted in personal freedom can harness the self-organizing power of markets to elevate living standards. Seventeen years earlier, Smith also wrote *The Theory of Moral Sentiments*, a book about the human disposition to care about others, without regard to self-interest. Most people have ignored or forgotten this earlier book. If we had integrated those two dimensions—the human need to care and the drive for self-interest—into the practice of business, we would have created a much richer humanistic and intellectual foundation for capitalism than what we ended up with. Resting on the single pillar of self-interest alone, capitalism evolved into a powerful and dynamic system that, unfortunately, hurt the well-being of many workers and the environment, even as it generated great material prosperity.

The pursuit of self-interest and the need to care—these two qualities should have been the two engines of capitalism. But for too long, the plane of capitalism has been flying with just one engine.

The fundamentals of capitalism—the rule of law, private property rights, and the voluntary exchange of goods, services, and ideas—remain as important as ever. But we need to bring in what has been missing: the human dimension.

Searching for a Better Way

To a large extent, businesses are still operating under the ideals of the Industrial Revolution and are using an operating system that was developed in the industrial age, using the military as the organizing metaphor. Little has changed in this way of thinking. The idea that the sole purpose of business is to make profits for shareholders and that everything else is a means to that end remains the dominant mental model for business. We still teach this in business schools.

But the traditional narrative of business and capitalism—that it is exclusively about maximizing profits—is increasingly being recognized as inadequate, uninspiring, and often toxic. Particularly in the West, there is a broad reform movement around capitalism, with terms like creative capitalism, inclusive capitalism, breakthrough capitalism, sustainable capitalism, capitalism 2.0 and 3.0, to mention a few. Conscious Capitalism, part of a growing movement that recognizes the tremendous value and potential of capitalism, is seeking to elevate this powerful force for potential good to a new level. We, and you in reading this book, are a part of an effort to reframe the dialogue around business and capitalism as a force for good in the world.

Today we are at a tipping point, where the old model is rapidly collapsing. As exemplified by companies like Southwest Airlines, Patagonia, Google, Unilever,

Danone, and Zappos, business is becoming more conscious about the many impacts that commerce has on people's lives and on the planet. These and other companies are recognizing that the decisions they make affect more than the bottom line.

Conscious Capitalism is a response to these concerns, suggesting that there is a better way for businesses to operate—a way for organizations to be as human as the people who work in them. It offers a new model that can help society move forward in a harmonious and productive way to bring about broad-based flourishing for all.

The Concept

To many, the terms *conscious* and *capitalism* are unlikely bedfellows.

Thinking in terms of psychologist Abraham Maslow's classic hierarchy-of-needs framework, business and capitalism have mostly operated at the lower levels, which have to do with survival, safety and security, and self-esteem. But we humans are capable of and care about so much more than that. Many more of us are now driven by higher-level needs such as building community, finding meaning and purpose, and serving humanity.

In choosing the phrase *Conscious Capitalism*, we are very deliberately leaning in to a more basic form of entrepreneurial capitalism, where the entrepreneur acts to create value and address issues that people care about and that make a difference in the world. When we refer to Conscious Capitalism, we are looking at the heroic potential of business and entrepreneurs to do well and to do good in the world.

When conducted with higher consciousness, business is the ultimate win-win-win game in the world. Businesses' potential to create value is extraordinary, and it does not come at the expense of our health or the health of our planet.

The *conscious* part of Conscious Capitalism refers to businesses' and their leaders' growing awareness of commerce's potential to do far more than make money and of mindsets and business models they choose to operate with. Conscious Capitalism means being aware of your purpose as an organization, seeing the interconnectedness of all stakeholders, and striving to create workplaces infused with dignity, meaning, and joy.

Conscious Capitalism has four key pillars or tenets: higher purpose beyond profit, creating value for all stakeholders and integrating their interests, conscious leadership, and conscious culture. These tenets work together and reinforce each other.

- **Higher purpose:** As suggested by Simon Sinek's book title *Start with Why*, every business should have a higher purpose that transcends making money. A company's higher purpose is the difference the firm is trying to make in the world. By focusing on its higher purpose, a business inspires, engages, and energizes its stakeholders. Profit is not the purpose, although it is one of the many important measures of a business's functioning and is necessary to enable a business to achieve its purpose. The business does not exist merely to generate profits, but also aims to generate multiple kinds of value for all its stakeholders (profit is a specific value for one of its stakeholders, the shareholder).

- **Stakeholder orientation:** Recognizing the interdependent nature of life and the human foundations of business, a business needs to consciously create value with and for *all* its stakeholders (customers, employees, suppliers, investors, communities, the environment, etc.). We need to shed the trade-off mentality and look for synergies, for simultaneous wins for each stakeholder. Creating win-win-win relationships between stakeholders becomes the modus operandi of the business.

- **Conscious leadership:** Conscious leaders transcend narrow self-interest; they are primarily motivated by purpose and service to people rather than by power and personal enrichment. They mentor and motivate, develop and inspire people. A firm that uses financial incentives alone to attract and motivate leaders will get precisely what it pays for: leaders who are primarily motivated by money. Such leaders are far less capable of inspiring their employees to extraordinary levels of engagement, creativity, and performance.

- **Conscious culture:** Most businesses run on fear and unhealthy levels of stress. They pay little attention to their culture, allowing it to evolve on its own. Conscious organizations intentionally foster cultures with high levels of trust, authenticity, transparency, and genuine caring.

Conscious Capitalism represents a comprehensive rethinking of what business can and should be. The movement seeks to change the narrative of business in accordance with these principles.

The tenets of Conscious Capitalism reflect universal human values, transcending any differences in history, language, religion, and culture. At their core, these ideas are rooted in human dignity, freedom, and caring. They speak to the deep inner striving toward meaning and purpose that is a hallmark of the contemporary zeitgeist. The ideas reflect the hunger and determination of enlightened leaders to not be confined by the tired "dogmas of the quiet past" (in Abraham Lincoln's elegant phrase), especially when it comes to how we should think about and practice business.

The Conscious Capitalism Credo

We believe that business is good because it creates value, it is ethical because it is based on voluntary exchange, it is noble because it can elevate our existence, and it is heroic because it lifts people out of poverty and creates prosperity. Free-enterprise capitalism is the most powerful system for social cooperation and human progress ever conceived. It is one of the most compelling ideas we humans have ever had. But we can aspire to even more.

Conscious Capitalism is a way of thinking about capitalism and business—a way that better reflects where we are in the human journey, the state of our world today, and the innate potential of business to make a positive impact on the world. Conscious businesses are galvanized by higher purposes that serve, align, and integrate the interests of all their major stakeholders. A business's higher state of consciousness enables it to see the interdependencies that exist across all stakeholders and to discover and harvest synergies from situations that otherwise seem replete with trade-offs. Conscious businesses have conscious leaders who are driven by service to the company's purpose, all the people the business touches, and the planet we all share. These businesses have trusting, authentic, innovative, and caring cultures that make working there a source of both personal growth and professional fulfillment. They endeavor to create financial, intellectual, social, cultural, emotional, spiritual, physical, and environmental wealth for all their stakeholders.

Conscious businesses can help evolve our world in such a way that billions of people can flourish, leading lives infused with passion, purpose, love, and creativity in a world of freedom, harmony, prosperity, and compassion.

Source: Conscious Capitalism, Inc.

The Case

In the end, Conscious Capitalism is simply a better way to do business. This approach includes but is not limited to generating superior financial returns over the long run. A conscious business is still a business; it must have a good business model, sound competitive strategies, and the discipline to execute and run the business well. To these basic good business practices, Conscious Capitalism adds the four tenets described earlier. The combination of good business practices and the four pillars of consciousness elevates businesses to greater operational success and makes them agents of societal flourishing.

There is strong and growing evidence that conscious companies significantly outperform the market financially. For example, the first edition of *Firms of Endearment: How World-Class Companies Profit from Passion and Purpose* (2007)

TABLE 1-1

Performance of conscious and other companies against the S&P 500

Cumulative returns	5 years	10 years	15 years	20 years
S&P 500	86%	96%	301%	269%
Good to Great companies	106%	54%	234%	422%
Non-US firms of endearment	49%	93%	961%	1,509%
US firms of endearment	**109%**	**231%**	**901%**	**2,077%**

Note: data calculated as of June 30, 2017.

reported that conscious companies outperformed the S&P 500 index by nearly nine to one over a ten-year period. In the second edition (2014), the ratio was fourteen to one over a fifteen-year period for an expanded set of companies. Table 1-1 shows updated financial performance numbers for those companies as of June 30, 2017.[2]

The financial dimension of corporate performance depends on a company's ability to increase its revenue and efficiency. Conscious businesses are superior on both these dimensions, because they are better aligned with the true needs of customers and are focused on investing money where it makes a difference (such as on rank-and-file employees and high-quality suppliers) and saving money in non-value-adding areas (such as excessive marketing costs and high employee turnover).

The consequences of being a truly conscious company are many. These include much greater employee engagement, passion, and commitment; delighted and loyal customers who are advocates of the company; and suppliers that are loyal and innovative. Conscious firms also enjoy a strong reputation that improves their ability to attract customers, employees, investors, and support from citizens. These firms have a positive impact on the environment and good relationships with the media, governments at all levels, and many advocacy groups. They also enjoy higher levels of innovation. These outcomes are all positive in themselves; even if they have a neutral or slightly negative impact on financial performance, the firms would still be justified in pursuing these results.

However, as the following studies indicate, each of these factors is also *positively* correlated with financial performance.[3] When all the tenets are present in the same company, the collective and cumulative impact on financial performance can be dramatic.

- **Environmental responsibility and performance:** A study found that highly rated companies outperformed low-rated companies by 5.06 percent per year.[4]

- **Customer satisfaction and stock returns:** Researchers from the University of Michigan found that companies in the top 20 percent of the American Customer Satisfaction Index outperformed the Dow Jones Industrial Average by 90 percent, the S&P 500 by 201 percent, and the NASDAQ by 335 percent over a six-year period.[5]

- **Social responsibility and the cost of equity capital:** A study found that an increase of one standard deviation in a firm's social responsibility was associated with a decline of ten basis points in a firm's equity premium.[6]

- **Employee satisfaction and stock returns:** Alex Edmans of the London Business School and colleagues have found that the "Hundred Best Companies to Work For" in the United States outperformed all benchmarks by 2.3 to 3.8 percent per year between 1984 and 2011. He noted that there was a delay of up to four or five years for the market to reflect the impact of being an outstanding company to work for.[7] Subsequent research showed that returns are similarly high in fourteen countries around the world; the US returns ranked tenth-highest in that group. The higher the labor-market flexibility, the higher the returns associated with being a great place to work.[8]

- **Trust and growth:** Higher levels of trust lead to rapid growth; a one-standard-deviation increase in trust was associated with an approximately 30 percent increase in firm size. Greater trust also results in greater decentralization.[9]

- **Sustainability and organizational processes and performance:** Between 1993 and 2009, high-sustainability firms outperformed low-sustainability ones by

4.8 percent per year. High-sustainability firms were also found to be more stakeholder oriented.[10]

- **Corporate culture and performance:** Firms that simply advertise values on their websites or in their annual reports but do not reflect these in practice exhibit no financial outperformance. Firms with higher levels of integrity have higher profitability. Such firms are also more attractive to job applicants. Private firms were found to have higher integrity levels in publicly traded firms.[11]

- **Environmental, social, and governance scores and financial performance:** One meta-analysis examined 2,200 unique academic studies since the 1970s and found that approximately 90 percent of the studies report a neutral or positive relationship between environmental, social, and governance criteria and financial performance. Of the more sophisticated studies, 62.6 percent found a positive relationship. Environmental and governance scores were more positively correlated with financial performance than were social scores.[12]

- **Stakeholder orientation and innovation:** Between 1976 and 2006, thirty-four US states enacted constituency statutes, which enable corporate directors to consider the interests of stakeholders other than shareholders in their decisions. One study found that the number of patents increased by approximately 6.5 percent within twelve to twenty-four months of the enactment of such statutes, rising to 8 percent after forty-eight months. The study also found that these innovations are more potentially groundbreaking than those seen in shareholder-centric firms.[13]

- **Corporate social responsibility and market or systematic risk:** Firms with more social responsibility have lower systematic risk. This benefit was attributed to higher customer loyalty.[14]

- **Social capital and performance:** During the 2008–2009 financial crisis, firms with higher social capital had stock returns 4 to 5 percent higher than did firms with low social capital.

Given this wealth of evidence, anyone would be hard-pressed to credibly argue that companies should ignore these social and human-based objectives and simply revert to the traditional profit-maximizing, shareholder-centric approach. Businesses won't be able to afford *not* to practice Conscious Capitalism in the future. Why would you operate any other way? Conscious Capitalism is a far better way to do business, because it drives superior returns without imposing costs on humans or the planet. In fact, the conscious approach enables humans and the planet flourish while delivering superior financial results.

The Compass

The Journey Ahead

Leaders and entrepreneurs around the world are reimagining business as a vehicle for service, for the uplifting of humanity, rather than as a way to make as much money as possible. The profit-above-all mindset often results in cynically preying on people's ignorance or vulnerabilities. Companies of any age and any size in any sector, public or private, can choose to embark on the journey toward Conscious Capitalism.

Because the tenets of Conscious Capitalism are easy to understand, their power and relevance are rarely questioned. But the question that we hear around the world once people are exposed to these ideas is "How?" Entrepreneurs and business leaders want to know how they can implement these ideas, how they can transform existing companies and build new ones so that the tenets of Conscious Capitalism become part of the DNA of their companies.

The book you now hold in your hands is our contribution to that end. We hope this field guide will help inspire you and other leaders and their teams by bringing the principles of Conscious Capitalism vividly to life in organizations. The book brings theory, insights, and cases to help entrepreneurs, CEOs, and other leaders at every level start practicing the principles of Conscious Capitalism. The book will help you devise and implement new business models that simultaneously create financial, social, and environmental well-being for all stakeholders.

It will help people connect to their purpose and help you discover the unique purpose that your company can fulfill in the world.

Some Caveats

Leaders who seek to create conscious businesses *only* because such businesses might make more money will likely not succeed. An essential truth about life is that we must strive to do the right things for the right reasons. We can never really control the outcomes of our actions, but in business, we have created the illusion that we can. Most companies give managers hard targets for market share, profit, stock price, and so forth. To achieve those numbers—which are just abstractions—managers often make decisions that harm the interests of most stakeholders. By squeezing their employees or suppliers, the managers may deliver the desired numbers in the next quarter, but doing so plants the seeds for bigger problems in the long term. If we focus on the right actions as a person or as a company, positive outcomes will result over time.

Adopting a Conscious Capitalism approach cannot compensate for having a poor business model and an underdeveloped strategy. Business leaders and their organizations have to demonstrate that they have a strategy and an economic model that can survive and thrive in their chosen marketplace. We assume the basics of having found a market with a need, a viable value proposition, and efficient processes that can deliver in a self-sustaining and profitable manner. Conscious Capitalism then enables that company to succeed at a higher level and achieve lasting significance.

Bon Voyage

Human beings are not a resource; they are a source. A resource is like a lump of coal that burns to ashes, but a source is like the sun; it keeps on generating light, warmth, and energy. People can generate extraordinary amounts of creative energy, inspiration, love, and care. There is no more powerful source of creative energy in the world than an inspired and empowered human being. A conscious business energizes and empowers people and engages their best contributions in service of its noble higher purpose. By doing so, the business has a profoundly positive net impact on the world.

In 1925, President Calvin Coolidge famously said, "The chief business of the American people is business." Too many people have taken this observation to suggest that American people are and should be concerned only about the profits generated by business. Herb Kelleher, the legendary leader who built Southwest Airlines into the most successful airline in the history of the world, did it using the dictum "The business of business is people: yesterday, today, and forever." Of the three sectors of society (private enterprise, government, and civil society), business has the greatest role to play in bringing about a better future for all humanity and the planet as a whole. If we can indeed make business our chief business, but ensure that it is first, foremost, and forever about the well-being of people, we can bring about universal flourishing in the world.

Conscious Capitalism is not just about business reaching its potential. It is about how we will continue to thrive and bring the benefits of longevity, modernity, and our extraordinary human potential to the billions on this planet yet unborn or still struggling through life.

To paraphrase Lynne Twist, founder of the Pachamama Alliance, a nonprofit dedicated to empowering the indigenous people of the Amazon rain forest, those of us who are alive today have the opportunity to lead the most meaningful lives that human beings have ever led on this planet. Our challenges are tremendous, but so is our awareness of those challenges as well as our ability to tackle them. Business will have to lead the way, but they cannot do so if we continue to operate as we have in the past. Conscious businesses can release the extraordinary capacities that remain locked up in most human beings. By doing so, they unleash the most powerful form of renewable energy ever discovered on this planet: passionate, empowered, fully engaged, caring, and purposeful human beings.

You are now ready to begin the journey. The next chapter, your starting point, asks you to think about where your organization is now. How does your organization define success? Where does your organization want to go? To help you reflect on these questions, we include a candid, in-depth interview with the leader of one of the most conscious businesses on the planet—a century-old beer-brewing company in Costa Rica (yes, a company that makes and sells alcoholic beverages can be conscious!)—and the truly inspiring ways that leaders there evolved their thinking about their purpose and their role in bringing a better way of living to the world.

Chapter 2

Starting the Journey

It is almost a cliché that the longest journey begins with the first step. As with most clichés, there is some truth to this one. This book is designed to make that journey very practical, relevant, intimate, and real for you and your organization. When you complete this book, you should have a road map for your transition toward Conscious Capitalism.

Understand that there are no quick-fix solutions; we will not offer you some magic sauce that will transform the business. Rather, we'll help you develop a practical set of actions that will help you, your team, and your organization shift your mindset and change how you operate so that you can create an increasingly conscious company.

Remember, this is a long-term, comprehensive, and ongoing journey.

The Why of Your Business

The journey usually begins with a conscious leader (hopefully you, our reader) asking a series of questions about the business and what the leader hopes for it. Take a few minutes to respond to the following questions as an individual:

- Why is this journey important to you personally as a leader?

  _____

  _____

  _____

  _____

- How do you define success?

  _____

  _____

  _____

  _____

- How do you define greatness?

  _____

  _____

  _____

  _____

Next, work with your leadership team to develop your responses to the following questions as an organization:

- Why is this journey important to your organization?

  _____

  _____

  _____

  _____

- **How do we define success for your organization?**

  _____

  _____

  _____

  _____

  _____

  _____

- **How do we define greatness for your organization?**

  _____

  _____

  _____

  _____

  _____

  _____

  _____

- **Is our business positioned to thrive in the future while making the world a better place?**

  _____

  _____

  _____

  _____

  _____

  _____

Fundamentally, these are questions about why your business exists. This is the first tenet of Conscious Capitalism—higher purpose. Why does your company exist, and what is the impact you're trying to have on the world?

As you begin, remember that there is no right place or best place to start. Each company and each leader faces individually unique sets of business and organizational challenges. We will help you create a specific map for your journey as you go through this book.

Before embarking on this effort, we would like to present the transformation journeys of two conscious leaders. We start with Ramon Mendiola, a CEO who has taken a traditional business and transformed it into Costa Rica's most admired and highly conscious company. Next, we feature Steve Hall, CEO of Driversselect, a retailer of high-quality used cars, describing his experience since he embarked on this journey in 2011.

My Journey to Conscious Capitalism

By Ramon Mendiola, CEO, FIFCO (Costa Rica)

I joined FIFCO in 2004. Back then, the company was pretty much concentrated on brewing beer, which we've been doing for about 108 years. FIFCO is a very traditional, well-established company in Costa Rica.

2004–2006: Becoming More Efficient

I focused initially on becoming more efficient. I found many areas in which we could become more efficient and then pour the savings from those efficiencies back into the business, rather than just applying them to the bottom line. For example, we took out 18 percent of the total cost base at that time, which was

equivalent to $22 million, and repurposed it in much better ways.

I had to reduce many expenses that were not adding value to our revenues. This meant that I had to lay off employees who were adding only bureaucratic layers and complexity to our processes. I call it "putting the house in better order": making things more efficient. I put a lot of emphasis on innovation, on compensating ourselves for performance. Compensation was then 70 percent fixed and 30 percent variable. Over four months, I made the change to 70 percent variable compensation for the sales folks and

30 percent fixed. Along the way, many people left the company, because they were really not into what I was doing. But I thought we were making the right decisions to face the competition from the multinationals coming into our market. I created a business-unit organizational structure that was focused on alcoholic and nonalcoholic drinks, primarily juices and water. Previously, the beer business was subsidizing the losses we were carrying on the nonalcoholic side; I needed to bring more accountability to each of the business units.

2006–2008: Aggressive Growth

All those steps in my first two years were, I would say, what you're normally expected to do as a CEO. Then, in 2006, I put a new challenge to my team: to double the size of the business. Historically, it had taken us seven years to double in size. I said to my fifty top executives, "Okay, guys, I am very proud of what we've been doing around efficiency and productivity across the organization. I now want to put a new challenge to you: to double the size of the business in terms of revenues and profits—not in seven years, but in two years." I wanted 70 percent of the increase to come from organic growth and 30 percent from new business expansion. My goal in the beer category was to increase per-capita consumption. Previously, we had grown around 1 or 2 percent a year. From 2006 to 2008, we grew 9, 10, 11 percent, year after year. We were able to grow like this because we brought a

lot of innovation into the category in terms of pack sizes, flavors, portfolio management, and strengthening our distribution. I also put forward specific key performance indicators (KPIs) that I wanted: for instance, 10 percent of our total volume would come from new products every year.

While we were growing the beer category, we were also significantly diminishing our losses in nonalcoholic drinks by strengthening our portfolio and entering new segments. For instance, we entered the iced-tea category, which was more "good for you" and in line with healthy trends.

2008: Becoming a Triple-Bottom-Line Company

After a year and a half—in 2007—I knew we were going to double the size of the business, including profits. I felt that my team was ready for a bigger challenge. As my management team (now around seventy-five top leaders) and I celebrated that achievement toward the end of 2008, we made a visionary decision. I gave the team a new challenge: to become a triple-bottom-line-oriented company. That meant that we would need to merge our business strategy with our environmental and corporate social-responsibility strategies. We set out to improve on our social and environmental dimensions with the same rigor that we used to improve our financial performance.

The impetus for this challenge was the signals we were getting from the public—especially signals about alcohol. When we started growing our business by 10 or 11 percent a year, we overheated a little in terms of the consumption of alcoholic products. For example, there were concerns about drinking and driving. I really started paying attention to the messages the public was sending to us. Inspired by the stakeholder model, we decided to do a comprehensive stakeholder mapping—a qualitative and quantitative consultation with all our stakeholders. We normally do a very good job with our consumers and customers, but I decided to expand our focus to nongovernment organizations (NGOs), society in general, regulators, our shareholders, and our employees.

When we asked those stakeholders what they expected from us as a responsible company, they mentioned four things. These expectations addressed both our social and environmental footprints. First they told us, "You have to do something about the excessive consumption of alcohol." That was by far our biggest footprint. Number two was waste; they said they saw our bottles floating in the rivers and beaches. Number three was water, because they believed that we were taking water away from our communities to produce our products. Fourth, they were concerned about carbon emissions from our distribution system and manufacturing facilities.

We went forward on these concerns very boldly. Assembling my team, I said, "Okay, guys, we need to do something about excessive consumption of alcohol." I didn't know exactly how to go about it, but we eventually teamed up with a Canadian NGO that has been changing alcohol consumption patterns in Quebec for the past twenty-five years. We adopted this NGO's philosophy. First, we measured the consumption patterns in our society. We found out that in Costa Rica, on average, consumers were drinking 1.75 times a week—meaning Friday and Saturday. Every time they drank, they consumed an average of 5 drinks. After five drinks, a person is typically intoxicated, depending on how many hours the drinker has waited and other factors. In the Canadian example, drinkers had much better consumption patterns, because they drank on average four times a week, but each time, they only had 2.25 drinks. Comparing the data, we had an aha moment. We realized that we should focus on changing the consumption patterns. We could continue increasing per-capita consumption, but could do it responsibly by recommending greater frequency but fewer drinks per occasion.

Changing consumption patterns takes generations; it doesn't happen overnight. I went to the minister of health, who never wanted to see me, because I was the opposite of the kind of person she wanted to meet. But I sent the research to her anyway, and after she saw it, she called me to her office. "Ramon," she said, "this is the best piece of information I've ever seen in my life, and I'm willing to work with you to find a solution."

Subsequently, I became president of the Latin America Brewers Association. It took me three and a half years to mobilize the industry in Latin America—from Argentina to Mexico—to do the same research we had started here in Costa Rica. With some exceptions, the consumptions patterns were pretty much the same in all the countries. With that data, I then went to the World Health Organization in Geneva. The WHO wanted to do what it had done with the tobacco industry: reduce per-capita consumption. I said to the organization, "We can prove to you that it's okay to increase per-capita consumption if we do it in a responsible manner, by changing the consumption patterns. Alcohol is not good or bad as a product. It depends on who consumes it and how (the consumption pattern)."

For four years now, we have been improving. Coming from little Costa Rica, we have tried to encourage the industry in a positive way to embrace these principles of smart consumption, as we call it, and we are educating our consumer base in a different way. So this is what we have been doing about the number one footprint that we create as a business: the excessive consumption of alcohol.

Also in 2008 we made an environmental commitment: by 2011, we would become a zero-solid-waste company. This meant that we would send no more garbage to the landfills. We met that commitment and became a zero-solid-waste company by 2011.

We also committed to become a water-neutral company by 2012 and a carbon-neutral one by 2017. All these commitments can be measured. As a publicly traded company,

we have been audited by Deloitte on these Global Reporting Initiative principles. We're very pleased and proud that we achieved our goals and became a zero-solid-waste and a water-neutral company. We are on our way to becoming a carbon-neutral company by the end of 2017.

Why those years, you might ask? Our goals were based on our stakeholders' point of view. For instance, because waste was much more of a concern to the public than were emissions, we focused on waste first.

We became a water-neutral company by first reducing the amount of water we use in our manufacturing processes. We measure everything—even the water in the toilets! We started with fourteen hectoliters of water used for each hectoliter of beverage produced and sold. Now we use less than four hectoliters per hectoliter of beverage. Then we set out to compensate for the water consumption we couldn't reduce. We adopted the Water Footprint Network guidelines and teamed up with other companies and NGOs to bring water to Costa Rica communities that lack access to potable water. We've done four such projects so far. For other ways to compensate for the water we use, we also harvest rainwater in schools and contribute to efforts to protect the rain forest here in Costa Rica.

2012–2014: Growth through Acquisitions
In 2012, we decided to continue expanding our business dramatically. We made four

acquisitions in eighteen months, entered the US market, and continued expanding our beverages, adding new categories like wine and spirits. We vertically integrated our processes and set up small convenience stores. When I joined FIFCO, it had eighteen hundred employees. Now we have sixty-three hundred: four thousand in Costa Rica, a thousand in Guatemala and El Salvador, and about thirteen hundred in the United States. When I joined the company, our turnover was $150 million; currently we're at $1.3 billion. We started with $70 million in profit, and now we're closing in on $320 million. But if you were to ask me the most important decision I have made, it was in 2008, when I merged our business strategy with our corporate social responsibility and we became a triple-bottom-line company. For me, that was the most important decision we have ever made as a company.

2014: The Search for a Higher Purpose

The second-most important decision was in 2014, after the very long expansion of new businesses that I mentioned. To be honest, I think we lost some connection with our employees, because we had stretched them too far, with all the initiatives and four acquisitions in eighteen months. We were missing something very important to me: the higher purpose of FIFCO. So we went out to search for our purpose. We have a very good vision and mission and very good strategies, but a purpose is different. It must answer the question "Why? Why

are we here? Why do we wake up every day and come to work?" I wanted something that could truly unify all our employees, no matter which businesses they were with. I wanted them to wake up every day aspiring to get to a higher place.

So we literally went up to a mountain for a three-day retreat. Twelve people joined me on this quest, and we discovered the higher purpose of our organization. Finding the purpose should not be an exercise delegated to an advertising agency; it was very introspective for each of us. The purpose is so important because it really touches the hearts of the employees. Strategies and vision all affect you mentally, in the mind. But a purpose is very different. We needed to open our hearts to our employees.

I believe very strongly that if we can win the hearts of our employees, we will have their minds forever. When my team members and I became more human, we were able to open a new way of doing things and embrace this principle of a higher purpose, which also led us to refresh our values: what we do and don't stand for. Over the past few years, we have become more human in this way.

Here is how we articulated our purpose: we bring a better way of living to the world.

I live a daily tension between living my purpose and complying with the performance I am expected to deliver. It may sound weird, but I love that tension. I've embedded this tension into my leadership team: that we are the guardians of this purpose for the company, and for every decision we make daily, we have to put the purpose in front of us. Sometimes, our purpose goes against performance, but overall, we always try to make the right decision. We live in that tension of fulfilling our purpose while still achieving the performance that is expected of us.

Making the Purpose Real

One strong example of the tension between purpose and performance occurred when I was sharing the higher purpose with all our employees. I started with the twelve people with whom I had gone on the mountain retreat. I then shared the purpose with my hundred top executives, then with five hundred middle managers, and eventually with the whole organization. I went to every country and region to share our purpose. In one of those meetings, an employee grabbed the microphone and said to me, "Ramon, listen. I am very proud of everything this company has been doing in terms of water, emissions, our policy on alcohol, all that. I read about it, I see you on TV, I see what you're doing. But you know what, Ramon? Do you know that we have employees living in poverty?"

I was stunned by that comment. "You're right," I said. "I don't know how many of our employees are living under poverty conditions, but give me six months to work out a comprehensive plan with my management team. I'll come back to this."

Being confronted with the reality of many of our workers' lives was an absolutely incredible thing. We looked around and took the best benchmarks and practices from other companies and from the UN's protocols. It took us six months to create our program, which we call FIFCO Opportunities.

In Costa Rica, about 22 percent of our total population lives in poverty, as measured by the United Nations. We hired social workers to help us. I went with the social workers and interviewed the people living in poverty—not only our employees but also their families. I wanted to find out how many employees were in this vulnerable condition and, more importantly, the reasons behind it. It's not because we pay bad salaries; FIFCO actually has some of the best salaries in the entire country and beyond in Central America. But an employee might be in a vulnerable situation for many reasons: bad financial decisions, debt, health issues, having more than one companion, and so on. We heard about all these things along the way. Ultimately, we discovered that 3.6 percent of our four thousand employees were living in conditions of poverty. I publicly promised the company, these employees, and their families that although it takes the government ten years to bring a person out of poverty, we would do it in three.

We developed a 360-degree program to help each of these families, with their agreement and input. We don't say "You're poor" or "You're in a vulnerable situation" or anything like that. They have to participate in counseling, and more importantly, they learn how to manage their finances. Many of them also have issues with health or education. We launched this program less than a year and a half ago, and we have already brought twenty-seven families out of poverty. Every single employee has a mentor, who is one of our executives. I gave the most complicated and difficult case to our chief financial officer. I said to him, "Carlos, if you cannot bring this guy out of poverty, nobody can!"

What I did not realize at first was the effect that this whole thing would have. Not only did we gain the loyalty and engagement of the employees and families participating in this program, but the program had a huge effect on the other 97 percent of our employees. They really felt like, "Wow, the company is doing all this to help our fellow employees who are living in very difficult situations." Our engagement, commitment, and indexes on Great Place to Work all skyrocketed. I'm told that normally, when you do something right in terms of improving the organization's culture, you go up at most three points a year. Last year, we improved twelve points on our Great Place to Work scorecard! In fact, the people at the regional Great Place to Work organization didn't believe the score at first, so they redid it. When they interviewed me, I said, "Do you know why I think we had such an incredible bump this year? I think it's all related to our purpose initiatives."

In addition to the example about poverty, we have done many other initiatives in the entrepreneurial area and are fostering new ideas among our employees.

Changing the Compensation System

Back in 2008, one of our most important decisions was to change the way we were compensating our executives and other leaders. We changed from 100 percent economic KPIs, which was related to our variable compensation. There were the usual suspects: earnings per share, market share, and so on. We lowered the economic indicators from 100 percent to 60 percent and incorporated 30 percent social KPIs and 10 percent environmental KPIs. It's a much more balanced scorecard, and it is accessible and visible to all employees.

Right now, this compensation system is for top executives. Out of some six thousand total employees, twelve hundred really have an influence on the well-being of the company today. Currently compensation is based on KPIs that are 60 percent economic, 30 percent social, and 10 percent environmental; the idea for me would be to lower the 60 percent economic to 50 percent—but that decision has to be made by the Compensation Committee.

By the way, when we acquired the business in the United States, we used 100 percent economic KPIs for the first year, because we really needed to bring the financial side under control. This year, it is down to 80 percent. An economic-based KPI is especially important when you are acquiring a new business, because you have to get the financials, the economics, all sorted out. Once you have a solid base, then you can start bringing in all these other elements.

Putting People First

We have explicitly used Conscious Capitalism ideas in this journey, without calling it that—we call it holistic capitalism instead. That's our own term for it, but it embraces the same principles that Conscious Capitalism holds.

I strongly believe that you can have the best production facilities and technologies, but ultimately, it's all about the people. The more your people are engaged, motivated, and committed to you—the more they believe in what you're trying to do—the better off you will be. They will do anything for you; they will climb Mount Everest, because at the end of the day, they believe in what we are trying to do. We are evolving in how we do business; we are evolving way beyond what we were taught in business school, which was to maximize shareholders' profits.

As business leaders, we need to evolve our thinking. We have an obligation to better share among all stakeholders, not just shareholders, the value we create. The more companies can embrace this fundamental principle, the better off we will be as a society. We can build a better planet all together, and I think it will start by all of us being humble in recognizing our social and environmental footprints. No matter which industry you work in, we all have to start by recognizing the footprints we generate. From there, you can move on and make a different kind of impact: a positive impact on society and the environment.

Often when I speak with businesspeople, they say, "Okay, Ramon, I generate so much employment, I pay all my taxes—what else do you want me to do?" We all need to go much further.

I'm a firm believer that more and more companies will come to embrace these principles.

Why is this journey important to you as a leader?

I think it's important because we need to be an example of the idea that companies can do much more than just generate employment and pay taxes. We're living in a society that has not quite failed yet, but we have so many social and environmental issues to cope with, and our governments—especially in this part of the world—do not have all the resources or competence to deal with them. We from the private sector must play a role in this and try to be part of the solution. I also firmly believe that we need to adjust our business practices and bring our skills to help out where it is most needed.

How do you define success?

For me, success will be the day that all businesses (especially the 145 businesses that control 45 percent of the world's wealth) can embrace the triple-bottom-line principles and become more conscious. That is how I would define success.

How do you define greatness as a business? What makes a great business?

Greatness is when we do the right thing, not only for the business but also for society in general. I can share with you how we're moving toward our 2020 vision: from neutral processes to a net positive. It's a fascinating topic that I'm working on with my management team as we speak. My intention now is not merely to move to water-neutral or carbon-neutral processes. We want to have positive footprints. We don't just want to do less harm; we want to do more good. That's a fascinating concept going forward.

Why I Am a Conscious Capitalist

By Steve Hall, CEO, Driversselect

There are many reasons I am passionate about the journey to Conscious Capitalism. I could refer to the fact that since we integrated this philosophy into my company six years ago, revenues have grown from $47 million to over $240 million and net profits have increased ninefold. But it's not the financial performance alone that makes this journey worthwhile. The journey to Conscious Capitalism has made me realize that the most essential part of my business is my relationship with my stakeholders. And the more I clearly define the type of relationship I want to hold with each of them, the more fulfilling the journey becomes for me.

One of the most important things this journey has taught me is *who* comes on the journey with me matters more than what I am building or how much I achieve. I have learned to recognize the difference that comes from thinking about my business in decades rather than quarters—the impact it can make on people and the sheer joy of leading a company when it reflects my personal values. Figure 2-1 shows how we present our core values and mission to customers.

In building my business on the tenets of Conscious Capitalism, I have come to realize that what stops most companies from scaling in a sustainable way is not capital, customer demand, or any other outside factor in the marketplace. Companies fail to reach their full potential mostly because of internal factors: places where they don't realize the interdependency of their stakeholders. Therefore, the firms can't find a path to create enough value to keep these stakeholders engaged and

Figure 2-1: Driversselect's core values and purpose, as presented on the company's web page

purpose

to infect the *workplace* with highly contagious C.A.R.E.
(Caring Acts Randomly Expressed)

customers   tribe members   consultants   key suppliers   community

driversselect

FUELED BY C.A.R.E.

core values

be transparent   refuse to be normal. just be yourself

take ownership   apply your talents to owning something that creates impact

learn to earn   there is opportunity to learn and grow inside every experience

celebrate small successes   find someone or something to celebrate every day

Source: Driversselect, "Core Values," accessed August 17, 2017, http://driversselect.com/custom/experience_our_core_values.

committed long enough to fulfill the company's mission, purpose, and vision. Conscious Capitalism has helped me recognize the importance of creating real and lasting value for all key stakeholders and how to balance the right amount of equity to invest in each group of stakeholders at various life cycles of the business.

Before embracing Conscious Capitalism, I found it is easy to overlook certain stakeholders, like the truck drivers who deliver our vehicles from auctions across the country. I didn't appreciate the value these people were providing us. But when you consider that the aging of vehicles affects our margins more than any other factor does and how trucking time plays a big role in how quickly a vehicle is ready for sale, I started to see this group of stakeholders differently. If we treated our trucking partners like key members of our tribe, they would be more committed to getting our cars to us quicker, safer, and at lower costs. It is simple things like greeting the truck drivers with water and food when they arrive after a fifteen-hour drive, making them feel welcome and appreciated for their efforts, and showing them that the work they are doing matters to us. We want them to feel a sense of pride in what they do for a living.

I now see business as a way to fulfill my purpose of infecting the workplace with highly contagious care. The more my business grows, the more profits we have to invest in helping our stakeholders fulfill their mission, purpose, and vision. Something magical happens when the stakeholders in a business show up caring about creating meaningful value for each other.

Conscious Capitalism can change not just your own life for the better by focusing on what really matters but also the lives of every person your business touches. There is nothing more rewarding for an entrepreneur, a CEO, or any other top executive.

What You Can Expect from This Journey

Becoming a conscious company has many rewards, starting with the realization that you are on the right side of society, that you are a force for good, and that you are part of the solution instead of adding to the pile of problems some mythical "future" generation will have to deal with. Figure 2-2 lists some of the likely outcomes you will experience as you move along on this journey.

Figure 2-2: Tenets and benefits of Conscious Capitalism

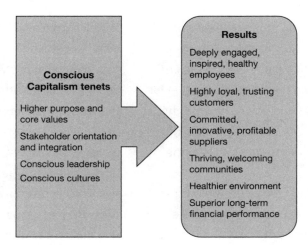

Conscious Capitalism tenets

Higher purpose and core values

Stakeholder orientation and integration

Conscious leadership
Conscious cultures

Results

Deeply engaged, inspired, healthy employees

Highly loyal, trusting customers

Committed, innovative, profitable suppliers

Thriving, welcoming communities

Healthier environment

Superior long-term financial performance

Benefits to Being a Conscious Company

There are many other benefits to being a conscious company. This infographic from *Conscious Company* magazine captures many of them.

URL: https://www.ccfieldguide.com/benefits

Search Words: Conscious Capitalism Field Guide Benefits of Conscious Companies

Assessing Where You Are on the Journey

In our experience working with companies, we often find that although most people are inspired by the concepts of Conscious Capitalism, they struggle to focus on the three or four things that will make the biggest difference in their organizations. We will bring structure to this process for you so that you have a clear strategic and tactical agenda for your business over the next three to five years. You will uncover the actions you can take both to produce the biggest impact on your business's performance and to accelerate your transformation to Conscious Capitalism.

Nowadays, when we take a trip, we have GPS to help us find the shortest possible route from where we are to our destination. Similarly, to become a conscious company, we need a clear understanding of where we are today. To assess where you are, you can complete the questionnaire for a conscious business in the following assessment.

Conscious Business Summary Audit

SCORE

Purpose

1. Our organization fulfills the deep-seated *needs* of our customers, not just their wants or desires.

2. Our customers would be genuinely distraught if we ceased to exist.

3. Our investments and R&D priorities reflect a higher purpose beyond profits.

4. We have a clear vision of how the world would look if we fulfill our purpose.

5. Our employees find in their work intrinsic satisfaction that goes beyond their salary. The best ones would leave if we ceased being true to our purpose.

Stakeholder Orientation

6. For all major strategic decisions, we explicitly consider the short-term and long-term impacts on each of our key stakeholders: customers, employees, suppliers, investors, and communities.

7. We use metrics to track the well-being of each of our stakeholders, and these are monitored at the highest levels within the company.

8. We routinely engage stakeholders in dialogue and give them a voice in the company's direction.

9. We recognize the interdependencies between our stakeholders, and we explicitly seek solutions that satisfy multiple stakeholders simultaneously. At the very least, we ensure that no stakeholder is harmed so that another may gain.

10. Our company's relationships with all our stakeholders are characterized by frequent communication and high degrees of mutual trust and goodwill.

Conscious Leadership

11. Our leaders are deeply self-aware individuals who are in their roles because they passionately believe in the purpose of our organization and in service to our people.

12. Our leaders are intuitive systems thinkers and systems feelers. They not only think in systems terms but also feel the connectedness and interdependence between stakeholders.

13. In our company, power and virtue go together. In other words, we consciously seek to promote individuals with the greatest integrity and capacity for caring and compassion.

Conscious Leadership (continued)

14.	Most senior positions in our company are filled by promotions from within.	
15.	In our company, accountability between employees and managers runs both ways; employees are accountable for their performance, and managers are accountable to ensure that employees have what they need to perform at a high level.	

Conscious Culture

16.	Our company's culture has a high degree of trust and transparency internally and externally. There is high trust among employees, between employees and management, and between the company and its external stakeholders.	
17.	In our culture, we say what we mean and we mean what we say. There is no sugarcoating of tough reality, and there is a high level of commitment to truth and integrity in all matters.	
18.	We operate within a culture of genuine caring and compassion for all stakeholders. When times get tough, our company exhibits an even higher level of caring and compassion than in prosperous times. There is a real sense of altruism in our culture. People do things for others with no expectation of a return, reward, or recognition.	
19.	Our people and our organization are continually evolving to higher states of capability and consciousness.	
20.	Employees in our company are empowered to always do the right thing. We use self-managing, self-motivated, and self-directed teams to accomplish our work.	
	TOTAL	

SCORING

5: We are exceptionally good at this, to the point that others should learn from us.

4: We demonstrate this most of the time, but there is room for improvement.

3: This is true for us sometimes, but our record overall is mixed.

2: This is rarely true for us.

0: We seem to embody the opposite of this, or it is missing entirely.

Starting the Journey   31

Once you and your leadership team have individually completed this assessment, you should get together to discuss and compare the results, to understand the gaps, and to learn from each other. In this way, you and the team can identify actions that need to be taken. You should refer back to this assessment after reviewing each of the tenets of Conscious Capitalism.

Take a look at your composite score for each tenet. If one score is exceptionally lower than the others, you should strongly consider starting with that tenet, instead of following the sequence of the tenets presented in the book. If all the scores are comparable, you can stay with the sequence as presented.

Now let's move on to the following four parts of this book and examine each of the tenets.

TEDx Talk on a Journey to Conscious Capitalism

By Thomas Eckschmidt, cofounder of Conscious Capitalism Brazil and coauthor of Fundamentals of Conscious Capitalism

This is a brief message on how the consciousness of Conscious Capitalism principles can leverage a business for its community, stakeholders, and environment.

URL: https://www.ccfieldguide.com/thomas

Search Words: Conscious Capitalism Field Guide Thomas Eckschmidt's Journey

Part One

HIGHER PURPOSE

*T*he first tenet of Conscious Capitalism is that a business must have a higher purpose, distinct from making money.* The simplest way to explain purpose is that it is a definitive statement about the difference you are trying to make in the world.

For far too long, the conventional wisdom has been that the purpose of business is to maximize returns for shareholders. Business thinkers and leaders of highly successful companies are coming to realize that this way of thinking is flawed and harmful.

Austrian psychiatrist and Holocaust survivor Viktor Frankl's landmark work *Man's Search for Meaning* powerfully articulated the importance of purpose for individuals. As he wrote, happiness cannot be pursued; it *ensues*. It is the outcome of living a life of meaning and purpose. Such a life comes from three things: doing work that matters, loving without condition, and finding meaning in our suffering. You could change the title of Frankl's book to *The Corporation's Search for Meaning*; the lessons are the same. Companies pursue profits the way humans pursue happiness. But like happiness, profits cannot be pursued; they ensue. They result from operating a business with a higher purpose, something that truly

*Part 1 of this book was primarily written by Haley Rushing, cofounder and chief "purposologist" of the Purpose Institute, Austin, Texas (see https://thepurposeinstitute.com).

matters; building the business on love and care instead of fear and stress; and growing from adversity.

Part 1 is composed of four chapters that address why every organization needs to have a purpose (see figure P1-1). The chapters present a methodology to help you reveal the purpose of your organization, and they give guidance on articulating that purpose and how to embed the purpose throughout the organization.

Figure P1-1: Overview of part 1

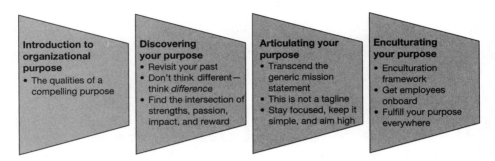

Introduction to organizational purpose
- The qualities of a compelling purpose

Discovering your purpose
- Revisit your past
- Don't think different— think *difference*
- Find the intersection of strengths, passion, impact, and reward

Articulating your purpose
- Transcend the generic mission statement
- This is not a tagline
- Stay focused, keep it simple, and aim high

Enculturating your purpose
- Enculturation framework
- Get employees onboard
- Fulfill your purpose everywhere

Assessment of Purpose for a Conscious Business

RESPONDENTS: C-level executives, managers, and frontline employees

DESIRED NUMBER OF RESPONSES: 10 C-level executives, 10 managers, and 10 frontliners; do not merge responses.

INSTRUCTIONS: Distribute this assessment to members of your company as noted. Have them assess the company's purpose, and do so yourself, using the scoring key at the bottom of the assessment.

QUESTION	SCORE
1. Our organization fulfills a deep-seated *need* of our customers, not just their wants or desires.	
2. Our customers would be genuinely distraught if we ceased to exist.	
3. Our teams have a deep understanding of how our higher purpose translates into the tasks they do and the decisions they must make every day.	
4. We routinely encourage employees to make business decisions on their own when their initiatives are aligned with the company's purpose.	
5. Our investments and research priorities reflect our purpose.	
6. Our company prioritizes purpose over short-term profits.	
7. The intrinsic satisfaction that our employees find in their work goes beyond the salary that they earn. The best employees would leave if we ceased being true to our purpose.	
8. We have a clear vision of how the world would look if we fulfill our purpose.	
9. Our organization is characterized by high levels of energy and creativity.	
10. We actively seek suppliers and other business partners who share a commitment to our purpose.	
TOTAL	

SCORES

5: We are exceptionally good at this, to the point that others should learn from us.

4: We demonstrate this most of the time, but there is room for improvement.

3: This is true for us sometimes, but our record overall is mixed.

2: This is rarely true for us.

0: We seem to embody the opposite of this, or it is missing entirely.

Add up your scores to identify the overall gap between your company and best practice (50 points). How did you score? What surprised you? What did not? Why? What are the implications?

_____

_____

_____

_____

_____

_____

_____

How to Feel the Purpose

By Roy Spence, chairman and cofounder of advertising agency GSD&M and author of It's Not What You Sell, It's What You Stand For: Why Every Extraordinary Business Is Driven by Purpose

URL: https://www.ccfieldguide.com/purpose

Search Words: Conscious Capitalism Field Guide Higher Purpose

Chapter 3

Introduction to Organizational Purpose

Purpose is the common ground, the intersection between your passion and talents and the needs of society. It is your vocation, the sweet spot where you can find true meaning and fulfillment. This idea applies to organizations as much as it does to individuals.

The authors of *The Purposeful Company* articulate the essence of purpose as follows: "The purpose of a great company is its reason for being. It defines its existence and contribution to society. It determines its goals and strategy. Underlying it is a set of values and beliefs that establish the way in which the company operates. Purpose is as fundamental to a corporation as our purposes, values and beliefs are to us as individuals. This purpose must be sufficiently compelling and inspiring to invigorate all members of the company community."[1]

Purpose fosters meaningful innovations and visionary ideas and helps your business navigate turbulent times. It injects greater power into your brand's message, helps attract the right talent and keeps that talent longer with the organization, contributes to personal fulfillment and a life well lived, and generates higher financial results in the long run.

Having a clear and inspiring organizational purpose makes a huge difference. It focuses a company's energies and illuminates the path forward.

Here are some examples of purpose-driven companies.

Google's purpose from the beginning was to "organize the world's information and make it easily accessible and useful." This purpose could seem like an infinitely arduous task, as information expands every day, with more discoveries, more research, and more history being made. After making sure their algorithms captured all the new information generated on the web, Google addressed the nondigital world. The company started to scan books; shoot images from the analog world; map streets, the countryside, and, eventually, the whole planet; and made this information universally and easily accessible. Now it has started a new wave of innovation that, for example, includes driverless vehicles.

Barry-Wehmiller, an industrial machinery company based in St. Louis with operations around the United States and in several other countries, defines its purpose in terms of its impact on people: "We measure success by the way we touch the lives of people." During the financial crisis of 2008, many US companies downsized, firing part of their workforce. Barry-Wehmiller faced a huge challenge then. New orders dried up almost completely, and many of its clients canceled existing orders. Financially, there was no easy fix to make up for those lost sales; the cost structure had to be reassessed. The company's leadership team came up with an idea. If every employee took four weeks of unpaid vacation, the company would save enough to make it through twelve months of the downturn. Leadership allowed the employees to decide when to take these four weeks off. Many employees altruistically stepped forward to take even more time off so that some of their colleagues could take less. Those who could not afford to take unpaid vacation because of higher financial commitments took fewer weeks, and those who could afford to took longer periods off to reach the four weeks' unpaid time off per employee.

The idea was extremely well received by employees and even embraced by the unions. Morale actually rose during the downturn as fear evaporated and a sense that "we are in this together" took hold. As a result, once the economic downturn was over, Barry-Wehmiller was in a much better position to recover and address rising market demand. The year 2009 was one of the best years in terms of financial results in the history of the organization.

For Southwest Airlines, the company's purpose has long been to "give people the freedom to fly." In 2008, while most other airlines decided to start charging for checked bags, Southwest Airlines, which had more than thirty years of profitable quarters, decided not to do so, despite recommendations from consultants and a possible $300 million upside in revenue. The decision was based on the company's purpose: enhance people's freedom to fly. Would charging for bags move the purpose forward or detract from it? The answer was pretty obvious. Helped by an effective ad campaign that celebrated its decision to let "Bags Fly Free," the airline found that sticking to its purpose helped it generate close to $1 billion in incremental revenue at a time when the airline industry was losing sales.

The Qualities of a Compelling Purpose

While there are as many potential purposes as there are companies, great purposes have some common characteristics. We capture several of these qualities in the acronym HEALING (heroic, evolving, aligning, loving, inspiring, natural, and galvanizing).

In a world filled with suffering and ill health, healing is noble work. A conscious business creates value by meeting some real, tangible needs of its stakeholders. By doing so, it improves the quality of their existence and makes them better off than they were before. It alleviates suffering and brings more joy, with positive impacts on stakeholders' physical, emotional, and spiritual well-being. Ultimately, we believe, every great purpose must be a healing purpose.

HEALING also represents seven essential qualities of a great purpose:

Heroic: Any worthy purpose has the potential to be heroic, to have a positive transformational impact on the world, affecting not only the company's stakeholders but also its industry and perhaps even society at large. Southwest Airlines has not only made air travel more affordable and enjoyable for its US customers, but has also helped bring the benefits of air travel to billions around the world by inspiring countless other airlines to emulate its philosophy and refine their approach.

Evolving: A conscious business aligns its purpose with the evolutionary impulses of its times. As we humans progress on our journey toward greater consciousness and higher states of being, companies will have to adapt and elevate their purposes to remain in harmony with our evolving aspirations and motivations. Whole Foods Market has evolved along with the changing needs, dreams, and concerns of its stakeholders. Its recent initiatives in holistic wellness for team members and customers and in improving school nutrition are examples.

Aligning: A great purpose acts like a powerful magnet that aligns all stakeholders. Stakeholders retain their distinctive roles and identities, but also voluntarily become part of a harmonious whole. The aligning power of a great purpose largely eliminates the conflicts that commonly arise between stakeholders and enables the discovery of win-win resolutions when conflicts do crop up. When they share a common purpose, stakeholders literally cease to be at cross-purposes with one another. In the absence of a shared higher purpose, all stakeholders default to profit maximization as their purpose. In so doing, each member becomes a taker from the system, rather than a contributor to it.

Loving: People are increasingly recognizing the tremendous power and centrality of love in all human endeavors, especially in business. A company's purpose must emanate from the deep reservoir of love and caring largely untapped in most of us. A purpose built on love and care creates a powerful and vital force throughout the organization. It is in harmony with the deepest essence of what it means to be human.

Inspiring: A great purpose inspires all the stakeholders of an enterprise to rise above their self-imposed limitations and self-serving agendas and strive for the seemingly impossible. It electrifies and animates the organization, giving it a sense of urgency and focus. At Millennium Pharmaceuticals, every employee every day embodies the company's inspiring purpose: "We aspire to cure cancer." Drivers, building attendants, and scientists alike come to work inspired by their company's noble purpose.

Natural: Every great purpose must reflect a mindset of living in harmony with nature rather than conquering or dominating it. A metaphor for the old way of business is the powerboater who muscles the vessel straight through the water, bent on overpowering all but the most extreme conditions. Powerboats consume a lot of fuel and are highly polluting and noisy, and the boaters pay little attention to the damage left in their wake. A conscious business is more akin to a sailor who continuously adapts to the environment and harnesses the superior power of the surrounding elements. Such a sailor draws the power to move the vessel forward from the wind and current, whose energy is boundless. Yet, he or she can move the vessel in any direction desired.

Galvanizing: A great purpose is not just conceptually and emotionally appealing; it moves people to action. It embodies "the fierce urgency of now," to use a phrase of Martin Luther King Jr.

Purpose and the Search for Meaning

By Miki Agrawal, successful entrepreneur and author of Do Cool Sh*t: Quit Your Day Job, Start Your Own Business, and Live Happily Ever After

Miki Agrawal shares her journey in the search for meaning and purpose.

URL: https://www.ccfieldguide.com/miki

Search Words: Conscious Capitalism Field Guide Purpose and Meaning with Miki Agrawal

In the next chapter, we will help you discover your company's unique purpose in the world.

Chapter 4

Discovering Your Purpose

In this chapter, we offer a series of exercises to help you uncover your organization's purpose. You aren't going to write a purpose statement just yet; rather, the exercises in this chapter will get you and your team to think creatively and broadly and to analyze and understand what's really special about your company. With a little excavating, some structured questioning, and a little inspiration, you can discover (or rediscover) the authentic purpose at the heart of your organization.

As with all the exercises in this book (unless indicated otherwise), you should do these in conjunction with your leadership team. Each member of the team should answer the questions individually first; you should then come together to discuss and integrate your perspectives into a single set of responses. As the leader, you need to listen more than speak. If you state your opinion or position too soon, other members of the team might be tempted to fall in line with your thinking. Such groupthink diminishes the value of bringing in diverse perspectives from all the members of the team.

For the purpose-discovery exercises in this chapter, we recommend reaching beyond the leadership team to include a cross-section of twenty to thirty highly engaged people from across the organization. For some of the questions, you should include long-term customers and suppliers as well (these questions will be evident).

Figure 4-1 lays out the steps to discovering your purpose. You will explore the company's past, including its origins, and will consider the hearts of the founders. You will contrast your company's successes and failures in the search for patterns. And you will explore what makes the business unique and the difference it can make in the world. Another area you'll examine is the intersection between your passions, your strengths, and the impact the organization can make in society to reveal its purpose. Discussions with your biggest fans, those who promote the company, will also uncover your company's strengths. You have to understand what you do at a functional-benefit level, and of course, you need to listen to your heart.

If the founders are no longer part of the leadership team but are still alive, this is a great opportunity to invite them to share their story of why they created the business.

Let's start this journey from the past forward and explore the origins of what you do.

Figure 4-1: Discovering your purpose

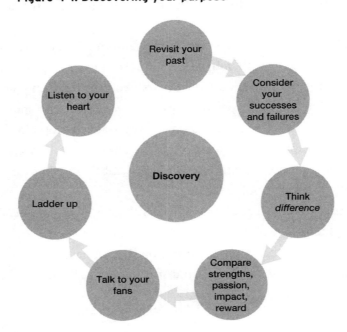

Revisit Your Past

Explore the genesis of the organization. Talk to the founders, review the founding documents, look for news and recordings from the time the company was created, and find the motivation that was present at the inception.

Explore the following questions to revisit your past:

- **Why was the organization originally founded?**

  _____

  _____

  _____

  _____

  _____

  _____

  _____

  _____

- **What were the guiding principles that this organization was founded on?**

  _____

  _____

  _____

  _____

  _____

  _____

  _____

  _____

- **What spirit or intention must be preserved and captured in our purpose at all cost?**

_____

_____

_____

_____

_____

_____

To see how one company went about revisiting its past to rediscover its purpose, let's look at GE Aviation.

As GE Aviation worked to identify its purpose, the leaders started by revisiting the wisdom of arguably one of the most purpose-driven, visionary founders a company could have: Thomas Edison, who once said, "I never perfected an invention that I did not think about in terms of the service it might give to others." GE Aviation leaders responded to this attitude: "We knew the purpose had to capture the spirit of innovation that drove Edison and has been core to GE since day one. We also needed to capture how that innovation was designed to serve the greater good." The company contributes to lifting people up (literally and figuratively, as aviation has lifted emerging economies and contributed to a more connected world). And the engines GE Aviation builds are also responsible for bringing millions of people home safely, from commercial-flight passengers to fighter pilots making it across enemy lines. For GE Aviation, the magic of the purpose was in the intersection of the spirit of Edison and the company's impact in the world both yesterday and today. GE Aviation's purpose is captured in the company motto: _To invent the future of flight, lift people up and bring them home safely._

Take a few minutes at this point to review your answers and reflect on the insights from the GE Aviation example. Make sure you have added enough details to your answers so that you and your team can understand your history.

Contrast Your Successes and Failures

Deconstruct your successes and failures—move beyond obvious variables to find both the tangible and intangible factors that are present when you are at your best and when your people are proudest of the organization. Notice where your energy and talent naturally tend to gravitate.

Answer the following questions to explore insights from your successes and failures:

- **When we are at our absolute best, what is going on?**

_____

_____

_____

_____

_____

_____

_____

- **When we love what we are doing, what is going on?**

_____

_____

_____

_____

_____

_____

_____

- **When we're failing, just getting by, in a slump, or not that interested in our work, what is going on?**

_____

_____

_____

_____

_____

_____

_____

_____

To explore the issue of successes and failures a little further, consider the example of GSD&M and one of its founders, Roy Spence.

GSD&M is one of the top advertising agencies in the United States. About twenty years ago, Roy Spence—one of the founders—asked, "What's going on that some of the brands we help build are phenomenally successful and everyone loves working on them . . . and others, not so much?" This question led to the discovery that the people of GSD&M were at their very best when they were using their creativity to help purpose-driven brands win in the marketplace—brands like Southwest Airlines, John Deere, BMW, the US Air Force. These brands actually stood for something. The people of GSD&M didn't want to just deliver visionary ideas that build sales or build brands. That's table stakes for any agency. They wanted to deliver breakthrough ideas with impact. Hence, the agency's purpose: _To deliver visionary ideas that make a difference._

Don't Think Different—Think *Difference*

Very often, companies spend an enormous amount of time and energy trying to differentiate themselves from the competition through their *unique selling propositions*. Rather than battling it out in the land of attributes, turn your attention away from being different just for the sake of being different, and focus on what difference you're trying to make. What difference are you ultimately trying to make in the world? When you can clearly answer that question, it becomes a powerful filter to determine where you should or shouldn't be spending your time, energy, and resources.

Ask yourself the following questions:

- **What is the ultimate impact we hope to make?**

_____

_____

_____

_____

- **When we're at our best, what difference do we make in the lives of the people we serve?**

_____

_____

_____

_____

_____

_____

_____

Here is another short story of how Southwest Airlines changed what a traditional industry had done for years and how this difference influenced the way we travel around the world.

After Southwest Airlines had spent over a decade educating the marketplace about how it was different from other airlines—low fares, frequent flights, friendly people—it decided to ask a new question. Herb Kelleher, the insatiably curious founder of Southwest Airlines, said, "By now, everyone knows how we're different. What I want to know is . . . what difference do we make?" When GSD&M started asking that question for Southwest, the ad agency started hearing people talk about the freedom that they had been given because of those low fares, frequent flights, and friendly employees. GSD&M went back and told Kelleher, "Holy smokes! You're not in the discount airline business. You're in the freedom business!" And the purpose of Southwest Airlines was revealed: *To give people the freedom to fly.*

Take the opportunity to go back to your answers and make sure you have included all the possibilities and impacts your organization can make in the world.

Find the Intersection of Strengths, Passion, Impact, and Reward

Your purpose resides in the intersection of your strengths, your passions, the company's impact, and the rewards your stakeholders receive from your company (figure 4-2). Knowing what intrinsically motivates your people, what you're built to do better than anyone else, and where you can deploy that passion and talent to serve a need or solve a problem in the world is extremely powerful.

Ask yourself several questions:

Figure 4-2: Where purpose resides

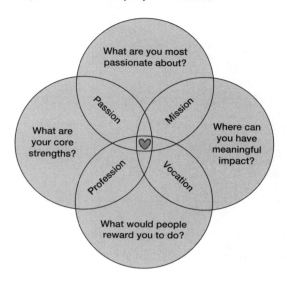

- What is our organization's greatest strength; what do we have the potential to be the best at in the world?

_____

_____

_____

_____

_____

_____

_____

_____

- What are we most passionate about? What do we love the most about what we do?

_____

_____

_____

_____

_____

_____

- Where can we have the most meaningful impact? Which big problems or needs in the world are we capable of and passionate about solving?

_____

_____

_____

_____

_____

_____

- What would people reward you for? What products and services would your customers happily purchase from you?

_____

_____

_____

_____

_____

_____

The purpose of an organization should be rooted in a set of strong beliefs. Here is how Whole Foods Market describes the process and states its purpose.

Over thirty years ago, sixty leaders of Whole Foods Market came together and wrote a document called the "Declaration of Interdependence." It contained the DNA of the company's purpose (and, in many ways, reflected the core tenets of Conscious Capitalism). When you read this document, the passions, strengths, and desire for meaningful impact come through loud and clear and have since been echoed in the voices of team members throughout the organization. One of the core strengths enabling Whole Foods to become not only a world-class grocer but also a world-class advocate for change is its mastery of the multi-stakeholder mindset. This strength enables the company to develop ideas that actually work because everyone affected is included in the creation of the idea. Whole Foods team members are some of the most passionate people you will ever meet. They embody the hero archetype and act with great courage and determination to change things for the better. From preparing a better store display to eradicating poverty, these are people on a mission. As for meaningful impact, they believe in creating a system where everyone can flourish—team members, customers, vendors or suppliers, communities, and shareholders. Its purpose is bigger than food, and yet the food is what makes everything possible. So a purpose that leaves food behind wouldn't be quite right. Whole Foods Market takes all these ingredients into account and brings them together in a powerful purpose statement that captures the strengths, passions, and ultimate impact of the company: *With great courage, integrity and love, we embrace our responsibility to cocreate a world where each of us, our communities and our planet can flourish. All the while, celebrating the sheer love and joy of food.*

Talk to Your Fans

Talk to your most evangelical employees, your most loyal die-hard customers, your vendor-partners who would do anything for you, and community leaders who love having your business in their community. Find out why they love your organization. What do they believe you stand for? What difference do they believe you make in their lives? These stakeholders know the real deal and are ultimately the heartbeat of the organization.

Ask your fans several questions:

- **What do you love most about this company or this brand?**

  _____

  _____

  _____

- **What does this company or brand do for you that no one else does?**

  _____

  _____

  _____

  _____

  _____

  _____

  _____

- **If this company or brand ceased to exist, what would be lost? What would you miss the most?**

  _____

  _____

  _____

The story of BMW might inspire you to search for your fans' honest and deep feedback about your business.

Anyone who has ever driven a BMW knows that there is nothing quite like it. It's fast. It's tight. It's fun. It's exhilarating. In the words of thousands of BMW owners over decades of driving experiences, it's pure joy. And that's precisely how people producing "the ultimate driving machine" think about their purpose. They have taken the idea of joy and made it the central idea that drives everything they do (pun intended). Certainly, the company wants people to experience the joy and thrill of driving a BMW. It also wants to do business in a way that makes people joyful—whether the company is creating a great work environment or pioneering sustainable ways of doing business—joy is what fans believe is at the heart of BMW.

Thus, we understand the purpose of BMW: *to enable people to experience the joy of driving.*

Look back at your answers, and make sure the ideas collected are what the fans believe you offer and not what your team would like to hear from them or what you think you are selling them. The truth in these answers could lead you to a much stronger position. Consider using independent researchers to collect this feedback.

Ladder Up

What's the ultimate value of what you're offering? At the most basic level, describe what you do. Moving up the ladder, identify the *functional benefits* of what you offer. Next, identify the *emotional benefits* of what you deliver. With these benefits mapped out, ask yourself, What's the ultimate value of these benefits in the life of the customers we're trying to serve?

Ask yourself these questions:

- At the most basic level, what do we have to offer people?

  _____

  _____

  _____

  _____

- Functional benefit: What does our offering enable people to do?

  _____

  _____

  _____

  _____

- Emotional benefit: How does our offering make people feel?

  _____

  _____

  _____

  _____

- Ultimate value: What is the ultimate value of these functional and emotional benefits in their lives?

  _____

  _____

  _____

  _____

  _____

  _____

  _____

To better explore these ideas, we bring you a case of a clothing company.

Most people know Life is Good as a socially conscious clothing and lifestyle brand. At the most basic level, it sells T-shirts, other clothing, and lifestyle-related merchandise with a message that life is good. The brand offers several benefits:

The functional benefit: Life is Good merchandise enables people to outfit themselves with a nice article of clothing, but much more importantly, it outfits them with a message that runs counter to the often-prevailing view that life is hard and messed up. It lets people advocate a different worldview.

The emotional benefit: Through its messaging, music festivals, community, contributions to nonprofit organizations, and its use of play to overcome trauma, the Life is Good brand is designed to stimulate good feelings—gratitude, hope, creativity, fun, compassion, openness, compassion, humor, and love.

The ultimate value: The company spreads optimism. Even if life isn't perfect and even when life is hard, it's still good.

Life is Good is not in the T-shirt business, as its chief executive optimist, Bert Jacobs, would tell you; it's in the business of optimism. And that's its purpose: *to spread the power of optimism.*

With the story of Life is Good in mind, go back to your answers, and add a second statement about each of the benefits and values you create. This is an important exercise, which will contribute to other sections in this journey.

Listen to Your Heart

In the end, purpose is a heart thing. What is your heart calling you to do? What problem, need, or other issue do you have a burning desire to address through your business? No market research study or SWOT (strengths, weaknesses, opportunities, and threats) analysis can dictate what your purpose should be. A purpose is only right and effective if it resonates with the leaders and employees of an organization in a deep and meaningful way.

To better listen to your heart, ask yourself these questions:

- **What is your heart calling you to do?**

  _____

  _____

  _____

  _____

  _____

  _____

  _____

  _____

- **What is absolutely essential for the purpose to be truly meaningful?**

  _____

  _____

  _____

  _____

The following story will bring to life a strong heart-driven purpose. It should inspire you and help you touch the deeper side of your heart.

A perfect example of tuning in to your heart to find your purpose comes from Interstate Batteries. As a battery company, it is in the business of providing dependable power. But for the leaders of Interstate Batteries, the most dependable source of power in the world is not *of* this world. Interstate Batteries is a faith-based company that strives to run its business in accordance with biblical principles. It practices servant leadership and lives by the Golden Rule. It honors its commitments and does all it can to serve those in need. When time came to articulate its purpose, there was almost no debate about what should be uppermost in the statement. The idea was a nonnegotiable, because it was so central to the company's sense of who its people are: *to glorify God and enrich lives as we deliver the most trustworthy source of power to the world.*

In this chapter, you explored the different dimensions of your organization's purpose. This is preparation for the next chapter, a warm-up to start the work ahead. Take a moment now, before we head into chapter 5, to reread all the questions and your answers. Complete the thoughts as you think necessary.

We will next work on articulating your purpose. You will use insights from the answers you gave in this chapter and then will dive into a deeper expression of purpose than what you have explored so far.

Articulating Your Purpose

Many companies have mission statements and a vision. Now we want you to work on your purpose. How do these three elements—mission, vision, and purpose—add up? How are they related?

- Purpose describes *why* we exist. What impact do we want to cause? What moves us to do what we do? What difference do we want to make in the world?

- Vision describes *what* the world will look like once we have fulfilled our purpose.

- Mission describes *how* we will get from our purpose to our vision of the future world. What is our strategy to fulfill our purpose?

In this chapter, we will focus on articulating our purpose.

Now that we have connected with our deep insights and emerged with a strong sense of where we are coming from and why we are here, it's time to put pen to paper.

We will share with you our experience from a decade of working through this process with our clients. We have identified three key building blocks of a powerful purpose:

- **Stay focused:** Make sure your purpose is connected to the reality of who you are. Otherwise, the purpose will divert attention and could be misread by your audience.

- **Keep it simple:** Don't use long statements and complex words, or some people won't understand you.

- **Aim high enough:** Make sure you are aiming for big changes, but not utopia; don't end up in the ether.

For this part of the process, we suggest that a smaller group be responsible—typically the CEO and the leadership team. It is difficult to write anything meaningful and compelling with a large number of people. As a group, devote a few hours a day for up to two weeks to this process. If you haven't arrived at a clear and compelling statement of purpose at the end of two weeks, you need to go back to the drawing board; redo all the exercises in the previous chapter.

Transcend the Generic Mission Statement

A great purpose statement goes far beyond the modern-day mission statement. Mission statements are often no more than a basic category description wrapped in corporate performance goals. Many of them are shareholder focused and give a clear sense that the business is focused on profits and costs. Be clear and definitive about the difference you are trying to make in the world, and leave the category descriptions and sales goals for the annual report. Compare the following two statements:

Generic aspiration: Our purpose is to be the most beloved brand in the world.

Definitive purpose: Our purpose is to use our imagination to bring happiness to millions.

Remember, a Purpose Is *Not* a Tagline

A great purpose statement errs on the side of clarity over creativity. It is intended to inspire your internal constituents by giving them a clear sense of purpose for all that they do. It should engage your external constituents in a way that they want to be part of your journey. Leave clever taglines for the branding process.

Nike's purpose: To bring inspiration and innovation to every athlete* in the world. (*If you have a body, you are an athlete.)

Nike's tagline: Just do it.

Stay Focused

A great purpose is focused. Prune away multiple ideas that can end up cluttering and sucking the life out of a great purpose. Remember, if you have a purpose statement that is too long, most people might not remember the first line or paragraph. Compare the purpose statements of these two hotel chains:

Not focused (hotel chain A): We succeed only when we meet and *exceed the expectations* of our customers, owners and shareholders. We have a *passion for excellence* and will deliver the highest standards of *integrity* and *fairness*. We celebrate the *diversity* of people, ideas and cultures. We honor the *dignity* and *value of individuals* working as a team. We improve the *communities* in which we work. We encourage *innovation*, accept *accountability* and embrace *change*. We seek knowledge and growth through *learning*. We share a *sense of urgency, nimbleness* and endeavor to have *fun* too.

Focused (hotel chain B): Be hospitable.

Keep It Simple

A great purpose statement should be immediately understandable and easy for anyone to repeat in an elevator without the aid of CliffsNotes. As the following examples show, if it's too complicated or clever for a child to understand, you may need to go back to the drawing board.

Too clever: Improve the quality of life by lowering the cost of living.

Clear and simple: Save people money and help them live better. (Walmart's statement of purpose)

Aim High . . .

A great purpose statement should feel like a lofty and noble goal worthy of putting your life's work into. Don't water it down by taking stock of all the ways that you may not be living up to the purpose every day (no company is living its purpose 100 percent of the time—that's the point: there's work to do!). A purpose is the ultimate reason for your organization's existence and not a wholly accurate assessment of all your current operations.

Say this: We transform lives for the benefit of society. One discovery, one student at a time. (American Council on Education)

Not this: Sometimes we transform lives in a way that might or might not be beneficial to the world, and sometimes we do breakthrough research, but sometimes we don't, but we make a genuine effort to give students useful skills for operating in the world.

. . . But Don't End Up in the Ether

A great purpose statement should have enough definition that people readily understand what you're actually doing or the space in which you operate:

In the ether: Our purpose is to make the world a better place.

Grounded: Our purpose is to create a healthier America, one person at a time.

Now it's time for the hands-on exercise. Go back to chapter 4, "Discovering Your Purpose." Review your answers, and start a list with ten ideas on why your company exists. Each member of your leadership team should compile this list individually.

NO.	MY COMPANY EXISTS TO . . .
1.	
2.	
3.	
4.	
5.	
6.	
7.	
8.	
9.	
10.	

Once each of you has listed ten possibilities, work with your team to narrow the list down to your collective top three—the ones you feel are closest to your heart.

NO.	MY COMPANY EXISTS TO . . .
1.	
2.	
3.	

Next, start sharing these ideas with people outside your leadership team. Ask each of them to write down the first thought that comes to mind when you present your tentative purpose statements.

- What is their gut reaction to the statement?

- Try to identify elements of inspiration, meaning, relevance, irrelevance, or confusion in their feedback.

- Rank these top three purpose options according to this initial feedback.

This is a good time for a break. Take a deep breath, and allow yourself to experience a change of scenery before coming back for the second round.

This time, write down your purpose in one shot:

What difference are we trying to make in the world? Be as simple and clear as possible.

The purpose of our organization is:

_____

_____

_____

_____

Go back and find people for feedback on this statement. Test it with a small group, and reevaluate this feedback. Remember, if you are the business leader, founder, and "creator," you should have the ultimate say on what the purpose of your business should be. But if the statement of purpose does not resonate with other stakeholders, you know you haven't found it yet. The statement might not be clear, or it might not be engaging others in the cause.

There is a limit on how many interactions you should do right now. At some point, you will have to go with a statement. Test it with the following questions:

- Does the statement motivate people? (Ask them; read their body language.)

- Does it inspire? (Ask how it inspires them.)

- Do people understand it? (Ask them to state it in their own words.)

- Does it foster innovation? (Ask them how it would do so.)

And live this purpose before starting to change or adjust it again. Remember, while the purpose is designed to be a North Star for your organization, it may need to evolve over time. Consider reassessing the purpose statement every five to ten years, depending on how much the business environment has changed, how much you've evolved as a company, or whether there have been major leadership changes.

To assess whether the purpose statement and philosophy you have arrived at meets the HEALING criteria described earlier, ask the following questions:

- Is it **heroic** enough? Are we really challenging ourselves to have the greatest impact possible?

- Is it **evolutionary**? Does it align with our journey as human beings, and how can we ensure that it remains relevant and compelling to all our stakeholders?

- Does it strongly **align** our stakeholders?

- Is it rooted in genuine **love** and care for all the people whose lives our business touches?

- Is it **inspiring** enough? Will it get people out of bed on Monday morning eager to face a new day of making a meaningful difference in the world?

- Is it in harmony with **nature**—our nature as a business and the world around us?

- Is it **galvanizing**? Does it have the "fierce urgency of now" to move people to action?

In the next chapter, we discuss how you can enculturate your purpose into your organization's daily life.

Chapter 6

Enculturating Your Purpose

After a great deal of soul-searching and through a structured, inclusive process, you have landed on a clear and inspiring articulation of your purpose. Now what? How can you make that purpose come to life? What should you do so that everyone understands and embodies the purpose? Our goal in this chapter is to help you create a road map to bring your purpose fully to life in your organization.

Enculturating your purpose ensures that it is not just words on a piece of paper but an idea that excites the people in your organization and generates visionary ideas that will move the organization forward. We'll lay out some general principles followed by specific tactics for you to consider as a part of purpose activation and enculturation.

Enculturation Framework

The framework to enculturate your purpose will help you focus on three key phases to speed up making the purpose a part of the fabric of your organization: getting your employees onboard; determining where you are and aren't fulfilling your purpose (gap analysis); and fulfilling your purpose everywhere (figure 6-1). What follows is a detailed set of best practices for each of the three key phases to ensure an effective and efficient implementation and organizational transformation.

Figure 6-1: A framework for enculturating purpose in your organization

Employees on board		
Inform	Inspire	Engage

↓

Where we are not fulfilling
Purpose gap analysis

↓

Fulfilling everywhere
Review all decisions and to-dos through the purpose's lens

Get Employees Onboard

You have to bring the purpose to life inside the organization. If your employees aren't clear about what you stand for or they don't know what you're preaching to the world—look out! Your customers will be in for some frustrating experiences when their expectations aren't consistent with their interactions with the organization. Think about all the ways that you could inspire your people, and put as much energy into those initiatives as you will put into those that you will eventually create for your customers.

This first phase includes five practices that will help you design your own program to align your employees with the organization's purpose.

Internal campaign: Create an internal employee campaign designed to inform, inspire, and engage internal constituents with the newly articulated purpose.

- **Inform:** Ask employees, What is the purpose, and why do we believe in it?

- **Inspire:** Celebrate examples of how your organization is fulfilling this purpose and making a real and meaningful difference today.

- **Engage:** Indicate how each individual can contribute to the fulfillment of the purpose. Be clear about how people are personally responsible for fulfilling the purpose, and invite them to contribute new ideas.

List a few ideas on how to communicate your purpose, and list a few channels currently available in your organization.

Ideas on how to communicate the purpose	Communication channels currently available

Letter from the leader and a purpose anthem video: A letter from the leader of the organization celebrating the purpose of the organization and the employees' role in fulfilling it sends a clear message that the purpose is the North Star of the organization. When it's accompanied by an inspiring *anthem video* that brings the purpose to life, the effort can truly inspire your stakeholders and fundamentally change the way people think about their work. These two pieces of communication can be great vehicles for informing and inspiring employees. You can see four examples of purpose anthems on the following site: http://thepurpose institute.com/index.php/our-offerings/#anthems.

Write a draft letter to your employees to communicate your purpose.

Draft letter to communicate the purpose

_____

_____

_____

_____

_____

_____

_____

_____

_____

_____

_____

_____

_____

_____

_____

_____

Purpose-inspired nomenclature: Develop internal nomenclature that reflects the spirit of the purpose. For example, Southwest Airlines is in the freedom business, and it created internal nomenclature to reinforce this purpose at every turn: HR benefits and policies became *employee freedoms*, employees became *freedom fighters*, and the launch of a new market was referred to as *liberating a market*. You can explore nomenclature that reflects the purpose or values of your organization to help it penetrate the organization on a daily basis.

Brainstorm some words and phrases that could become part of your organization's internal terminology and that could reflect your purpose in action.

Key words and phrases to consider

_____

_____

_____

_____

_____

_____

_____

_____

_____

_____

_____

_____

_____

_____

_____

_____

Purpose-driven talent management: Ways to make your talent management more purpose-driven include modifying recruitment strategies, onboarding of new hires, training and development programs, and how you recognize and celebrate people in the organization.

- **Recruitment strategies:** Recruitment strategies should be adapted to screen for individuals who demonstrate sincerity of interest, excitement, and commitment to serving the purpose of the organization.

  List here a few recruitment strategies you currently have in place, and then describe what needs to be done to adjust those strategies to the purpose.

Current recruiting strategies	Adjustments needed

- **New-hire orientations:** Don't settle for new-hire orientation that just includes HR benefits and a tour of the facilities. Include a purpose module into the orientations to ensure that all employees are steeped in the purpose from day one. The module might include the anthem video, the letter from the leader, stories about the difference that the organization has made in the world, and an invitation to share ideas on how the new hires might contribute to the purpose.

List here a few of your onboarding strategies and the adjustments you need to make to align those strategies with your purpose.

Current onboarding practices	Adjustments needed

- **Training and development programs:** Every individual in a purpose-driven organization needs to understand how his or her role and day-to-day work contribute to the purpose. Identify the training that people need to understand their role and to fulfill their part in the purpose.

  Select two or three of the most popular training programs in your organization, and evaluate how they should be adapted to fit the purpose.

Training programs	Adjustments needed

Employee evaluation, recognition, and celebration: Employee evaluations should include a section on contributions to, and alignment with, the purpose. Where has the person demonstrated initiative and a passion for fulfilling the purpose? Along with this type of purpose-driven evaluation, create purpose awards to celebrate the people who have gone above and beyond to fulfill the purpose of the organization.

What are the current evaluation criteria for your employees? Could you think of at least three more that you would consider contributions to the purpose?

Current evaluation criteria   New criteria

_____

_____

_____

_____

_____

What are your current recognition and celebration programs? Are they sufficiently meaningful and distinctive from incentive programs? How can you improve them?

Current programs   Ways to enhance

_____

_____

_____

_____

_____

Initiative overhaul: Initiative fatigue is a real phenomenon, particularly in larger corporations. Employees may have a hard time getting onboard with the purpose of the organization if they feel it is just the latest in a series of never-ending initiatives. People can only digest so much before they shut down or just give up trying to decipher the real priorities of the organization. Before the purpose is launched, keep in mind all the initiatives under way, and look at them through the lens of the purpose. With the purpose in mind, what can be scrapped? What should be elevated? How could these initiatives be simplified or, better yet, brought together in the context of the purpose so that employees can see how various initiatives work together to support the larger purpose?

Now it is your turn to define the initiatives and actions you will take to start enculturating your purpose into your organization. By answering the following questions, you will define your own enculturation plan.

1. **Which of these enculturation steps feels like something you should do first?**

   _____

   _____

   _____

   _____

2. **Which steps would give you the greatest return on your efforts?**

   _____

   _____

   _____

   _____

3. **Who would you need to get involved to make it happen?**

   _____

   _____

   _____

   _____

4. What commitments will need to be made in the next three months to make it happen?

_____

_____

_____

_____

_____

_____

_____

_____

Use these ideas to work on a structured plan, establishing initiatives and leaders, tasks, deadlines, and owners.

Initiatives	Leaders	Tasks	Deadlines	Owners

Determine Where You Are and Aren't Fulfilling Your Purpose

You need to conduct some research to assess where and how your purpose is currently being fulfilled, and where it's not. Look at all the ways that your stakeholders experience your brand. Ask yourself if those experiences align with the purpose. By identifying where the purpose is currently being fulfilled, you can begin to build the momentum necessary to get the purpose flywheel turning, while you plan to close the gaps wherever you are falling short.

A purpose wouldn't emerge as a purpose if it weren't being meaningfully expressed in the organization. Nevertheless, there will always be work to do. The final thoughts of the Whole Foods Declaration of Interdependence express this well:

> *When Whole Foods Market fails to measure up to its stated vision, as it inevitably will at times, we should not despair. Rather let us take up the challenge together to bring our reality closer to our vision. The future we will experience tomorrow is created one step at a time today.*

Start by identifying all the ways that you are currently living in alignment with the purpose. You want a good sense of what living your purpose looks and feels like in your organization today. You can use those stories and examples to get the purpose flywheel going in your organization. The difficulty of this first step will often give you an indication of just how much work is in store for you.

Use the following space to write down how your purpose is being fulfilled. Use concrete examples, citing people, processes, decisions, and other hard evidence.

_____

_____

_____

_____

_____

_____

_____

Now consider how you are not living up to your purpose. Solicit input using means that are appropriate for your organization (internal surveys, one-on-ones, committees, focus groups, town halls, etc.). Ask employees the following questions:

- **Where are we not living up to our purpose?**

_____

_____

_____

_____

_____

_____

_____

- When do we lose sight of our purpose?

  _____

  _____

  _____

  _____

- What must we do to live in greater alignment with our purpose?

  _____

  _____

  _____

  _____

  _____

  _____

  _____

- Are our performance evaluations and incentives aligned with our purpose? How should they be improved?

  _____

  _____

  _____

  _____

  _____

  _____

  _____

In pretty short order, you should be able to identify the gaps between the aspiration and the reality. Now, you can set a course for bringing your reality closer to your vision. For each gap—or challenge—that you've identified, ask the following questions:

- Who would you need to get involved to tackle that challenge?

- What resources are needed to make meaningful progress?

- What is a realistic time horizon for closing the gap between the reality and the aspiration?

Work with your team to answer these questions on the following chart:

Prioritized gap	Who should be involved	Resources required	Time frame

Consider bringing the appropriate people together in a workshop format to discuss and brainstorm ideas that would enable the organization to close each gap and begin operating in greater alignment with the purpose. A well-designed workshop can generate dozens of viable and valuable ideas for making meaningful progress.

Fulfill Your Purpose Everywhere

Purpose takes the idea of integration to a new level. It transforms integration from an exercise in consistency to an exercise in creation; it's about looking at everything on your plate as an opportunity to deliver another dimension of your purpose.

Think about all the initiatives on your to-do list. How many contribute to the overall purpose of the organization? How much more powerful would your brand be if everything you were putting out into the world was attempting to fulfill the promise of your purpose in some compelling and exciting way?

In this last phase of enculturation, we tackle all the daily activities and current running projects and evaluate how we can apply the purpose to each decision and action.

What's right in front of you: Look at your current to-do list through the lens of your purpose. As you look at what's right in front of you, search for opportunities to fulfill the purpose of the organization beyond what you're already doing. How could that HR initiative, that sales promotion, that corporate responsibility effort, that new product in development, the website redesign, be an opportunity to express the purpose in a new and interesting way?

Southwest Airlines' purpose, "Give people the freedom to fly," was originally held up by the core business model that delivered low fares and frequent flights. But once the good people of Southwest knew that they were in the freedom business, they set about looking for ways to deliver freedom in everything they did. They developed "employee freedoms" that gave their own people a sense of freedom in how they went about their jobs. A new loyalty program had the fewest blackout dates and the greatest seat availability so that people were actually free to use their rewards. The airline also created promotions like Friends Fly Free, which gave people the freedom to bring a friend along. And when everyone else in the industry started charging for bags, Southwest Airlines continued its bags-fly-free policy. And, of course, freedom was celebrated in its advertising: "[*Ding*] You are now free to move about the country."

To consider how you could enculturate your everyday activities, ask yourself these questions:

- Which tasks on my to-do list could provide a great new opportunity for expressing our purpose? How would that initiative change if we were looking at it through the lens of our purpose?

  List below three actions on your to-do list. Right next to each action, write down how you would modify this action through a decision or an action designed to fulfill your organization's purpose:

To-do list	Revised action or decision to fulfill the purpose

- Which actions on my to-do list shouldn't be there, because they have nothing to do with furthering the purpose of our company?

  List below which actions should no longer be on your to-do lists, and explain the reasons behind this decision. Use this list to show other team members how to eliminate activities not aligned with your purpose.

Item to be removed from to-do list	Why this activity no longer fits your purpose

Imagining the future and making it happen: While it's a good idea to start with the reality right in front of you, it's also useful to envision what's possible. A vivid and compelling vision of success is essential for ensuring that everyone is headed in the same direction.

Keeping the purpose in mind, imagine the most successful version of your organization. In this version, the purpose is in full throttle. Everyone in the organization is deeply connected and committed to the purpose. Customers' lives are being changed for the better. All your stakeholders feel it. What does this level of purpose-driven success look like for your company? Ask yourself these questions:

- **If we lived our purpose and were making the difference that we aspire to make, what would that look like three to five years from now? In the space below, describe what successfully living your purpose looks like in your mind's eye.**

_____

_____

_____

_____

_____

_____

_____

_____

_____

_____

_____

_____

_____

_____

_____

_____

- What measures of success—measures that align with the purpose—would we use to know that we had succeeded? List below three to five metrics that would capture the success of your purpose.

_____

_____

_____

_____

_____

_____

_____

_____

_____

_____

_____

_____

_____

_____

_____

_____

- With that vision in mind, what would we need to do over the next five years to make that vision a reality? List below the potential resources required and the changes that might have to happen for you to reach your vision.

_____

_____

_____

_____

_____

_____

_____

_____

Final Thoughts

Becoming a purpose-driven organization is a thrilling journey. But there is no button you can press to magically transport yourself to the final destination. How you choose to get there may evolve over time as your landscape and your leadership evolve over time. You might take some detours along the way. The destination you originally envisioned might even begin looking different the further you go on the journey. But if you keep your purpose as your North Star, if you remain determined to use your business as a force for good, you're in for the ride of your life. It's a path that will let you make money, possibly make history, and certainly make a difference.

In the following chapters, we will cover the other three tenets of Conscious Capitalism—stakeholder engagement, conscious culture, and conscious leadership—and connect them to purpose.

How to Discover the Purpose of Your Business

By Haley Rushing, cofounder and chief "purposologist" of the Purpose Institute.

URL: https://www.ccfieldguide.com/haley

Search Words: Conscious Capitalism Field Guide the Impact of a Business Purpose

Part Two

STAKEHOLDER ORIENTATION

*I*n this part of the book, we will focus on the stakeholder-orientation principle of Conscious Capitalism. We will describe the basic stakeholder concepts and move deeper into stakeholder orientation. Following that, we will discuss how to identify your stakeholders. We conclude with guidance on developing a win-win stakeholder orientation throughout the organization (figure P2-1 summarizes part 2).

Figure P2-1: Overview of part 2

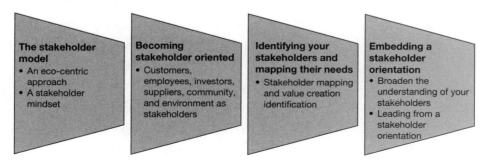

The stakeholder model
- An eco-centric approach
- A stakeholder mindset

Becoming stakeholder oriented
- Customers, employees, investors, suppliers, community, and environment as stakeholders

Identifying your stakeholders and mapping their needs
- Stakeholder mapping and value creation identification

Embedding a stakeholder orientation
- Broaden the understanding of your stakeholders
- Leading from a stakeholder orientation

A False Dichotomy

In a famous *New York Times* essay titled "The Social Responsibility of a Business Is to Increase Its Profits," economist Milton Friedman asserted in 1970 that a company's only real responsibility was to its shareholders. But that perspective separates human actors into two categories: means and ends. In this way of thinking, the well-being of shareholders is the end, and all other participants in the system are the means to that end. Such a mindset leads many companies to undervalue and underserve their employees, customers, suppliers, and other stakeholders.

Conscious businesses recognize that all stakeholders are means as well as ends. Each stakeholder contributes to overall value creation, and each needs to flourish for the business to achieve its purpose and its potential. Shareholders are important too, of course, but by reframing or zooming out to see that they are part of a greater whole, we can create more value for all.

As described earlier in the book, Ed Freeman frames the stakeholder approach thus: "Every business creates, and sometimes destroys, value for customers, suppliers, employees, communities and financiers. The idea that business is about maximizing profits for shareholders is outdated and doesn't work very well, as the recent global financial crisis has taught us. The 21st Century is one of 'Managing for Stakeholders.' The task of executives is to create as much value as possible for stakeholders without resorting to trade-offs. Great companies endure because they manage to get stakeholder interests aligned in the same direction."[1]

Executives do not merely serve the interest of shareholders; they have a direct impact on the well-being of other stakeholders. Business leaders are accountable to shareholders for returns, but are also accountable to employees, customers, and other stakeholders for different actions and results.[2] A shareholder-centric business consistently resolves most trade-offs in favor of shareholders, viewing them as the ultimate stakeholders. A stakeholder-oriented business keeps searching for creative options until it finds a way to simultaneously benefit both stakeholders and shareholders. POSCO, a highly admired South Korean steelmaker, has inscribed above the entrance to its steelworks in Pohang a message that summarizes this approach: "Resources are limited. Creativity is unlimited."

Stakeholder Management

By R. Edward Freeman, American philosopher and professor of business administration particularly known for his work on stakeholder theory originally published in his 1984 book Strategic Management: A Stakeholder Approach

URL: https://www.ccfieldguide.com/ed

Search Words: Conscious Capitalism Field Guide Stakeholder Management

Assessment of Stakeholder Orientation

RESPONDENTS: C-level executives and members of the board of directors

DESIRED NUMBER OF RESPONSES: 10

QUESTION	SCORE
1. In all our major strategic decisions, we explicitly consider the short- and long-term impacts on each of our stakeholders.	
2. We use metrics to track the well-being of each stakeholder, and these metrics are monitored at the highest levels within the company.	
3. We routinely engage stakeholders in dialogue and give them a voice in the company's direction.	
4. We recognize the interdependencies between our stakeholders, and we explicitly seek to achieve an integration of interests among them. In other words, we seek solutions that satisfy multiple stakeholders simultaneously.	
5. Our stakeholder-facing organization works to understand stakeholders deeply and serve them better over time.	
6. We overinvest in our stakeholders, devoting more time, money, and other resources to their needs than is typical in our industry.	
7. We actively engage with our most vocal critics so that we can learn from them how to realize our purpose and principles in a better way.	
8. Our company's relationships with all our stakeholders are characterized by great trust and goodwill.	
9. We realize that it is far better to engage with stakeholders and manage those relationships ourselves than it is to have the government involved in the process.	
10. We recognize that stakeholder needs and perspectives change over time. We have processes, therefore, that constantly monitor changes in the external environment so that we can better serve and respond to our stakeholders' needs as they evolve.	
TOTAL	

SCORES

5: We are exceptionally good at this, to the point that others should learn from us.

4: We demonstrate this most of the time, but there is room for improvement.

3: This is true for us sometimes, but our record overall is mixed.

2: This is rarely true for us.

0: We seem to embody the opposite of this, or it is missing entirely.

Add up your scores to identify the overall gap between your company and best practice (50 points). How did you score? What surprised you? What did not? Why? What are the implications?

_____

_____

_____

_____

_____

_____

_____

_____

Stakeholder orientation is typically one of the hardest diagnostics to score well on. Unless you have already introduced the concept and begun to bring it to life in the organization, you'll probably not score well here. You may have discovered in your organization some areas where you do this integration well, but others that need work.

Chapter 7

The Stakeholder Model

This chapter will cover basic stakeholder concepts as we move toward fostering a stakeholder orientation in the organization. We will explore the potential of basing value creation on a stakeholder approach, which is different from the traditional shareholder approach focused on profit maximization alone.

Stakeholders are all the entities connected to, and impacted by, the business. We can classify them as *inner circle* and *outer circle*. The interaction between the company and its inner-circle stakeholders is relational (i.e., two-way, sustained, and mutually value-creating) and voluntary, whereas relationships with outer-circle stakeholders are more episodic and often involuntary. Figure 7-1 gives examples of inner- and outer-circle stakeholders.

Figure 7-1: Stakeholder classification framework

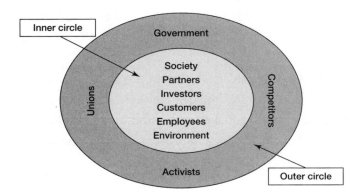

Our primary emphasis in part 2 will be on inner-circle stakeholders. Note that the term *society* includes the local communities in which the business operates as well as society as a whole.

Historically, relationships in the business world have been based on bargaining. This *trade-off* approach assumes that someone has to lose so that the other party involved can gain. As Ed Freeman has said, "Managing for stakeholders is not about trade-off thinking. It is about using innovation and entrepreneurship to make all key stakeholders better off and get all their interests going into the same direction."

Trade-offs have been explored in game theory and economic theory and defined through mathematical representations in which the utility gains from the winning participant are exactly balanced out by the losses of the losing participant. This is called a *zero-sum game* or a fixed-size pie approach. If one takes a larger slice, others will end with smaller slices. Conscious Capitalism is based on the belief that business has the power to create surplus value; it is the ultimate positive-sum game.

How we frame our connection with our stakeholders matters. We can view the connection in terms of the time frame we consider and the nature of that connection—a transaction or a relationship. Clearly, we interact with stakeholders differently in a long-term relationship than we do in in a short-term transaction. A transactional approach results in a zero-sum game, while a relational approach generates collaboration, innovation, and incremental value.

A long-term relationship is rooted in win-win thinking, by definition. It leads to greater trust and connection and hence to a more creative and innovative approach to business opportunities and challenges. Long-term relationships offer more opportunities for each party to invest in creating shared value. One might trade off a short-term gain for greater benefit in the long term. The explicit understanding is that by investing in the relationship now, both parties can potentially enjoy larger longer-term gains.

In committing to a stakeholder orientation, we must pay a minimally acceptable level of attention to each stakeholder. However, it is not possible or desirable to treat all stakeholders with equal attention and care. Therefore, it is important to identify those stakeholders where improvements in the relationship will yield greater impact on the business and the creation of shared value. This is a good working definition of what we mean by primary stakeholders.

A Failure of Imagination

US Supreme Court Justice Oliver Wendell Holmes Jr. once said, "I would not give a fig for the simplicity on this side of complexity, but I would give my life for the simplicity on the other side of complexity." The shareholder-centric view lies on this side of complexity; the stakeholder mindset exists on the other side.

A shareholder-centric view is not wrong per se; businesses do need to create value for shareholders, or they will not long endure. Nor can they achieve their purpose in a sustained and scalable way without paying attention to shareholders. But this view is simplistic and reflects a lack of imagination. It presumes a world filled with inevitable and unavoidable trade-offs. It underestimates the extraordinary capacity of human beings to find creative solutions to seemingly intractable dilemmas.

If you accept the idea that shareholders are the only end, you would deem it acceptable to squeeze other stakeholders to benefit your shareholders. Such a narrow, mechanistic view of a business considers financial, natural, and human resources as inputs and profit for the owners as the output. But a business is in fact a complex, living, adaptive system. Any unhealthy part of it can bring down the whole system, in the way that if one part of your body gets a serious infection, the whole body can die. Pioneering naturalist John Muir observed, "When you tug at a single thing in nature, you find it attached to the rest of the world." Such is also the case with the world of business, which is an intricate, interconnected, and interdependent web of relationships.

When you start to think about business this way, you recognize the inherent interdependence of stakeholders. In the long run—and it must always be about the long run—investors cannot profit unless customers are truly happy and satisfied. Customers cannot be truly happy and satisfied unless employees are fulfilled and have a sense of meaning in what they're doing. You cannot do any of that unless you have high-quality inputs, which is where suppliers come in. Because no business can flourish as an island of prosperity amid a sea of despair, the community's health and well-being is vital.

The acknowledgment of such concepts allows us to understand the impact of a disempowered, unengaged stakeholder. Some business leaders think they run a stand-alone organization that does not depend on anyone else. This egocentric mindset is losing its grip and giving way to the emergence of an ecosystem-centric mindset. The recognition of the interdependency of all stakeholders is the first step toward a more conscious stakeholder orientation.

One of the fundamental debates between Wall Street and Main Street over the next few years will be about either narrowing this potential disconnect between shareholders and stakeholders or allowing it to continue to grow. With the growth of activist investors looking to force short-term financial returns to boost short-term stock prices, the question of how best to create long-term value will move stakeholder orientation to the forefront of this debate. *How* one makes profits matters, and we believe the research will continue to provide solid evidence for a stakeholder-oriented, longer-term, systems view of value creation.

Key Principles

- Business is an interconnected, interdependent living organism, not a linear machine.

- In such an organism, it is folly to seek to maximize one aspect of its functioning. Rather, we must focus on the benefit of the whole.

- All the components of this system (the stakeholders) are both the means and the ends; they contribute to value creation in the system and receive different kinds of value from the system.

- Motivated by shared values and shared purpose, stakeholders are *givers to the system* rather than *takers from the system*. Paradoxically, they receive far more in return than they give. In summary, in order to win-win-win, you must give-give-give.[1]

Think Win-Win: Creation of Value versus Dividing Value

A stakeholder orientation must come from a win-win perspective. When we view stakeholder relationships as transactional or as win-lose interactions, then the result fails to create optimum value for the business. If we look for trade-offs, we are guaranteed to find them. If we see the world as a zero-sum game, we will find ourselves constantly facing and even creating these dynamics in our business.

On the other hand, if we look for synergies, we will probably find them. This shift in mindset is based on a more systematic view of the business ecosystem that we operate in. When we look to create value, we expand the total size of the pie, instead of arguing about how to divide the pie as it currently exists. This is a mindset of creation and innovation. John Mackey of Whole Foods Market captures this notion well: "Trade-offs and win-lose scenarios are fundamentally the result of a lack of creativity." Win-win is a fundamentally different way of approaching business problems—and it is not easy to do. However, tremendous value creation and innovation can result from approaching our stakeholder relationships with this mindset versus looking to maximize one stakeholder's position at the expense of others.

> Win-win is based on the paradigm that there is plenty for everybody, that one person's success is not achieved at the expense or exclusion of the success of others. Win-win is a belief in the Third Alternative. It's not your way or my way; it's a better way, a higher way.
>
> —Steven Covey, *The 7 Habits of Highly Effective People*

An Eco-Centric Approach

One way to understand the interdependency of the business ecosystem is to use systems thinking, which has its foundation in the field of system dynamics, originated by MIT professor Jay Forrester in 1956. Traditional analysis separates the individual pieces from the whole to study. In fact, the word *analysis* means to break something into its constituent parts. Systems thinking takes into account the interactions between the elements of the system.

To explore the idea of an eco-centric approach to stakeholders in more detail, consider the Declaration of Interdependence, which has been a guiding philosophy for Whole Foods Market since 1985, when the statement was crafted by sixty team members.[2] The interdependent elements at Whole Foods Market are depicted in figure 7-2.

The virtuous circle starts with the company's purpose and values. The company hires employees (referred to as team members) with values like its own;

Figure 7-2: Whole Foods Market's interdependent stakeholder approach

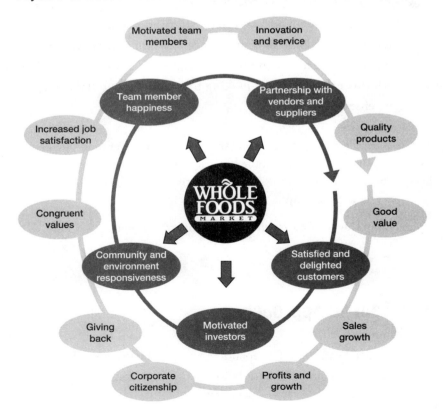

team members are also passionate about food and health. It makes sure team members are happy with the work they do and what the company offers them in terms of working conditions, benefits, and compensation. A motivated team will be creative and search for innovation on service and products offering. The team's creativity and innovation will lead it to form partnerships with vendors and suppliers. These suppliers contribute with better quality and innovative products with more value. Better products and outstanding service generate greater customer satisfaction, which results in better growth and profits for the organization. The improved financial results motivate investors and enable the company to give more back to its communities and environmental causes. These contributions generate strong responses from communities. The congruent values increase community and employee pride and elevate job satisfaction. And again, we start the virtuous cycle of shared value creation and strengthening the network through the strengthening of interdependencies.

In the business world, acknowledging and leveraging interdependency leads to the possibility of win-win value creation. It becomes a value-based exchange, in which stakeholders search for innovative ways to create more value. Note that like a clock, this virtuous circle only runs clockwise. The financial results are a consequence of the value created for and by the different stakeholders.

A Stakeholder Mindset

How we look at the world affects what we see. If I ask you to look around the room and notice everything that is red, you will pay attention to what is red. If I ask you to close your eyes and recount all the things that are green in the room, you are unlikely to recall any. When you open your eyes, you can immediately identify several green items that were in your environment, but because you weren't focused on them, you didn't see them.

So too with stakeholder orientation. When we look for win-win opportunities to create shared value, we are much more likely to find them. If we look for trade-offs, we will find ourselves surrounded by them.

Thus, a critical element in the implementation of a stakeholder orientation is that the leadership team take a long-term, systems, and relational view of the connection with stakeholders. A stakeholder orientation begins with thinking about our stakeholders differently and making them an integral part of how we operate as a business. The next chapter addresses the practical elements of identifying and working with stakeholders differently by getting clear about what their needs are and what this means in your organization.

Chapter 8

Becoming Stakeholder Oriented

In this chapter, we will navigate through some of the key stakeholders and explore value-creation opportunities with each of them. We will examine customer trust and loyalty, employee engagement, committed and patient investors, collaborative suppliers, welcoming communities, and healthy environments.

In a capitalist world, where all exchanges are voluntary, value needs to be created constantly between all stakeholders so that the relationships persist over time and the business experiences long-lasting results to benefit all its stakeholders, including society (figure 8-1).

Figure 8-1: Stakeholder interdependency map

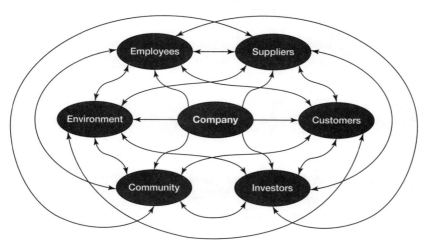

Customers as Stakeholders

In the traditional view of business, customers are seen as targets—the objects of our attention as a business. They are the means to an end of generating revenues and thus profits.

What does it mean to think of customers as stakeholders instead? We recognize that customers are the reason the business exists. Their well-being should be an end in itself, not merely a means to generate profits. Serving customers well means that we deeply understand their real needs, not just cater to their desires. We recognize the growing potential for the cocreation of value with customers; our customers can help us expand the frontiers of what is possible with our products and services. We use the tools and techniques of marketing to better serve customers instead of manipulating them. As auto retailer Herb Chambers in the Boston area proclaims, "We don't sell cars. We help people buy them."

Treating customers as stakeholders also implies two-way loyalty and advocacy. Satisfied and delighted customers become advocates on the company's behalf, making others aware of what the company has to offer. Companies act as advocates on behalf of their customers. In the extreme, this means that if you realize that your competitor's offering will best serve your customer's needs, you should steer the customer to that competitor. You lose the transaction but build trust and strengthen the relationship.

Adopting a stakeholder orientation toward customers implies a duty on the part of the company to employ these practices:

- Continually innovate on behalf of the customer; expand what is possible.

- Educate the customers by informing and inspiring them to improve the quality of their lives.

- Refrain from taking advantage of the customers' vulnerabilities. This practice includes not engaging in opportunistic pricing.

- Focus always on what you believe to be best for the customer.

- Earn the customer's trust by always operating with complete integrity.

- Take full responsibility, and stand behind your offering.

This approach has other economic benefits. Conscious businesses generally rely less on paid marketing than most firms. The book *Firms of Endearment* explores how highly loved companies operate with minimum marketing budgets.[1] Their strength lies in positive word of mouth based on the daily experience that customers have with the company's products and services, rather than bombarding messages to convince people to consume.

Assessment of Customer Orientation as Stakeholders

RESPONDENTS: C-level executives, marketing executives, and representative customers

DESIRED NUMBER OF RESPONSES: 10 executives, 100 customers; do not merge responses

QUESTION		SCORE
1.	We place great emphasis on providing a high level of value to our customers.	
2.	We strive to create a great experience for customers when they interact with us.	
3.	Our goal is to be the most reliable supplier possible for our customers.	
4.	When our customers have unusual requirements, we work with them to make sure that they are fully satisfied.	
5.	Our customer-facing employees are highly skilled at being empathetic listeners to customers.	
6.	We place great emphasis on making it as convenient as possible for customers to do business with us.	
7.	Rather than looking to maximize the quantity of sales, we are more focused on enhancing the quality of life for our customers.	
8.	We have designed our systems and created a culture in which we are constantly becoming better at understanding our customers and serving even their unrecognized needs.	
9.	Our approach with customers is based on building, growing, and enriching a mutually beneficial relationship with them, rather than focusing on individual transactions.	
10.	We operate as advocates and trusted advisers on behalf of our customers. In practice, this means that sometimes we may advise a customer to buy products from other suppliers when we believe it is in the customer's best interest.	
11.	Our customers are so satisfied with us that they routinely recommend us to other potential customers.	
12.	We are very authentic and transparent in all our dealings with customers. We never overpromise in order to win a sale, and we always own up to our responsibility when something goes wrong.	
13.	We believe that educated customers make the best choices for themselves and for us in the long term. We make sure that every customer is fully informed before every business transaction.	

QUESTION	SCORE
14. Our customer satisfaction levels are significantly higher than the norm in our industry and have been increasing in recent years.	
15. Our customer loyalty levels are significantly higher than the norm in our industry and have been increasing in recent years.	
16. Our customer trust levels are significantly higher than the norm in our industry and have been increasing in recent years.	
17. Even though they may not own any shares in our business, our customers exhibit a sense of ownership in their dealings with us.	
18. We understand our customers so deeply that we meet the needs that they did not even know they had.	
19. Our marketing efforts are deeply focused on uncovering and serving true customer needs, not just catering to desires.	
20. Our customers are a significant source of new ideas for our business, and we have a formal process of involving them in long-term strategic planning.	
TOTAL	

SCORES

5: We are exceptionally good at this, to the point that others should learn from us.

4: We demonstrate this most of the time, but there is room for improvement.

3: This is true for us sometimes, but our record overall is mixed.

2: This is rarely true for us.

0: We seem to embody the opposite of this, or it is missing entirely.

Add up your scores to identify the overall gap between your company and best practice (100 points). How did you score? What surprised you? What did not? Why? What are the implications?

_____

_____

_____

_____

_____

_____

_____

_____

Employees as Stakeholders

Traditional businesses treat employees as a resource, alongside other resources such as financial capital and raw materials. Employees are seen as a cost to be minimized, and their value begins and ends with their ability to help the company make more money.

One of the corporate world's most serious and enduring problems is employee engagement—the extent to which employees care about their work enough to do more than the bare minimum needed to keep their jobs. Year after year, the Gallup organization releases new data about employee engagement. In the United States, engagement has been in the 30 percent range for over a decade, with few signs of improvement. It is a shockingly low 13 percent worldwide. This trend places a tremendous drag on the organization and on all other stakeholders. It is also an extraordinary waste of human potential. The fault doesn't lie with the people; responsibility for disengagement rests squarely with managers and leaders.

What does it mean to treat employees as stakeholders? First, we need to recognize the central role that they play in creating value. We must appreciate that human beings are not a resource; they are a source. They are capable of extraordinary acts of innovation, creativity, and caring. Employees deserve to be cared for, inspired, recognized, and celebrated. Their well-being and that of their families is inherently important. It means recognizing that their work is an inherent part of their identity and can be a source of deep fulfillment and meaning.

A stakeholder orientation toward employees implies a duty on the part of the company to adopt certain practices:

- Treat each employee as a precious human being.

- Strive to be a good steward of their lives.

- Give them opportunities to grow and evolve.

- Help heal them and make them whole.

- Empower them to share their gifts and realize their potential.

As Bob Chapman, CEO of Barry-Wehmiller, says, "Take care of the people, and they will take care of the business." How you treat people will ultimately dictate how much contribution you get in return.

Assessment of Employee Orientation as Stakeholders

RESPONDENTS: C-level executives, HR executives, and representative employees

DESIRED NUMBER OF RESPONSES: 10 executives and 100 employees; do not merge responses

QUESTION		SCORE
1.	Our frontline employees are better paid than their peers in the industry.	
2.	We provide generous health benefits (including incentives for employee wellness) and reasonable and prudent retirement benefits to all our employees, including part-time workers.	
3.	We encourage our employees to maintain a healthy balance between their work and personal lives.	
4.	Our company has many family-friendly policies, such as flextime, parental leave, and on-site day care.	
5.	There is a high degree of collegiality and caring in our work culture. This includes a great deal of teamwork and team-based operations.	
6.	Our employees are a significant source of new ideas for our business, and we have a formal process of involving them in long-term strategic planning.	
7.	We encourage reasonable risk taking. Failures are not frowned on, but employees are expected to learn from them.	
8.	Our employees are given much autonomy to pursue projects that are personally relevant and reflect their own passions.	
9.	We routinely recognize and celebrate employee efforts and achievements.	
10.	We design jobs in such a way that they offer employees rich opportunities for growth and mastery.	
11.	We are extremely careful in the hiring process to ensure that we bring in employees for whom the work that we do as a company has inherent meaning and value.	
12.	We share with our employees a great deal of information, including information about our financial performance, our strategic priorities, and our areas of greatest concern.	
13.	We provide employees opportunities to engage in meaningful community development projects on company time.	
14.	Our company operates with fewer layers between the CEO and frontline workers than there are for the industry norm.	

QUESTION	SCORE
15. When we hire employees, we try to assess their emotional, cultural, and social intelligence.	
16. Our internal research shows that our employee engagement levels are much higher than the norm.	
17. We generally promote people from within rather than hiring from the outside.	
18. We actively foster diversity in ideas, backgrounds, and experiences.	
19. A high proportion of our new hires comes through referrals by our own existing employees.	
20. We provide our employees with training and resources to help them collaborate better and to develop win-win solutions rather than settling for compromises.	
TOTAL	

SCORES

5: We are exceptionally good at this, to the point that others should learn from us.

4: We demonstrate this most of the time, but there is room for improvement.

3: This is true for us sometimes, but our record overall is mixed.

2: This is rarely true for us.

0: We seem to embody the opposite of this, or it is missing entirely.

Add up your scores to identify the overall gap between your company and best practice (100 points). How did you score? What surprised you? What did not? Why? What are the implications?

_____

_____

_____

_____

_____

_____

_____

_____

Investors as Stakeholders

When a founder's passion and people's talents meet the needs of the society, a purposeful business is born. When capital joins this equation, it can amplify and accelerate the impact and success of the business. Investors have a fundamental importance in the capitalist system. However, capital often distorts the process. An approach predicated on the relentless extraction of financial results in the short term does not serve people, the company, or the larger societal system well. As Tom Gardner, CEO and cofounder of the Motley Fool, says, "Short-term investing is an oxymoron. It is not investing at all; it is just speculation. Investing, by definition, is for the long term."[2]

Traditional companies treat investors or shareholders as the only stakeholders who matter. These companies cater to their shareholders' short-term expectations, often manipulating the numbers, delaying investments, squeezing their suppliers and employees, cutting corners with customers, and externalizing burdens onto society and the environment. They treat all investors the same way, exercising no discretion in whom they choose to bring in as investors. They assume that all investors are looking for the same thing: the highest possible returns in the shortest possible time.

What does it mean to treat investors as stakeholders? It means recognizing and respecting their role as enablers of the growth and expansion of the business and as legitimate claimants on its residual profits. It means understanding that not all investors are looking for the same things and that not all investors have the same time horizon. Treating shareholders as stakeholders may require more time to find the capital sources that are aligned with your vision, but in the longer term, this alignment is critical. True investors are in it for the long haul, and they view their capital as a way to have an impact and leave a legacy, in addition to generating a good return. Conscious companies maintain strong relationships with true investors and are selective in whom they choose to partner with.

To adopt a stakeholder orientation toward investors, a company should follow these practices:

- Be transparent about the company's purpose, plans, constraints, risks, and opportunities.

- Engage in ongoing and frequent communications with key investors.

- Be a good steward of the financial capital the firm has been entrusted with.

- Seek alignment on the time frames and the mindsets related to how the business builds value over time.

- Focus on creating superior long-term value for investors without hurting other stakeholders.

One of the defining moments in the history of the Motley Fool's business was the decision that the founders, Tom and David Gardner, made to buy out the venture investors who had funded the firm's early growth. The Gardners had a fundamentally different perspective on how to run the business and the time frame for value creation then did the VC investors. The resulting tension was not healthy for the organization. The initial period after the buyout created some financial challenges, but in the long term, the buyout enabled the longer-term success of the business. The decision has enabled the Gardners to manage with a stakeholder mindset and to create value through long-term relationships.

Investors are slowly changing despite the legacy of the financial services industry. New funds being created now consider subjective indicators as well as objective financial metrics for decision making. Another idea receiving significant attention is impact investment. Impact investing begins with a focus on the impact an organization is trying to have on the world. This fulfillment of purpose or impact becomes the main indicator of success. Sometimes, though not always, investors put less focus on the overall financial return on the investment and more emphasis on creating this social impact on the world. We need to understand what true investors, not speculators, expect in terms of value creation, if we are to better serve them as stakeholders.

An important trend over the past several years has been the rapid rise of the *benefit corporation*, or B Corp, movement. This movement is an important mechanism for companies to enshrine a stakeholder orientation into their legal charter. See the sidebar "B Corps and Conscious Capitalism," by Jay Coen Gilbert, and appendix A, which provide further details on B Corps and the assessment methodology they use to track the stakeholder orientation of companies.

Benefit Corps and Conscious Capitalism

By Jay Coen Gilbert, cofounder of B Lab and the B Corp movement

One of the most powerful tools available to conscious capitalists . . . is to adopt a corporate structure like the benefit corporation.* The benefit corporation legal structure embeds a stakeholder orientation into the legal DNA of the company through an expansion of the fiduciary duty of the corporation's board of directors and officers (i.e., C-suite management). This expansion of fiduciary duty creates a legal obligation for all directors and officers to consider the impact of their decisions on all stakeholders, not just shareholders. This legal change means that stakeholders can rely on the law, not just a higher state of consciousness in heroic leaders, to ensure that their interests are considered when the company makes decisions. Among other benefits, this legal commitment creates additional room for boards and directors when dealing with activist investors who are focused on short-term share

Source: Jay Coen Gilbert, "Can Conscious Capitalism Survive Amazon? Or the Public Capital Markets?" *Forbes*, June 27, 2017, www.forbes.com/sites/groupthink/2017/06/27/can-conscious-capitalism-survive-amazon-or-the-public-capital-markets/#2cfa98dd4629.

price and not long-term stakeholder value creation. This might have been useful, for example, for Whole Foods. And it may be a big part of why Danone recently adopted the benefit corporation legal structure for its US subsidiary, DanoneWave (the entity with more than $6 billion in revenues that was created after Danone acquired WhiteWave for $10 billion last year and merged it with its existing US business—WhiteWave is the owner of brands Silk, Horizon Organics, Wallaby, and Earthbound Farms). Danone's plans may not stop there as Danone became the first *Fortune* 500 company to publicly state its intention to adopt this legal standard as part of its long-term goal to become a Certified B Corporation. Lorna Davis, CEO of DanoneWave, said: "In 10 years' time, people will say it's inconceivable that business was done any other way. The notion that a company can only care about profit will be seen as old-fashioned and irresponsible."

In addition to this increased legal accountability, benefit corporations are obligated to meet higher standards of public transparency by publishing an assessment of the company's overall social and environmental performance. (In best practice, this assessment is verified against a credible, third-party standard.) By increasing accountability and transparency, benefit corporations align and reinforce conscious-capitalist corporate cultures, build trust among all stakeholders, and, as a result, create more long-term value for shareholders and society.

An increasing number of large, institutional investors believe this to be so. As one example, here is an excerpt from the most recent annual letter sent to S&P CEOs by Larry Fink, CEO of Blackrock, the world's largest asset manager: "Environmental, social, and governance (ESG) factors relevant to a company's business can provide essential insights into management effectiveness and thus a company's long-term prospects. We look to see that a company is attuned to the key factors that contribute to long-term growth: sustainability of the business model and its operations, attention to external and environmental factors that could impact the company, and recognition of the company's role as a member of the communities in which it operates."

The benefit corporation legal structure is the strongest corporate governance tool yet available to meet these stated needs of long-term value creation, and to address the virus of short-termism that plagues the public capital markets. It is this short-term mindset that can be especially challenging for conscious capitalists like Whole Foods, Etsy, or Unilever. (For a more detailed legal analysis on how the benefit corporation structure can support long-term value creation and stakeholder orientation, read "Saving Shareholders from Themselves," originally published in the Harvard Law School Forum on Corporate Governance and Financial Regulation.)

That being said, best-in-class ESG governance may be necessary, but it is not sufficient for conscious capitalists to thrive "under new ownership" or in the public capital markets.

Conscious capitalists (and their investors) need best-in-class management tools to assess their performance in managing their business with a stakeholder orientation. One such tool, currently used by more than 60,000 businesses; recommended by Conscious Capitalism, Inc. and The B Team; and used by scores of impact investors is the B Impact Assessment. It is a free, confidential tool that makes it easier for companies to assess, compare, and improve their performance in creating value for all their non-financial stakeholders—their workers, suppliers, customers, communities, and the environment. The B Impact Assessment is being used by small businesses and by multibillion-dollar multinationals, including Danone and BanColombia.

If the Conscious Capitalism movement is to survive, let alone thrive, over the long term in the public capital markets, then conscious capitalists will be best served not only to hope that new owners will "make good on their promise," but also to employ best-in-class stakeholder governance and management tools to help them live fully into their values under any ownership.

Which brings us back to whether Whole Foods' conscious capitalist practices will survive inside Amazon. John Mackey is hopeful: "One thing I absolutely love . . . about Amazon is they think long term. They have had the courage that almost no other public company has had . . . to . . . resist the drumbeat of short-term, quarterly earnings that have had us trapped here for a couple of years."

That may be true. But, for Conscious Capitalism to thrive—not only inside Amazon but also more broadly inside the public capital markets—it might be helpful if John Mackey and Jeff Bezos combined their visionary leadership to inspire countless conscious capitalists to embed their principles into the legal DNA of their company by turning Whole Foods into the largest benefit corporation in the world. This would not only benefit Whole Foods and Amazon, but it would also benefit the Conscious Capitalism movement by demonstrating how a conscious company can be built to last and by offering all of their stakeholders a credible, comparable, third-party-verified assessment of their progress in maintaining, or even unleashing more of, their heroic spirit.

What kind of investors does your organization have? How much do they agree with your approach to a longer-term value-creation model based on a stakeholder orientation?

_____

_____

_____

_____

_____

_____

_____

_____

What are their expectations regarding the business and its results?

_____

_____

_____

_____

_____

_____

_____

_____

Assessment of Investor Orientation as Stakeholders

RESPONDENTS: C-level executives and investor relations executives

DESIRED NUMBER OF RESPONSES: 10

QUESTION	SCORE
1. We look for investors who take a long-term perspective rather than those looking for quick returns.	
2. As a general principle, we do not believe that it is good corporate practice to buy back our own shares.	
3. The leaders of our company are motivated to create sustainable long-term value for investors, not to increase the short-term stock price.	
4. Our largest shareholders have a deep and close understanding of our purpose, culture, and long-term strategic vision.	
5. We engage in honest, direct, and regular communications with our key investors.	
6. We believe in great transparency in reporting financial results and potential business risks.	
7. Stock ownership is widely distributed among our employees.	
8. Our customers and suppliers own a significant amount of stock in our company.	
9. The interests of our key investors go considerably beyond making a good return; the investors are also interested in helping us fulfill our purpose of having a positive impact on society.	
10. Our key investors do not interfere in the day-to-day operations of our business and do not pressure us to engage in short-term actions.	
TOTAL	

SCORES

5: We are exceptionally good at this, to the point that others should learn from us.

4: We demonstrate this most of the time, but there is room for improvement.

3: This is true for us sometimes, but our record overall is mixed.

2: This is rarely true for us.

0: We seem to embody the opposite of this, or it is missing entirely.

Add up your scores to identify the overall gap between your company and best practice (50 points). How did you score? What surprised you? What did not? Why? What are the implications?

_____

_____

_____

_____

_____

_____

_____

_____

_____

Suppliers as Stakeholders

Of all the stakeholders, suppliers have traditionally been the most neglected and abused. Even somewhat conscious companies often view suppliers as outsiders and do not prioritize their well-being. Traditional companies see suppliers as completely interchangeable and make getting the lowest price their highest priority. They have little concern for the supplier's ability to generate a profit, stay in business, and invest in the future. Supplier relations at many companies are an exercise in brute power and domination. Many companies try to unilaterally dictate terms to their suppliers, threatening to walk away if the suppliers do not comply. Such companies seek to enhance their own profits at the expense of their suppliers.

In the 1990s, a "purchasing czar" at GM made a unilateral decision that the company would simply pay all its suppliers less as a way to reduce supply costs and boost profits. In the short term, this decision generated significant incremental profit for the company and was well appreciated by analysts and shareholders. Most suppliers could not afford to abandon the relationship and had to endure the short-term consequences. But in the medium and long term, higher-quality suppliers refused to cooperate on the development of innovative products with GM. The automaker's focus was on cutting costs year after year—seeking to substitute increasingly cheaper parts and materials to meet the unrelenting cost pressure. This approach affected car quality and greatly harmed GM's market position and boosted the perception of its brand as one of lower quality than that of Japanese and German competitors.

What does it mean to treat suppliers as stakeholders? It is primarily about mutual respect and the recognition of interdependence. Suppliers today make up an ever larger proportion of the total value that a company offers to its customers. The quality of those inputs and suppliers' ability to continuously innovate are crucial to the success of every business. Treating suppliers as stakeholders requires openness on both sides, dedicated investments in facilities and processes for mutual benefit, long time horizons, and the desire to work together to help the partner improve and search for innovative ways to create value.

> *"Fill the other guy's basket to the brim. Making money then becomes an easy proposition.*"*
>
> *This is a quote from Andrew Carnegie, the famous industrialist and philanthropist, who attributed all of his success to this simple adage. It has become our business philosophy, encouraging us to creatively craft mutually beneficial relationships with our vendors. New vendors are typically shocked when we explain this principle to them and ask them, "What can we do to fill your basket to the brim? How can we help you succeed?"*
>
> *Many of our vendors are thriving small businesses who say they wouldn't even be solvent today without our support. And this is how The Container Store can compete on pricing with some of the mass merchants. Somebody has to get that last pallet of the vendors' hottest product—and it's usually us, because of our great relationships. Some businesspeople think they have to exploit the other party to succeed. (Then they say, "Don't take it personally—it's just business.")*
>
> *How can you separate your personal and business values? Do you treat your business relationships differently than you would treat your friendships? Simply put, the more win-win situations you can create, the more you'll*

succeed in everything you do. After all, business is not a zero-sum game. Nobody has to lose for someone else to win.

—**Kip Tindell, cofounder and chairman, The Container Store**

Source: This article is from "What We Stand For: Organization with Heart," The Container Store web page, accessed August 17, 2017, http://standfor.containerstore.com/our-foundation-principles/fill-the-other-guys-basket.

Adopting a stakeholder orientation toward suppliers implies a duty on the part of the company to take these approaches:

- Have a commitment to co-prosperity.

- Be fair and transparent in all interactions.

- Refrain from making sudden, unilateral decisions.

- Engage with key suppliers at the leadership level and in the formulation of strategy, not just through the purchasing department.

- Have a commitment to mutual learning and growth.

- Help suppliers become conscious businesses themselves.

What have been the biggest contributions that your suppliers made to your business in the last twelve months? Can you identify their motivations for this assistance? How can you create more such contributions?

_____

_____

_____

_____

_____

_____

_____

_____

What have you done to create more value for your suppliers?

_____

_____

_____

_____

_____

_____

_____

What more could you do?

_____

_____

_____

_____

_____

_____

_____

Assessment of Supplier Orientation as Stakeholders

RESPONDENTS: C-level executives, purchasing executives, and key suppliers (keep the responses from each group separate)

DESIRED NUMBER OF RESPONSES: 5 from each category

QUESTION	SCORE
1. Our relationships with suppliers are not based on power or domination but are based on mutual trust and respect. We are committed to being the best customers we can be.	
2. When there is a disagreement, we don't settle for a compromise; we search for a mutually satisfying, win-win outcome.	
3. We are committed to the long-term success of our business partners.	
4. We have a transparent process that enables suppliers to understand how well they're doing in meeting our needs. When there is a problem, we work with them to help resolve it, rather than simply walking away.	
5. We have a strong commitment to fairness in our dealings with all suppliers.	
6. We view our suppliers as long-term strategic partners, not just as vendors of standardized commodities. Through this process, we and our suppliers grow as companies and can increase the scale and scope of our business as well.	
7. There is consistent ongoing communication between us and our partners, including at the level of senior executives. We strive to build mutual trust.	
8. We exercise great care in selecting our business partners. We look to do business with suppliers with which we feel there is a strong level of cultural fit. As we grow as a company, our suppliers grow with us.	
9. In recent years, we have reduced the total number of suppliers and increased the amount of business that we do with each.	
10. We have high and explicit standards for suppliers' conduct in terms of their ethical business practices and how they in turn treat their own suppliers.	
11. We collaborate with partners to develop a greater number of innovative solutions than we could develop on our own.	
12. We monitor and take responsibility for practices throughout our supply chain, including, for example, the suppliers to our suppliers.	
TOTAL	

SCORES

5: We are exceptionally good at this, to the point that others should learn from us.

4: We demonstrate this most of the time, but there is room for improvement.

3: This is true for us sometimes, but our record overall is mixed.

2: This is rarely true for us.

0: We seem to embody the opposite of this, or it is missing entirely.

Add up your scores to identify the overall gap between your company and best practice (60 points). How did you score? What surprised you? What did not? Why? What are the implications?

_____

_____

_____

_____

_____

_____

_____

_____

Communities as Stakeholders

Companies forget that they are part of the community. Communities start out with the assumption that business will not really participate. If you set aside old assumptions and truly listen, you can imagine a new relationship between a company and a community. You connect with them, you are part of them.

—**Walter Robb, former co-CEO, Whole Foods Market**

Traditional companies pay little attention to the communities in which they operate. They view communities as interchangeable with one another and seldom put down deep roots. They go to great lengths to secure favorable terms for themselves, pressuring communities for incentives and tax breaks. They do not hesitate to walk away from communities if an opportunity to lower the cost of doing business presents itself.

Purpose-driven companies exist to make a positive impact on society. They improve the community while carrying out their business. Even if they spend no money on philanthropy or lack a corporate social responsibility department, they still make a positive impact on society through their core business.

Nevertheless, companies that connect and share values with the community can also be strong philanthropists. The philanthropy doesn't come at the expense of investors; it goes toward leveraging the company's purpose, creating a sense of pride and improving the organization's reputation with all stakeholders engaged with the cause. This earned goodwill attracts new customers, employees, investors, and suppliers.

What does it mean to treat the community as a stakeholder? You have a real sense of belonging and a desire to be part of the community for the long term. You consult with community leaders and seek their inputs before making major decisions. The company is sensitive to both global and local concerns and elevates community standards to higher levels. You are committed to source locally to the extent possible and to encourage employees to become active members of the community.

When Whole Foods Market's only store was virtually destroyed in the Memorial Day flood of 1981, it was members of the community who showed up a day after the tragic night in Austin, Texas. They helped clean up the area and get their neighborhood grocery open again. This act elevated the community as a primary stakeholder. To this day, Whole Foods Market requires that each of its 450 locations donate 5 percent of its earnings to local community organizations chosen by the store.

Adopting a stakeholder orientation toward communities implies a duty on the part of the company to follow these approaches:

- Do what you can, within your realm of expertise and business focus, to improve conditions within the community.

- Create hope and opportunity in the local community by, for example, stimulating entrepreneurial activity.

- Have a commitment to stay in the community as long as possible, despite short-term pressures and inducements to move to lower-cost locations.

- Work cooperatively with community leaders and other companies to elevate business practices.

What is the state of your relationship with the communities you operate in today? Why is this? What are the community needs that you and the community could work on together?

_____

_____

_____

_____

_____

_____

_____

How could this cooperation impact your business? Your employees? What is one area where you might make a difference in the community?

_____

_____

_____

_____

_____

_____

_____

Assessment of Community Orientation as Stakeholders

RESPONDENTS: C-level executives and community affairs executives

DESIRED NUMBER OF RESPONSES: 10

QUESTION	SCORE
1. We can say with great confidence that our business is on the right side of society. In other words, our company creates a great deal of value and improves the welfare of the communities in which it operates and in society as a whole.	
2. Our employees are highly involved in thinking about and suggesting how our actions can be more closely aligned with the needs of society.	
3. Our commitment to environmental stewardship goes considerably beyond carbon neutrality. We seek to improve the quality of the natural environment wherever we are present in the world.	
4. Our company regularly provides more financial support than do others in our industry to organizations engaged in activities beneficial both to our business interests and to the interests of society.	
5. We make our capabilities and infrastructure available in the service of public goals when the need arises.	
6. As we grow as a company, our impact on and obligations to society also grow. We seek to address serious challenges and major opportunities that exist in the world, often in conjunction with governments and sometimes in partnership with our competitors.	
7. Our commitment to society is deep and heartfelt and includes the active involvement of former senior management as well as our board of directors.	
8. The leaders of our company live in the communities in which we operate and are active participants in civil society as fully engaged citizens.	
9. We work with our competitors and the government in support of enlightened regulations that create a level playing field as well as ensure high standards of conduct and a positive net impact on society.	
10. When embarking on any new initiative, we take care to involve members of the community at a very early stage of our discussions to ensure that we have taken all perspectives into account.	
TOTAL	

SCORES

5: We are exceptionally good at this, to the point that others should learn from us.

4: We demonstrate this most of the time, but there is room for improvement.

3: This is true for us sometimes, but our record overall is mixed.

2: This is rarely true for us.

0: We seem to embody the opposite of this, or it is missing entirely.

Add up your scores to identify the overall gap between your company and best practice (50 points). How did you score? What surprised you? What did not? Why? What are the implications?

_____

_____

_____

_____

_____

_____

_____

_____

_____

The Environment as a Stakeholder

For twenty-one years, I never gave a thought to what we would be taking from the earth or doing to the earth in the making of our product . . . I did not have an environmental vision . . . Unless we can make our carpet sustainable, we might not have a place in the world . . . One day in this journey, it dawned on me that the way I was running Interface is the way of a plunderer. Plundering something that is not mine, that belongs to every creature on earth.

> —Ray Anderson, late CEO of Interface Carpets,
> in the documentary _The Corporation_

Historically, businesses have tended to treat the planet as an infinite source and an infinite sink. They have acted as though there is no end to natural nonrenewable resources and no limit to the planet's capacity to absorb the harmful by-products of business, such as polluting emissions, toxic chemicals, or plastic waste. Many companies are starting to take a closer look at their ecological footprint. Truly conscious organizations go further, treating the environment as a key stakeholder. As they do with every other stakeholder, they consciously seek to create value for that stakeholder—not just do less harm. Patagonia, one company that considers the product's environmental impact in deciding what to launch or sell, has over time eliminated components, colors, and materials that hurt the environment.

It has been estimated that if all seven-billion-plus people in the world consume at the same rate and in the same manner as do people in the United States, we would require the resources equivalent to several planets earth. When you recognize the environment as a stakeholder, it releases the extraordinary creative potential of human beings to make a positive difference. See the sidebar "Sustainability as a Good Investment for Business."

Ray Anderson's Shift Toward a Conscious Business

By Ray Anderson, former CEO of Interface

Excerpt from the documentary *The Corporation* about Ray Anderson's shift toward a more conscious business.

URL: **https://www.ccfieldguide.com/ray**

Search Words: **Conscious Capitalism Field Guide Shift Toward a Conscious Business**

Sustainability as a Good Investment for Business

By Chuck Fowler, chairman of Fairmount Santrol Mining

Fairmount Santrol is one of the largest producers of industrial sand and value-add sand products in North America, serving the oil and gas, foundry, glass, water filtration, building products, and sports and recreation markets. I cofounded this company in 1986 with a deep understanding of our responsibilities to the communities in which we operate and the importance of treating them with great respect. Since early in our company's history, sustainable development (SD) has been important to how we do business. The leadership team believes SD is necessary and integral to who we are as an organization.

As Fairmount Santrol grew through acquisitions and organically, the leadership team established our legacy commitment to SD and appreciative inquiry, and this commitment endured as we united our merging organizations. Developed at Case Western Reserve University, appreciative inquiry is a strengths-based approach to whole-systems change. The approach is used by organizations worldwide to advance growth and engagement. We at Fairmount Santrol implanted the practices of SD and appreciative inquiry in our culture. Ignoring any boundaries in terms of hierarchy, we encouraged a diverse group of employees,

or "family members," to get together in one room to work on a common goal.

The knowledge and perspectives of our family members have been vital in shaping our company and its future. Every three or four years, we host a companywide Appreciative Inquiry Summit and invite important external stakeholders to participate as well. We held our first large-scale summit in 2005, bringing together more than 80 percent of our workforce. Including such a high percentage of family members was a significant undertaking since it meant that we had to stop production in the plants. We headed into this summit with the goal of collectively formalizing our SD program—a task so important that we thought it was imperative for as many family members as possible to participate. At every summit, we employ the appreciative-inquiry methodology to encourage family members to discover our collective core strengths, to dream of a possible future, and to design a plan to achieve our vision. From these dreaming sessions, our formal SD program emerged, with thirteen SD teams today organizing our efforts. These teams focus on zero waste, clean water, best practices, sustainable mobility, supply chain, energy efficiency, tree planting, safety, community volunteering, health and wellness, training and development, new product development, and innovation.

Our most recent Appreciative Inquiry Summit, in 2014, was facilitated by our partners David Cooperrider and Ron Fry of Case Western Reserve University. At the summit, almost five hundred family members representing every functional area within our business—as well as external stakeholders such as neighbors, partners, community leaders, and customers—united near Chicago. We dedicated our time to boldly cocreating our vision for the future and defining the necessary steps to realize it. Discussions initiated at the summit powerfully accelerate our collaborative, driven culture and support our original endeavor to be leaders in SD. The summit led to further growth of our thirteen SD teams, with approximately ninety family members joining a new SD team.

Each year, our SD advisory committee and SD teams set big and bold goals that benefit both our business and the world around us. Over the year, we closely monitor and measure progress on our goals. To reward our family members for staying true to our commitment, we provide financial incentives for collectively achieving SD goals as an organization, with 20 percent of the annual bonus determined by our success.

SD goals have a positive impact on the three pillars of SD—people, planet, and prosperity.

For example, in 2015, when one of our SD teams focused on training and development, the efforts ultimately resulted in over 80 percent of the company completing a financial wellness course.

Participating on an SD team, leading a subteam, and eventually becoming a team leader or coleader provides an excellent development opportunity and exposure to colleagues from across the organization. Through their participation on an SD team, family members can challenge themselves, deepen their skill set, and work with peers outside their department. The teams typically have at least one face-to-face meeting per year to design their future and set new goals. At the end of the year, team leaders and SD advisory committee members have an annual meeting to celebrate successes and plan for the new year.

Some 2016 SD achievements include the following:

- The company outperformed the industry-average lost-time incident rate and surpassed the record for its best-year total-case incident rate for safety, thereby improving morale and lowering the cost of insurance.

- More than ninety-eight hundred volunteer-hours were donated to the communities where our employees live and work. These numbers were achieved through the participation of more than

75 percent of Fairmount Santrol's family members. Volunteering strengthens valuable community partnerships that support our business activities.

- We achieved zero waste at twenty-seven of our thirty-one facilities in operation, including our largest facility, in Wedron, Illinois.

- To sequester 100 percent of our 2015 scope 1 and 2 greenhouse gas emissions, Fairmount Santrol funded the planting of over 102,000 trees, with 10 percent of the trees planted by our own family members.

- We donated $1.2 million to our communities through the Fairmount Santrol Foundation, with a significant portion funding children's health and wellness, and education.

Striving to be an employer of choice, we provide one key benefit to our family members: the opportunity to donate forty hours of paid volunteer time per year. Since 2011, our members have donated more than seventy-six thousand paid volunteer-hours. And, because of our commitment to being good stewards of the environment, we have planted nearly half a million trees since 2011 to annually offset greenhouse gases to neutral.

In the interest of transparency and maintaining our commitment to SD, Fairmount Santrol has voluntarily produced a Corporate Social Responsibility Report since 2006. Until 2013, we reported on 161 of 171 possible Global Reporting Initiative indicators (topics). Since then, the global initiative's move to materiality has added new focus and rigor to our SD efforts. Fairmount Santrol invested in a robust materiality assessment in the fourth quarter of 2014 to prioritize the SD topics of greatest interest to both our organization and our external stakeholders. We focused specifically on which of our significant economic, environmental, and social impacts, risks, and opportunities across our value chain could substantially influence the decisions of stakeholders. Our research identified seventeen priority areas, which we have been working to align with our annual SD team goals and bold Vision 2020 goals. Every three years, the Fairmount Santrol family plans to refresh the materiality assessment we use to make sure we manage our efforts with the greatest potential impact to people, planet, and prosperity.

Fairmount Santrol's steadfast commitment to creating positive change in society, the environment, and our overall economic health is an integral part of our company's approach to ensuring long-term growth and prosperity for all our stakeholders. SD investments not only benefit our family members, our communities, and the planet, but they also drive prosperity for our business through cost savings and improved profitability—a virtuous cycle we refer to as *SD Pays*. Annually, our SD Pays Standardization Committee manages our measurement methodology, clearly outlining which types of projects create SD Pays, the SD expenses to include, and how to calculate the project value. This practice helps our business and stakeholders clearly see how SD at Fairmount Santrol creates value. From 2011 to 2016, our yearly SD efforts produced approximately $5.0 million to $9.0 million of net tangible SD Pays value.

I'm proud of the Fairmount Santrol family's SD accomplishments and wanted to share with students our experiences in imagining new possibilities. After all, they are tomorrow's leaders who must take SD to the next level globally if we are to ensure a bright future for

Figure 8-2: Relative priority of sustainability topics at Fairmount Santrol

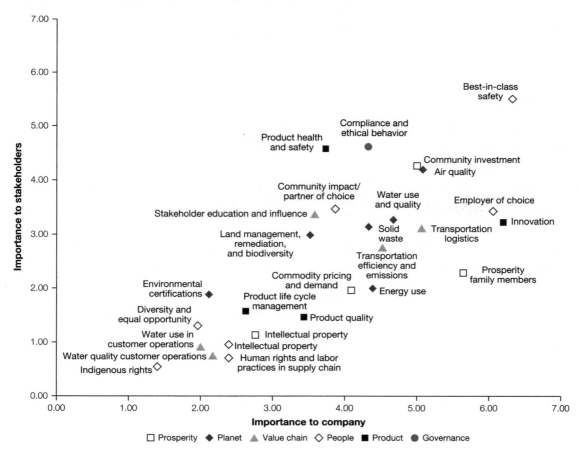

the next generations. That's why my wife, Char, and I support the AIM2Flourish initiative. It is housed at the Fowler Center for Business as an Agent of World Benefit at the Weatherhead School of Management at Case Western Reserve University in Cleveland.

AIM2Flourish's mission is to catalyze and celebrate inspiring examples of innovation that tackle humanity's greatest challenges. The initiative combines a curriculum for business school professors, the AIM2Flourish.com story platform, and the Flourish Prizes. Using the UN Sustainable Development Goals as a lens, students around the world sit down for one-on-one appreciative-inquiry interviews with business leaders in their communities. Students then write stories based on their experiences, and the stories are posted on AIM2Flourish.com as inspiration for others.

A successful AIM2Flourish initiative can help students see firsthand what business innovators can do to improve our world. More importantly, students report that they see themselves becoming these kinds of leaders when they graduate. As of May 2017, the AIM2Flourish website has over 535 student-written stories underscoring Fairmont Santrol's motto about leadership: "Do Good. Do Well." The seventeen best-of-the-best

stories from 2016—one for each sustainable development goal—were celebrated with the inaugural Flourish Prizes at the Fourth Global Forum in June 2017 at Case Western Reserve University. These annual awards honor the most flourishing innovations around the globe. Char and I believe that business leaders everywhere, and young people in particular, need to hear this message. We're glad to see it growing, and we wholeheartedly support it.

Since Fairmount Santrol became a publicly traded company in 2014, our family members have been asked if our commitment to SD will endure. The answer is simple: Yes. Sustainable development, one of our most important differentiators, is core to our values and vision. Family members are deeply engaged in the commitment to exceed all expectations while fulfilling economic, social, and environmental responsibilities. High engagement drives efficiency, innovation, hard work, commitment, and, ultimately, financial value and prosperity. Fairmount Santrol is committed to being bold, staying true, and leading by example, because we believe that business *can* be an agent of world benefit. It's simply good business. As I like to say, "Take care of the land, and the land will take care of you."

There is no large company that doesn't significantly affect the environment. Think of the amount of transport, packaging, and other natural resources that are used to run your business. Where is there room to improve your practices? What environmental side effects—or externalities—does your business create? How can you internalize these and mitigate their negative effects?

Externalities   **How do they affect the business in the long run?**

_____

_____

_____

_____

_____

The next step is to move from the discussion of why stakeholders matter to why they matter for you and what it means to have a stakeholder orientation and mindset in your organization. In the next two chapters, we will take these steps to understand the importance of stakeholders:

- Assess where you are on the journey to stakeholder orientation.

- Identify your stakeholders and their needs.

- Get the notion of stakeholders deeper into the organization.

- Build a stakeholder orientation in which people think and act win-win in your organization.

What are three key points you can take away from this chapter?

1. _____

2. _____

3. _____

Chapter 9

Identifying Your Stakeholders and Mapping Their Needs

Stakeholder orientation is fundamentally about a shift in how you think about your business: from a shorter-term, transactional approach to a systems and relationship model focused on creating greater long-term value among all stakeholders. PwC illustrates this transformation in figure 9-1. The critical shift is from thinking in terms of maximizing profit to focusing on maximizing value in the stakeholder system. This is a fundamental shift in focus and in mindset. By seeking to create maximum value in the system, the system itself is larger and therefore the share of that value, represented by profit, that comes to the shareholder is larger.

You can shift this mindset by better understanding both who your stakeholders are and how well you are presently working with them while also shifting how your top team and the rest of your organization think about stakeholders. We describe this shift in thinking as taking a win-win approach to business decision making—the key to a sustainable stakeholder orientation in your business. We will address the core issue of understanding and working with stakeholders in this chapter, and in chapter 10, we will illustrate possible ways to shift the broader organization's approach to stakeholders. A stakeholder-oriented culture can take years to build. The systemic approach we will discuss in these next two chapters can accelerate that transformation.

Figure 9-1: Profits maximization to stakeholder's value maximization model

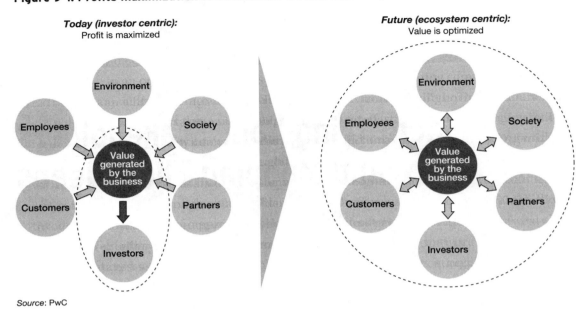

Source: PwC

In this chapter, we will help you to clarify three issues:

1. Where your organization is today on the journey to a stakeholder orientation

2. Who your stakeholders are, and what the opportunities are to improve stakeholder relationships

3. Where value-creation opportunities exist with underserved stakeholders

As described in the following case, one company in Brazil identified these three issues to its advantage.

Porto Seguro, a major Brazilian car insurance company, started its stakeholder-orientation journey focusing on insurance brokers. Jayme Garfinkel, at the time, CEO of the company, knew that if brokers had a good product and knew how to sell it to customers, the company would be strong. During one of Brazil's economic crises, the company almost went bankrupt. At that time, it learned about a US study on the impact of a third brake light, which had been found to reduce rear-end collisions by 25 percent. The finding was the company's impetus to launch a new insurance plan. All brokers were invited to come in and learn about the new plan, which would offer a third brake light for all insured cars. Every broker had to come in with his or her own car. During the presentation of the new product, all brokers got their cars upgraded. The upgrade turned out to be a great marketing tool. Everyone knew the cars with the third brake light had insurance, and as predicted by the study, collisions dropped by about 25 percent.

The company had a long-running practice of meeting monthly with brokers. The CEO decided to start monthly meetings with authorized repair workshops to listen to feedback from their interactions with customers. These monthly discussion forums uncovered more ideas to improve the insurance product. Customers were complaining that they needed their cars to get to work; being without a car for up to a week was really inconvenient for them. The company started to offer customers a loaner car during the repair process.

Another complaint that surfaced was that customers lost a lot of time trying to figure out how to tow the car to the workshop. Another improvement was added to the insurance service: towing service for any kind of car failure.

Next, the company started monthly discussions with another group of stakeholders: tow-truck drivers. This helped the company identify more improvements. One truck driver shared that he liked to offer a bottle of water to the person involved in a car incident. He found that this gesture would lessen the person's anxiety. The company decided that every tow truck working for the company should have water to offer; later, it decided to offer snacks as well, since most people involved in accidents ended up stuck for many hours trying to figure out a solution for the broken car.

Over time, more and more stakeholders have been identified, and the discussion forums have become fundamental to develop, innovate, and grow the business.

Introduction to Understanding Stakeholders and Their Needs

Introduce the stakeholder-orientation concept to your senior team. As a leadership group, work through the following exercises, and reflect on how stakeholder orientation applies to your organization. The goal is to identify your stakeholders and understand their needs.

The following case illustrates this process and is a good warm-up exercise for your team.

The leader of a business that distributes prostheses (artificial limbs) was concerned about potential new entrants into the market. As an exercise to explore stakeholder orientation, read the dialogue below, and then draw the stakeholder map on the following page.

Who is your customer?

I sell the prostheses to doctors.

Who do you buy them from?

From European manufacturers.

What is your major concern at this point?

I fear that a Chinese manufacturer might enter the market.

Can anyone come in and sell prostheses?

Not really. They need US Food and Drug Administration approval.

After the approval, can anyone sell it?

Well, customs are a bureaucratic burden on this product. You might need help from a specialist to clear customs.

Okay, once you clear customs, can you sell and deliver the prostheses to doctors?

It is not that simple. The doctors cannot carry them around. They have to be delivered to a hospital and need proper storage.

So, once it's sold, you send it to the hospital, right?

Almost. The insurance provider has to approve the surgery before we send it out, unless it is an emergency.

I see. The doctor buys in, the insurance provider approves the surgery, and the hospital receives the prosthesis. Then it's time for surgery, right?

Yes, but we have to have a technician available at the hospital who stands by in case there are any technical questions about the product. After the surgery, we have a physiotherapist specialized in our product to help the patient recover.

Throughout this discussion, a few stakeholders were identified. Work with your team to identify them, and list them in the space below.

Who are potential stakeholders for the prosthesis company?

1. _____

2. _____

3. _____

4. _____

5. _____

6. _____

7. _____

Compare your team's answers with the potential stakeholders that the prosthesis company listed:

1. Patients

2. US Food and Drug Administration

3. Customs officials

4. Insurance provider

5. Distributors

6. Hospitals

7. Doctors

Identifying Your Stakeholders

As a team, take ten to fifteen minutes to identify the primary stakeholders in your business. Most organizations identify five to seven of them. If you have more than seven, ask which ones are your primary stakeholders and which could be considered secondary stakeholders. In this exercise, we'll focus on only the primary stakeholders. Remember, primary stakeholders are those that your business affects and is affected by every day. Secondary stakeholders are not directly interacted with on a regular basis, but nevertheless can have an impact on your business. Examples might be media, government, or your competitors. Use the diagram in figure 9-2 to list your primary stakeholders.

The next step is to reflect on what the different needs of each of your stakeholders might be. The key to this exercise is to put yourself in the position of that stakeholder. What are this stakeholder's fundamental needs? Try to shift and see things from this perspective; walk a mile in the stakeholder's shoes.

Figure 9-3 presents an example from First United Bank.

Now try this with your team. List your stakeholders below. Identify at least three needs for each stakeholder.

Figure 9-2: Primary stakeholder map

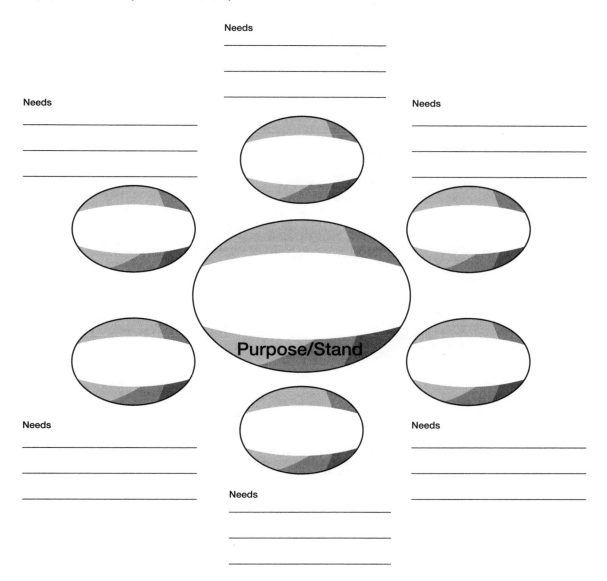

Needs

_____

_____

_____

Needs

_____

_____

_____

Needs

_____

_____

_____

Purpose/Stand

Needs

_____

_____

_____

Needs

_____

_____

_____

Needs

_____

_____

_____

Figure 9-3: First United Bank stakeholder map

Needs
1. Access to growth capital when my business needs it
2. To be able to save money for my children's education and my retirement
3. To improve my financial literacy and learn how to manage my money better

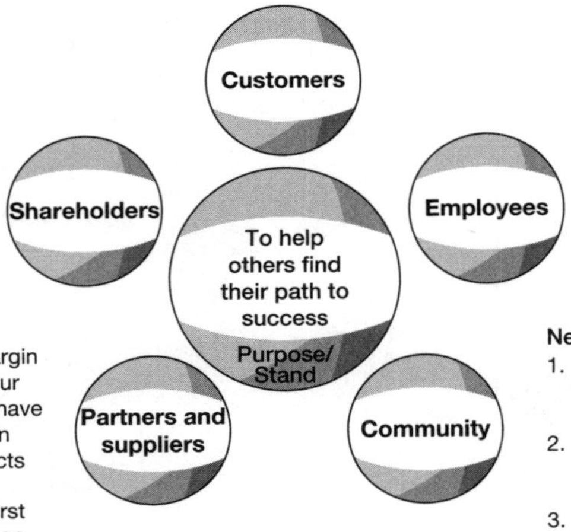

Needs
1. To receive fair returns
2. To see the value of my shares grow through time
3. To know that First United gives back to the community and acts as a good corporate citizen

Needs
1. To be paid fairly and have the opportunity to save for my retirement
2. Learning opportunities that will allow me to grow in my career
3. To find a deep sense of meaning and purpose in my role at work

Needs
1. To earn a healthy margin so that we can pay our employees well and have the capital to invest in improving our products and services
2. A relationship with First United that is based on mutual trust and respect
3. A real partnership, where our business and First United can grow together over many years

Needs
1. Engaged citizens working together to improve the well-being of our community
2. A strong tax base that can pay for infrastructure (roads, schools, utilities)
3. Partnerships with local businesses to promote economic development

Customers

Shareholders

Employees

To help others find their path to success

Purpose/Stand

Partners and suppliers

Community

Stakeholder	Primary needs of this stakeholder

How could you and your team "reality check" that you have correctly identified the needs of your primary stakeholders? What might be a next step to do this?

_____

_____

_____

_____

_____

_____

_____

_____

Now that you've identified your stakeholders and their key needs, lead a discussion with the team members about which stakeholders they feel are underserved.

1. Which stakeholder do you feel is most neglected, and why?

_____

_____

_____

_____

2. Identify the stakeholder relationship that, if we could strengthen it, would have the greatest impact on the business.

_____

_____

_____

_____

3. Do we have any "silent" stakeholders that we may not have considered?

_____

_____

_____

_____

Food for Thought:
Can All Stakeholders Win Equally All the Time?

Have we ever had to make a decision in which not all the company's stakeholders benefited? Probably, but I've never really thought of it that way. I usually try to think about how something will benefit all the stakeholders. And since they're interdependent, I don't like that question because it gets you thinking in a way I don't think we ought to be thinking. It means you start thinking about trade-offs and the assumption that if someone is winning, then someone else must be losing. Something about human nature makes us want to think that way; maybe it's our culture of competitive sports. We tend to think that if someone wins, then someone loses. But that is limited thinking. The stakeholders are in relationship with one another. It's like a relationship you have with a friend or a marriage. In marriage, one partner can't be always gaining whenever the other loses. If that happened, the marriage would fall apart. The couple has to be simultaneously winning and both be gaining. If that happens the relationship deepens and it grows. When you begin to exploit the other in a marriage or a friendship or in business, you're on the path to ruin. Instead, think about how you can create value for all your stakeholders and can create win-win relationships.

—John Mackey, CEO, Whole Foods Market

Deepen Your Stakeholder Understanding and Engagement

Having identified your stakeholders, their needs, and potential areas for improvement and business impact, you can now go deeper in your understanding of stakeholders and how you might engage with them.

Use the following chart to test how well you understand each of your stakeholders. Doing this exercise as a team has great value in making sure that you are aligned on what you know about the stakeholders, and what you don't. Undoubtedly, some members of the leadership team will know more about some of these stakeholders than will others on the team. The assessment is a great opportunity to share that knowledge and insight and educate the whole team on your stakeholders. You may not be able to fill in each section completely for each stakeholder, but do your best—and notice where there may be some significant gaps in the team's knowledge and understanding of your stakeholders. Do this assessment for each of your primary stakeholders. You may find it helpful to go through this quickly as a team and then assign members of the team to follow up and fill in the chart before your next meeting.

	NAME OF STAKEHOLDER:		
ISSUE TO CHECK	NEED 1	NEED 2	NEED 3
Our current strategy with this stakeholder (capture this in detail, in two or three sentences):			
How do we create value for them today?			
What is the opportunity to improve our relationship with them?			
What is the opportunity to create more value with them?			
What risks or threats exist with this stakeholder?			

As you go through this exercise, you will soon discover some things you know about your stakeholders and other things you don't. You will also start to see areas where you might work more closely with some of your stakeholders to create value and some areas where you are vulnerable to a business disruption if you don't manage and connect with these stakeholders differently.

Enlist and Engage with Your Stakeholders

Thus far, you have assessed your stakeholders from an internal perspective. The next step is to validate these assumptions directly with selected stakeholders and with others in your organization who might be closer and more knowledgeable about these stakeholders. While it would obviously be good to do the following approach with all your stakeholders, we recommend that you begin with one or possibly two stakeholders that you have initially identified as having the greatest potential impact on your business—to either create value or disrupt your business (or sometimes both). For example, you could choose your largest customer and most important supplier.

The enlisting process begins with holding an informal meeting with the management team (or equivalent) of the stakeholder. Your goal is to create two-way communication with this stakeholder. You want to both communicate what you are striving for with your stakeholder orientation and listen and confirm what their needs are and how they see the opportunities and threats to the relationship. The following is a suggested agenda for that meeting;

- Introduce your stakeholders to the notion of stakeholder orientation. Explain why it is important to your organization and what you hope to achieve in building stronger stakeholder orientation throughout your organization and with them (value cocreation, closer cooperation, greater efficiencies, and win-win opportunities and thinking).

- Seek to explore and better understand their needs and how well or poorly you have met them in the past.

- Show them your initial analysis of the relationship, and discuss where you see things similarly and where things are seen differently and why.

- Brainstorm areas in which you might work more closely together to co-create value and to improve the relationship and align your interests.

- Agree on some next steps, and establish a regular routine for future interactions.

After the meeting, debrief as a team. Use the following as a guideline for this:

- **What did you learn? What surprised you?**

  _____

  _____

  _____

  _____

- **How has your team shifted its thinking about the opportunities and potential threats with this stakeholder?**

  _____

  _____

  _____

  _____

- **What are your next steps to follow up on after this meeting?**

  _____

  _____

  _____

  _____

  _____

  _____

  _____

Document your findings from the meeting, and share them with the stakeholder—asking the stakeholder to add anything that might have been missed. Circulate this report to your organization's relevant team members who interact with this stakeholder.

Next, we recommend that you form an internal team to decide how and when to move forward with exploring these value-creation opportunities. This step moves things from simply good dialogue to action. In the next section, we outline how your internal team can brainstorm on what actions or projects could explore a strategic experiment with this stakeholder. In addition, you should review what else could be done to enhance the communication, connection, and coordination with this stakeholder? Have this team come back with recommendations on how to go forward.

This exercise generally creates a new sense of purpose and opportunity in working with various stakeholders. It can also lead to some hard discussions and decisions about which stakeholders are no longer in alignment with your company's approach to doing business. For one company, this process revealed that some of the financial institutions that it was working with on finance options were not acting with the same sense of purpose and values toward the company's customers. Other financial institutions were clearly in alignment with the company's values and purpose. This discovery led to a tough discussion about putting more time and resources into developing those better-aligned relationships and shifting business away from the institutions not aligned. The company's shifting relationships paid off. One of the selected partners double downed on its relationship with the company and placed the company in its strategic partner program, offering access to the partner's latest technology and preferred pricing.

Strategic Experiments to Create Shared Value with Your Stakeholders

Taking a stakeholder orientation can have great practical strategic value when applied to specific areas of your business. The goal is to identify areas where you can run small-scale experiments to see how to create additional shared value for your organization. These *strategic experiments* provide an important innovation opportunity for an organization. They can be a testing ground for a concept that can then be scaled up to have a significant impact across several stakeholders.

Finding and Executing Shared-Value Strategic Experiments

This exercise begins with the executive team's identifying a few areas in which various stakeholders might cooperate to create shared value. You need to be specific about the opportunities you want to pursue. The executive team should review the stakeholder needs in light of the strategic priorities of the organization. From this list of needs, the executive team needs to take the following steps:

1. Brainstorm a list of opportunities to work with single or multiple stakeholders to create shared value.

2. For each good idea generated, discuss two key questions: Why is this important to us? Why might this be important to them?

3. Prioritize the ideas and opportunities generated above to create a list of three or four potential experiments based on potential business impact and the likely ease (or difficulty) of aligning the interests of the stakeholders involved.

4. Set up strategic-experiment teams to follow up and explore the potential of strategic experiments, and propose a way to launch them. Once the executive team has identified the members of the strategic-experiment team and asked them to participate in this exercise, the strategic-experiment team should address the following:

   - Invite specific stakeholders to participate in a shared-value process to develop and test the experiment. The shared-value process entails both parties looking at the interface of their activities for ways in which they can identify areas of the business where working together can create additional value. In essence, it is looking for an opportunity to jointly create value where neither party could do so on their own. There may also be opportunities that involve bringing in a third party to help with this creation and realization of value. At the heart of this exercise is a brainstorming process and thinking outside of the conventional model in which organizations look at the world separately; for example, if we were one organization, what new opportunities might exist to create value?

   - Hold a series of working sessions with stakeholders to develop and flesh out a pilot program.

   - Pilot the concept, and gather feedback.

   - With the executive team, review the possibilities of scaling the effort.

In this chapter, we sought to make the notion of stakeholder orientation more relevant to you and your organization. You have identified your primary stakeholders and their most important needs. We asked you to focus on the stakeholders with the greatest opportunities for improvement and to identify what you can do with them to realize those opportunities.

We also challenged you to further examine your stakeholders' needs to uncover those that have the greatest potential to either create value or disrupt your business. For these high-priority stakeholders, we suggested a way to enlist and engage with them to create meaningful action plans.

In going through these exercises with your team members, you have no doubt increased their awareness and understanding of stakeholder orientation. In the next chapter, we discuss how to take this notion deeper into the entire organization by helping people understand what this orientation might mean to them personally and how they can think in terms of win-win opportunities every day.

Chapter 10

Embedding a Stakeholder Orientation

Having identified your stakeholders and their needs, the leadership team takes the next step in becoming a conscious company by sharing this information and way of thinking with the rest of the organization. Besides helping other people understand who the stakeholders are and what their needs are, the team needs to make this knowledge relevant to their day-to-day roles. Organizations that do this well go a step further. They work to help people understand what it means to think win-win.

Win-win has become a bit of a cliché in business. However, to make this concept real in an organization, you must foster your people's ability to approach problem solving and decision making differently. They need to think win-win within your organization. One way to instill the win-win attitude is to look for practical examples of how this can be practiced in the organization. Finally, you need to ensure that the policies and processes in the organization allow people to act this way. You'll want to check that there are not reward, performance management, or other practices that might be reinforcing types of behavior different from those you are trying to foster around stakeholder orientation.

This chapter focuses on four practices to sustain this new way of thinking and to make it relevant to the people at all levels in the organization:

1. Make sure people know who your stakeholders are and what their needs are.

2. Wean people off the adversarial mindset toward stakeholders that is an integral part of traditional business cultures and have them think differently about your stakeholders.

3. Make stakeholder orientation relevant by having people think about and look for win-win solutions in their daily work lives.

4. Ensure that the systems and policies you have in place are aligned with and reinforce this new way of thinking and acting.

Broaden Your Organization's Understanding of Stakeholders

It is very difficult to meet stakeholder needs when most people in the organization don't understand what these needs are or only have an abstract understanding that seems meaningless. This section provides an approach for cascading stakeholder orientation deeper into the organization. Depending on the size of the organization, you might integrate the approach into existing training programs for leaders and frontline team members, or you might create a stand-alone training module. The goal is to ensure that everyone in the organization understands stakeholder orientation and that everyone, regardless of specific role, can find ways to help meet stakeholder needs. There is an abiding commitment to co-prosperity; when stakeholders win, the company wins. That's the beauty of interdependence.

Stakeholder-Orientation Training

You can develop a stakeholder-orientation training module using the outline below. The goal of the module is to get participants to relate their role to the broader stakeholder issues or strategy of the organization.

Begin with a comparison of stakeholder and shareholder approaches. Use the material from chapter 8 to briefly introduce the concept, and watch the Ed Freeman video with them (www.ccfieldguide.com/ed).

- **Ask the group members what they think are the opportunities and challenges in taking a stakeholder approach. Why? (Depending on the size of the group, you may want them to do this in smaller groups of four to six people, and then have them share their group's takeaways with the larger group.)**

_____

_____

_____

_____

_____

_____

_____

_____

_____

_____

_____

_____

- **Ask people to identify who they think the stakeholders of the organization are. Share what the leadership team cited as the primary stakeholders and their needs. (Use the material that the leadership team developed in chapter 9, section "Introduction to Understanding Stakeholders and Their Needs," including figure 9-2, which we reproduce here as a blank figure 10-1 for your convenience.)**

Figure 10-1: Primary stakeholders map for team training

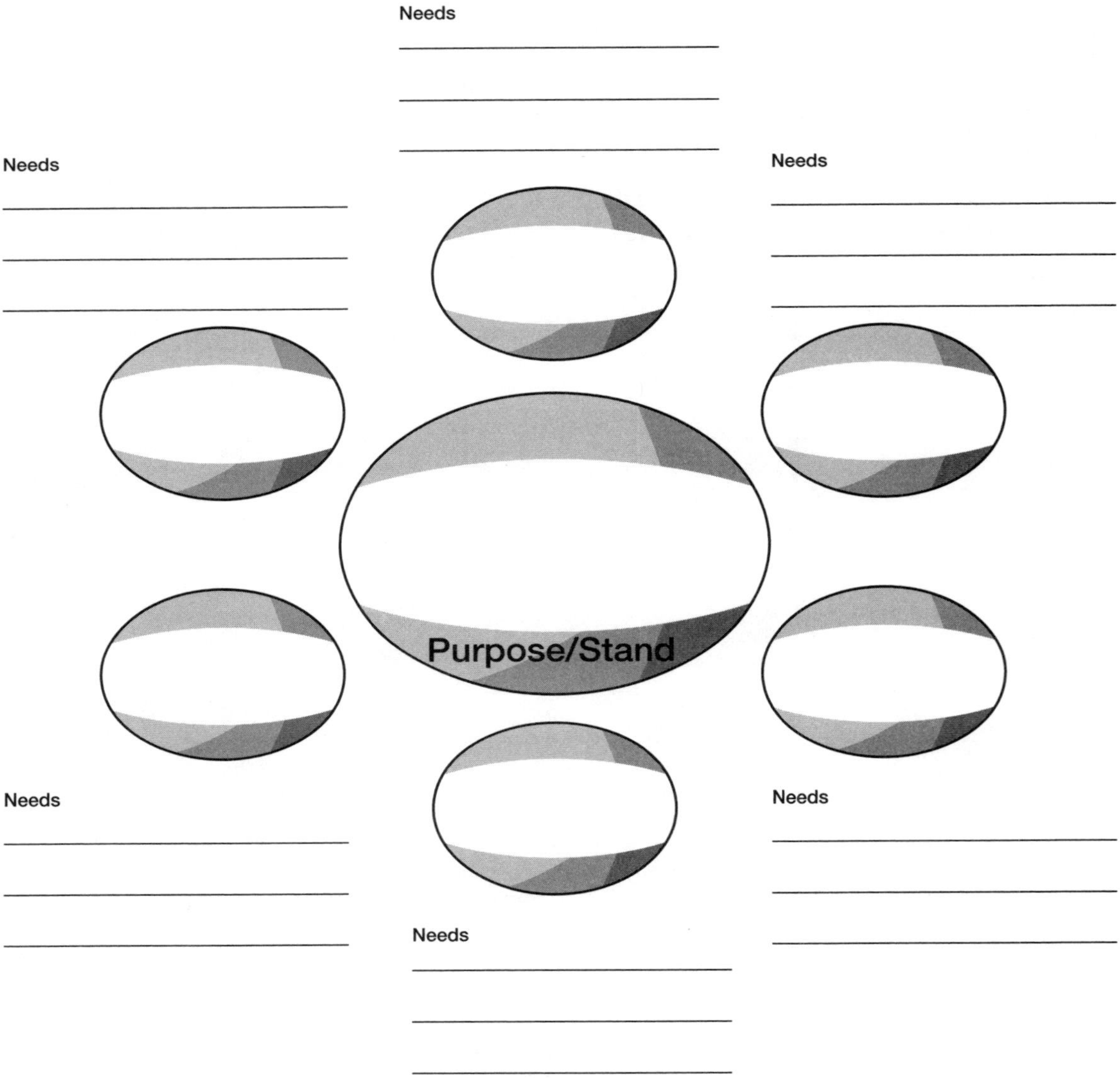

Needs

_____

_____

_____

Needs

_____

_____

_____

Needs

_____

_____

_____

Purpose/Stand

Needs

_____

_____

_____

Needs

_____

_____

_____

Needs

_____

_____

_____

- Ask the group, "Why do we think these are our primary stakeholders?" Did they miss anyone?

_____

_____

_____

The leadership team has listed some needs for the primary stakeholders. Show these to the group. Now break out into smaller groups—the same number of groups as there are primary stakeholders—and assign each group a stakeholder. Put flip charts up around the room with each stakeholder's name, and have the groups address these questions:

- What are the stakeholder's needs? Have the groups divide the flip chart page with a vertical line, and ask them to write down the needs of their stakeholder on the left-hand side.

- How can we best help meet their needs? These answers should be explored on the right-hand side of the flip chart.

- Where could we do more to meet these needs? (Note: collect these responses from each workshop, and provide them to the executive team in a consolidated and summarized form.)

The next step is to make stakeholder orientation personally relevant to people in the company. Ask them whom they consider the stakeholders in their own work lives. Have them fill in the blank stakeholder map in figure 10-2 to show who their primary stakeholders are for them personally.

- **How well are you meeting their needs? Which stakeholder have you most neglected?**

Figure 10-2: My personal primary stakeholders at work

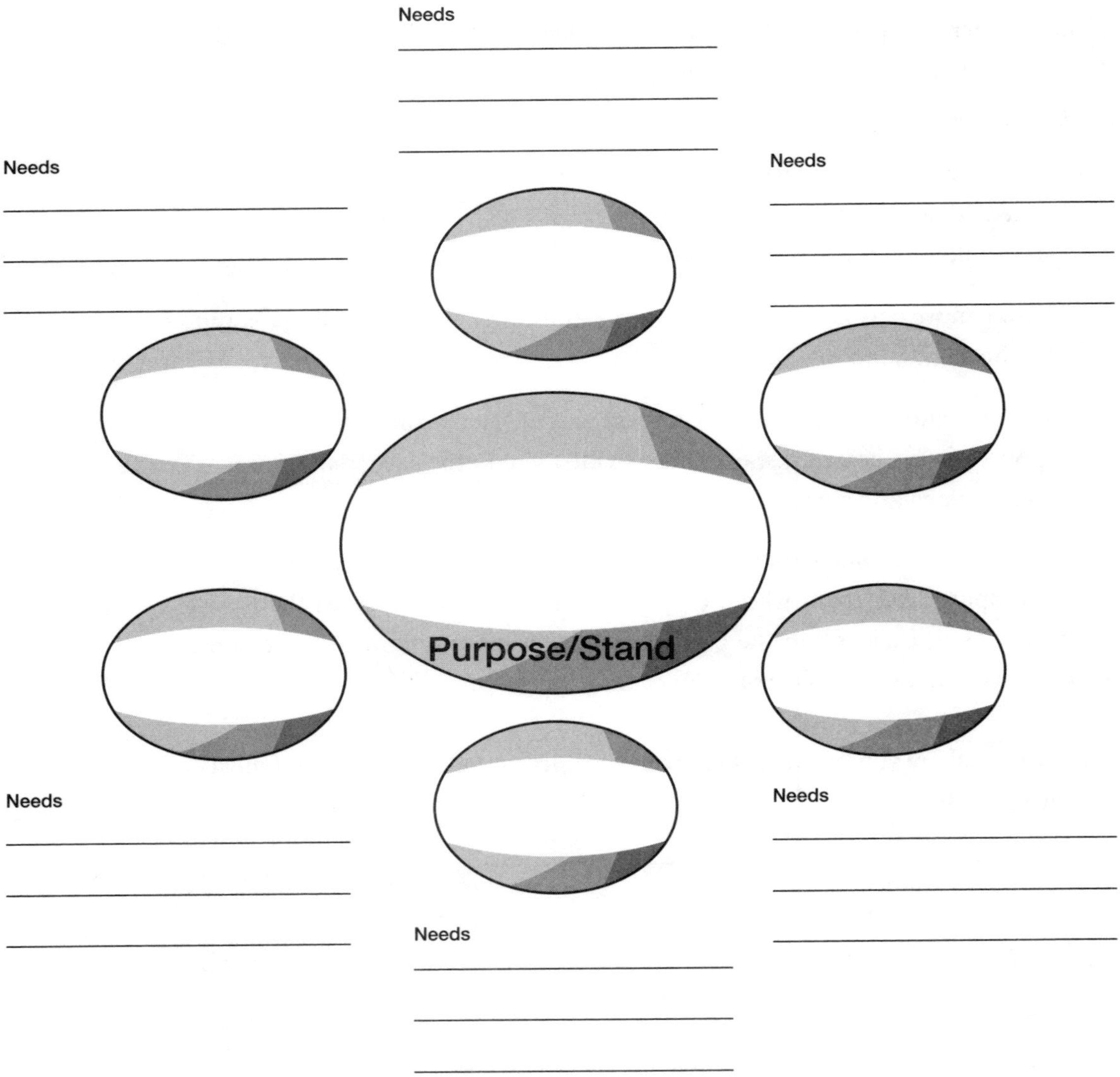

Needs

_____

_____

_____

Needs

_____

_____

_____

Needs

_____

_____

_____

Purpose/Stand

Needs

_____

_____

_____

Needs

_____

_____

_____

Needs

_____

_____

_____

- Are your own needs being met?

_____

_____

_____

- Given these reflections, what are two of the most important things you can do to improve your stakeholder relationships? Why?

_____

_____

_____

_____

_____

_____

_____

_____

Food for thought: Consider doing the preceding exercise for your life outside work. Identify your stakeholders in your personal life, and consider similar questions to those you just answered.

Embedding Win-Win Thinking

We now dig deeper into stakeholder orientation and take a twofold approach to making win-win thinking come alive in your organization. We do this first at the individual level and provide exercises on how to increase win-win thinking for individuals. These exercises can be interwoven into existing training programs or used as stand-alone exercises with teams or large groups of people participating in an off-site meeting. Second, we will examine some issues that the leadership team needs to consider to ensure that the organization is supporting and reinforcing the right behavior in the organization.

Fundamentally, win-win thinking requires a mindset shift. We have been conditioned to think win-lose—that any discussion, negotiation, or business relationship necessarily comes to a zero-sum game. If you win, I lose, and if I win, you lose. Win-lose thinking has often been ingrained in our thinking at an early age. Vince Lombardi, the Hall of Fame coach of the Green Bay Packers in the 1960s, is often credited with the well-known expression "Winning isn't everything; it is the only thing." In Conscious Capitalism, the fundamental shift from this attitude is toward abundance and a growth mentality. Looking for mutual gain increases the size of the pie for everyone; together we can create more. Such thinking begins with an ability to deeply understand the needs of others. Only from this place of mutual deep understanding can we begin to work together to brainstorm and find solutions to meet both our needs in the long term.

Thinking win-win means that we instill several habits:

- See challenges as opportunities—how you can create more value in this situation by engaging deeper with your stakeholders.

- Identify the key issues, interests, and motivations (not positions) for each stakeholder.

- Reframe your perspective. In organizations, it's easy to think that others know what challenges you face daily. Just remember, you only see your part of the system. We must communicate with each other to come to some semblance of the truth of the whole.

- See the challenge and opportunity from others' point of view. How can they benefit?

- Seek to create results that would constitute a fully acceptable solution or increase in value for both parties.

- Identify possible new options to achieve those results. The more options you have, the more likely you are to find a win-win. Not all stakeholders can equally benefit at once. This process is dynamic and evolves over time.

Creating a Win-Win Outcome: The Ugli Orange Exercise

Whole Foods Market used the following stakeholder exercise in its leadership development program. The exercise aims to reinforce with team members that if people understand each other's needs at a deeper level, they can find solutions that are more creative.

In appendix B, you will find instructions for a negotiation exercise involving two fictitious negotiators—Dr. Jones and Dr. Roland—who are competing for one resource: Ugli oranges. The pages are each to be copied and given to two halves of your group. Each side is asked to not share the instructions with the other side. The groups should be separated and given about ten minutes to discuss the questions they would like to have answered by the other team. In the end, the groups should have come up with questions that are respectful of the other team's objectives without asking them to give up all their information.

As the facilitator, you will arrange a meeting between delegates (two people) from each group. The rest of each group should attend the meeting, listen to the delegates, and be available to consult with and help their delegate. The meeting should last about five minutes.

The groups then go back and discuss what they have learned and what options may exist for negotiating with the other side. They pick a preferred solution and write it up on a flip chart with a rationale for why this is the best solution.

Now discuss with the group what the win-win looks like—each group needs only part of the orange. Often, each team is so focused on getting all the Ugli oranges that it fails to see that the two parties in the negotiation are after different parts of the fruit. For many people, a simple and fair solution would be to split the oranges and give each group one-half. But this solution is not the best approach, because you did not ask why each one needed the orange. As a result, both parties might be throwing half their oranges away.

If the right questions are asked, the negotiators are headed for a win-win situation, which is at the heart of the stakeholder interdependence and orientation model. By fully understanding each other's needs, groups can see that they if they work together, both groups will get all of what they need in this situation. We should notice the different level of conflict, from a domination position, to a compromising approach, to finally an integrated solution for the challenge.

Have each participant spend a couple of minutes writing down the key takeaways from this experience with their team. Then have them share these conclusions in pairs or triads.

_____

_____

_____

_____

_____

_____

_____

_____

_____

When Win-Win Seems Impossible

Sometimes a win-win outcome seems impossible. However, applying a win-win approach explores the possibilities in the situation and can result in unexpected outcomes. The following exercise is meant to test the mindset that considers win-win impossible. As we have said, a positive-sum-game approach is all about our mindset and our approach to a problem or an issue. The following exercise illustrates how when we use a win-win mindset to follow a systematic approach on an issue, we may see an outcome that could not have been predicted at the outset.

For this exercise, have the group break out into smaller groups of three or four people. Each group should discuss and identify two or three situations for which the group agrees that a win-win approach would be difficult in a given situation with a stakeholder. After they choose these few issues, ensure that the groups are clear about what is involved in each situation. Do this by quickly capturing on a flip chart (a separate flip chart for each situation) the key issues involved in that situation. Now in the smaller groups, ask each group to pick two of the three situations and fill in a flip chart using the exercise below. Use separate flip charts for each situation. Give the groups ten to fifteen minutes to do this exercise.

	SITUATION 1	SITUATION 2
Identify two situations in which win-win seems impossible.		
Why does win-win seem impossible?		
What are the obstacles?		
Moving toward a win-win, consider these questions:		
How can the obstacles be removed?		
Can a win be redefined?		
What can rebalance a loss?		
What's the long-term perspective?		
What unexpected win-win outcome may conceivably occur?		

Source: "The Conflict Resolution Network."

Now bring the small groups back together. Have one member of each group pick one situation and spend two minutes describing to the others the key takeaway from the exercise. After all the groups have presented their two-minute takeaways, reflect as a group on taking a win-win approach to these problems. What has shifted for them? Why?

A Conversation with William Ury

The book *Getting to Yes*, written by Roger Fisher and William Ury nearly thirty years ago, has become a classic in negotiation. One of its key tenets is looking for the win-win in negotiation. In 2015, Ury wrote a new book, *Getting to Yes with Yourself*. In the decades between the books, one of his big reflections has been that we always need to look for a third win. The third win is about a bigger win; it looks for something for the larger community, for the ecosystem, or connecting to a common purpose. In a sense, if you can identify or connect to the common purpose or intention that the involved parties have, then you move to a different space for the negotiation or discussion.

Nevertheless, Ury says that the ability to develop win-win solutions is affected by one's ability to understand oneself at a deeper level. What are my needs in this situation? The classic language that Ury and Fisher use around this question is the difference between positions and needs. Too often, people get caught up in positions they have in negotiations rather than going deeper and understanding their own needs and those of the other parties. Ury's experience has been that our level of self-understanding helps enormously in terms of developing a deeper understanding of our needs. Often, the issue is who can give you permission to get your needs met. Sometimes this is a self-fulfilling issue; you can give yourself permission to have your needs met. It also means being honest with yourself about this deeper sense of what is important to you. When you have done this homework, you then enter into discussions with others from a very different orientation.

In our conversations, Ury cited an example of two senior executives who had been battling over a multi-billion-dollar acquisition for years. What was really the need wasn't so much the money but the freedom that both people were seeking to act on their own accord. Once it was clear that this was what they both really needed at a deeper level, the financial side of the deal came together very quickly.

Ury makes some recommendations for approaches that help develop win-win thinking:

- "GOING TO THE BALCONY": In this way, you can step up a level from the "dance floor" and, from the balcony above the dance floor, see the big picture. Developing this ability to step away from things that are right in front of you and get a broader perspective helps you understand the needs of the different parties better.

- LISTENING BEYOND JUST THE WORDS: This ability helps you understand more deeply what somebody is saying. This is key to understanding their needs.

- CREATIVE METHODS OF BRAINSTORMING: Brainstorming and looking for unusual approaches help you see creative ways of solving issues that are in front of you. This approach includes running several what-if scenarios that allow you to, again, think differently. What if we did such-and-such?

When you fall back into win-lose thinking, it is a sign that you have not been imaginative and creative in thinking about how you might solve something. Win-win is not just a technique; it is a way of living and thinking. You cannot achieve win-win results with anything less than a win-win approach. The ends and the means must be the same. Therefore, win-win approaches grow out of proactive thinking, the level of personal maturity of the participants, well-established and maintained relationships, and goal-oriented, principle-centered strategies. Without these, the idea of win-win will quickly draw cynicism in your organization. The leadership team and leaders at all levels need to have a win-win mindset and encourage this as the "way we do things around here."

Developing Win-Win Capability in Your Organization

Embedding win-win thinking in an organization has several components (figure 10-3):

1. Establishing the value of win-win thinking in the organization— making sure everyone understands that this is how we do business and that the executive team acts as a role model for this approach to problem solving

2. Ensuring that people are trained and have the tools to understand how to implement win-win thinking

3. Embedding the idea of win-win thinking in the incentives and rewards system

Leadership must reinforce that win-win thinking is a core value and a key approach in the business and that it is the expectation and not the exception. Leaders must also set the expectations for win-win and model the win-win approach to value creation rather than focusing on short-term gains.

Figure 10-3: The win-win thinking framework

- Ensure that this is built into the evaluation process—are we recognizing people for doing this in their day-to-day jobs?
- Reward the right behavior—create informal and formal systems for recognizing when this behavior is demonstrated (e.g., "Stakeholder Academy Awards Night"once a year).

- Develop a training program for win-win thinking.
- Provide simple tools for people to use (consider simple checklists as reminders, or decision trees for addressing stakeholder decisions).

- Communicate clearly that this is the way we do things around here—this is a key value to how we do business (see Container Store foundation values).
- Leaders need to model this—begin the training at the top.

To give people the training and the tools to implement a win-win approach to stakeholder orientation, you can take these measures:

- Create checklists and other tools that people can easily use to remind them to follow this approach when they face challenging situations.

- Enlist trained experts on thinking win-win (use an outside training source if needed), and make them available to help coach people through difficult issues and to design and run your training sessions.

Finally, the evaluation and reward system needs to recognize and reward this behavior. Too often, organizations claim that they want a long-term stakeholder perspective and yet have in place internal systems that reward and recognize short-term financial gains in the business.

- Ensure that appropriate recognition of stakeholder-orientation practices is built into performance management. Are we evaluating and setting goals for people on this behavior? Do they get regular feedback when they do this well and when they have missed opportunities to think this way?

- Reward win-win behavior through formal and informal recognition programs. Consider holding a Stakeholder Academy Awards ceremony once a year.

Reflections for the Leadership Team

- What are we communicating about stakeholders and the win-win approach? Is this a constant theme in our communication?

  _____

  _____

  _____

  _____

- How are we reinforcing this message to our frontline employees? What could we do differently?

  _____

  _____

  _____

  _____

  _____

  _____

  _____

- What can we do as leaders to model this approach? How do we incorporate this thinking into our management meetings and decisions? When have we consciously decided to think win-win lately?

  _____

  _____

  _____

  _____

- Think of a recent case in which this team could have taken—but didn't take—a win-win approach to a stakeholder issue. Point out what we could have done differently.

_____

_____

_____

_____

_____

_____

_____

Stakeholder Thinking as an Ongoing Process: Future Search at Whole Foods Market

In its most advanced expression, a stakeholder orientation comes to life when you participate with your stakeholders to cocreate a strategic vision and operational capacity to build sustained competitive advantage for your organization. A good example is how Whole Foods Market has used a process called Future Search. Originally a method developed for community organizations, Future Search is a multiday event that brings together representatives from all stakeholder groups to "dream about the future." It recognizes external trends and each stakeholder's unique perspective and motivation. At the end of the process, the group reaches common ground on the organization's top goals, what actions need to be taken, and how success will be measured. Organizations that develop their vision and strategic agenda in cooperation with their stakeholders have an advantage in terms of both engagement and alignment. They are much more likely to see their strategic vision come to life. This has been Whole Foods Market's experience over multiple iterations of Future Search gatherings organized every five years.

Leading from a Stakeholder Orientation

The final step in stakeholder orientation is to integrate it into how you manage the business. If you are going to lead with a stakeholder orientation, then you must monitor and report on how you are doing in this area. You need to be clear on the state of your relationships with your stakeholders. Given that whatever management focuses on is generally what management gets, there are a couple of key things to consider around stakeholders.

For example, you should put in place metrics that track whether stakeholder needs are being met and whether there is transparency in reporting. You are probably already doing some of these things, for example, the net promoter score for customers. Extend this practice to suppliers and other stakeholders. For example, Whole Foods Market uses morale surveys, team leader surveys, and customer comment cards. There is much work going on regarding integrated reporting, including measurements of environmental, social, and governance impact.

In addition, the leadership team should build in processes and mechanisms that will regularly collect feedback from stakeholders:

- Put in place a process for collecting, addressing, and sharing ongoing feedback from stakeholders—for example, surveys or yearly pulse-check calls by executive team members. One company has each senior leader make one stakeholder call a week. These regular check-ins are appreciated by the stakeholders and are an invaluable source of information on the dynamics of the business.

- Be sure to use this feedback to change your programs or to address quality or other concerns. If you collect the information and then do nothing with it, you will waste everyone's time and lose credibility with your stakeholders.

Final Reflections

Stakeholder orientation is fundamentally about changing the operating system in an organization to focus on creating value and building competitive advantage in a fast-moving and evolving business environment. To borrow from the metaphor that it takes a village to raise a child, in a fast-moving and changing business environment, it takes an ecosystem to build an adaptable and agile organization. No company is smart enough, on its own, to know and see all the opportunities and threats in its business environment. Significant competitive advantage can be built through a stakeholder orientation. The bottom line is that, paradoxically, a stakeholder approach is how shareholders gain the most. In the twenty-first-century business environment, it takes twenty-first-century thinking and processes to succeed. Stakeholder orientation and its execution in an organization is a key part of this success. We should strive to do business in such a way that everybody matters and everybody wins.

Given the work we have done in this section, what are our three biggest stakeholder priorities, and why?

Priorities   **Reason**

_____

_____

_____

_____

In the next section, we will discuss developing and sustaining a conscious culture in your organization.

Part Three

CONSCIOUS CULTURE

The Volunteer Premium

If we are serious about becoming a truly conscious company, we must pay attention to our culture. Every company has a culture, whether the company pays attention to it or not. We need to build and sustain a culture in a conscious way.

A great culture creates employee engagement and passion. It leads to greater innovation, creativity, collaboration, and productivity. Instead of people saying "Thank God It's Friday," they may say (or feel) "Thank God It's Monday!" The workplace becomes a fun place of caring, meaning, and fulfillment. A strong culture becomes both an attractor and an immune system; it helps us bring in people who would be a great fit with the organization and dissuades others who would not.

A conscious culture is important because it creates a competitive advantage that is extremely difficult to replicate. Most strategies can be copied, but the culture of every organization is unique and cannot be copied. Peter Drucker famously said, "Culture eats strategy for lunch." Strategy matters, but culture matters even more. A strong and positive culture results in a *volunteer premium*: the difference between someone doing just enough work not to get fired and a person who comes in passionate and inspired to do a great job. You can't pay or coerce people to close that gap; you can only inspire and motivate them. Cultures that can create such motivated employees who care will have a huge impact on the performance of the business.

The purpose, brand, and culture have to work together to ensure the long-term, sustained success of the organization. The purpose has an impact on the external identity or brand and at the same time relates to the inner reality of the organization—its culture.

In this part, we will define and make the case for conscious cultures and discuss the attributes of such organizational cultures (see figure P3-1 for a summary of part 3). We will help you explore and understand where your culture stands today and how to evolve it to become more conscious.

Figure P3-1: Overview of part 3

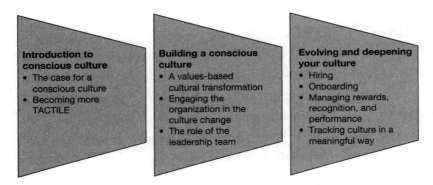

Introduction to conscious culture
- The case for a conscious culture
- Becoming more TACTILE

Building a conscious culture
- A values-based cultural transformation
- Engaging the organization in the culture change
- The role of the leadership team

Evolving and deepening your culture
- Hiring
- Onboarding
- Managing rewards, recognition, and performance
- Tracking culture in a meaningful way

Assessment of Culture for a Conscious Business

RESPONDENTS: C-level executives, senior HR leaders, and rank-and-file employees (keep the responses from each group separate)

DESIRED NUMBER OF RESPONSES: 5 from each of the first two groups, 20 from employees

QUESTION	SCORE
1. Our company's culture has a high degree of trust internally and externally. There is high trust among employees, between employees and management, and between the company and its external stakeholders.	
2. In our culture, we have authenticity; we say what we mean and we mean what we say. There is no sugarcoating of tough reality, and we are highly committed to the truth in all matters.	
3. We operate within a culture of genuine caring and compassion for all stakeholders. When times are tough for the company, we don't diminish our level of caring and compassion for our stakeholders.	
4. We operate with great transparency; we have few secrets and nothing to hide in our business.	
5. Our company has integrity. We have strict ethical standards, and we stand behind all our actions. We believe in dealing fairly and openly with all internal and external stakeholders.	
6. Our people as individuals and our organization as an entity are committed to learning, continually evolving to higher states of capability and consciousness.	
7. Employees in our company are empowered to always do the right thing. We make extensive use of self-managing, self-motivated, and self-directed teams to accomplish our work.	
8. Maintaining and growing the culture of our company is an important priority for us. It requires the attention of our senior executives and the active involvement of our employees.	
9. We place a high priority on recognizing and celebrating within our organization the individuals and teams that best embody our desired culture.	
10. There is a real sense of altruism in our culture—people doing things for others with no expectation of a return, reward, or recognition.	
TOTAL	

SCORES

5: We are exceptionally good at this, to the point that others should learn from us.

4: We demonstrate this most of the time, but there is room for improvement.

3: This is true for us sometimes, but our record overall is mixed.

2: This is rarely true for us.

0: We seem to embody the opposite of this, or it is missing entirely.

Add up your scores to identify the overall gap between your company and best practice (50 points). How did you score? What surprised you? What did not? Why? What are the implications?

_____

_____

_____

_____

_____

_____

_____

Chapter 11

Introduction to Conscious Culture

What do we mean by a conscious culture? In this chapter, we describe the qualities of a conscious culture and explain why a conscious culture is important. Later chapters in part 3 discuss how to assess and improve your culture. We have created the acronym TACTILE to represent the qualities of a conscious culture: trust, authenticity, caring, transparency, learning, and empowerment (figure 11-1). These qualities arise as outputs from a sustained conscious culture in an organization. Consider the seven qualities a checklist; make sure you're covering all these bases.

There are many ways companies can instill a conscious culture, but these seven qualities represent where you want to get to. When you walk into an organization, you can feel the difference between a conscious organization and a traditional one. The TACTILE attributes of a conscious company can be felt just by observing how people interact with each other.

Figure 11-1: Qualities of a conscious culture

T	Trust
A	Authenticity
C	Caring
T	Transparency
I	Integrity
L	Learning
E	Empowerment

In this chapter, we will look at each of these characteristics and ask a series of questions about them. We will also offer some examples of organizations that are very good in each of these areas. No company is perfect at all seven attributes. Each company will find its unique blend of these attributes, scoring higher on some more than on others. Collectively assessing yourself against these will offer you an initial snapshot of where you are on your journey to a conscious culture.

Too often people talk about the carrots and the sticks they use to encourage the right behavior in an organization. Our friend Ed Freeman asks the question "What kind of animal belongs between a carrot and a stick?" The answer is clear: a donkey, or a jackass. And the overwhelming characteristic of a donkey? Stubbornness. A donkey will only do what it is rewarded to do or what it is pushed and prodded to do.

We know enough about rewards and motivations to know that an approach that focuses mainly on extrinsic rewards (things outside of us like money and power) for behavior is not nearly as powerful and sustainable as one based on intrinsic rewards (passion, purpose, meaning, etc.) when the work requires any degree of creativity or out-of-the-box thinking. See Daniel Pink's book *Drive* for a further discussion on this point.[1] When conscious cultures tap into these intrinsic motivations and bring out the best in people, the result is a volunteer premium.

Now the challenge becomes a practical one. A conscious culture is easy to talk about but not easy to create. There are no silver bullets. If everybody could build a high-performing conscious culture overnight, then everybody would. But the sheer difficulty of the task is also why a conscious culture is a source of sustainable competitive advantage.

The Case for a Conscious Culture

The greatest impact of a conscious culture is on employee engagement. A positive culture leads to lower employee turnover and higher performance.[2] According to the Gallup Institute, businesses in the top quartile of employee engagement outperform the bottom quartile organizations by 10 percentage points or more on a multitude of metrics, including profitability, productivity, and customer satisfaction.[3]

Great cultures are great for business. If we analyze the share prices of publicly traded companies from the "*Fortune* 100 Best Companies to Work For" list, these companies outperformed the S&P 500 by three to one (12.32 percent versus 3.71 percent per year) from 1997 to 2011.[4] Other analyses have reflected the same trend. Don't confuse having a conscious culture with a trade-off versus high-performance standards. As illustrated above, great cultures enable superior returns.

Becoming More TACTILE

We recommend that you work through this section with your team. Ideally, the team members should work through the exercises on their own, and then all of you gather to share what you have done. As individuals, we often have blind spots on some of these issues and how they are manifesting in our organization. Having an honest conversation about each quality of TACTILE is a great starting point. We have seen leadership teams gather for an afternoon to work through the TACTILE section all at once (preferred). Other groups have picked one-hour slots over a few weeks and worked through each characteristic of TACTILE one at a time. The goal at the end of this chapter is to have an initial list of the top three to five TACTILE qualities you want to address in your current culture. If they are addressed, which cultural issues do you and your team believe will have the greatest impact on the business?

Trust

It all starts with trust. A high degree of trust permeates conscious businesses internally as well as externally with all their stakeholders. Internally, a strong trust exists vertically (between leaders and employees) and horizontally (between employees); externally, there is great trust between the company and all its external stakeholders: customers, suppliers, business partners, investors, the communities in which it operates, and the government.

At Nordstrom, CEO Blake Nordstrom has commented that trusting people to do the right thing has been critical to the store's success. The company drives this point home during onboarding. New hires receive a one-page statement that we reproduce here:

Welcome to Nordstrom

We're glad to have you with our Company. Our number one goal is to provide outstanding customer service. Set both your personal and professional goals high. We have great confidence in your ability to achieve them.

Nordstrom Rules: Rule #1: Use best judgment in all situations. There will be no additional rules.

Please feel free to ask your department manager, store manager, or division general manager any question at any time.

Looking at trust as a two-way street can create interesting opportunities for a company. Driversselect, a used-car retailer in Dallas, revamped how it worked with its financial partners. It went from working with over twenty financial institutions to going very deep with a handful. The result was a closer working relationship and deeper trust between businesses partners. Accordingly, one of the financial institutions, a major money-center bank, proposed to Driversselect a strategic experiment to speed up and otherwise improve how used-car loans are processed. With the trust they shared, both parties believed they could experiment with a different way of doing business together. Driversselect benefited from being a first mover in its industry in this area.

In discussions about trust with senior executives, the focus often quickly becomes "Do my people trust me and my leadership team?" This is clearly an important issue to look at. At the same time, we have observed that the question is rarely reversed: "Do we trust our employees?" By doing so, we start to understand trust as a relationship, a two-way street. If you don't trust your people, how much can they trust you? Conscious cultures manifest relational trust in the organization. People trust their leaders, and leaders trust their people.

An important caveat: strive to use objective means for gathering information as much as possible. As leaders, you may find it difficult to be truly objective in assessing how people experience the culture. For the exercises in this section, we suggest you reflect on the following issues and discuss them as a team. You can easily turn these questions into a quick online survey (for example, using Survey Monkey) and get feedback from a broader set of people in the organization. It is extremely useful to compare the scores of the executive team and others deeper in the organization.

You also need to assure those taking the survey that the results will be anonymous. Doing this—reassuring people that they can give candid feedback—is a first step in building trust within the organization.

On a scale of 1 to 5, where 5 is the highest score, how much do you trust your frontline people to do the right thing for the business? If you score less than 4, explain why you did not give a higher score. Do your people know what the right thing to do is? If not, why not? Do they have the resources, or believe they have them, to do the right thing? If not, why?

_____

_____

_____

_____

_____

_____

On a scale of 1 to 5 (where 5 is the highest score), is the leadership team trusted by the organization? If you score less than 4, explain why you did not give a higher score. Are people comfortable in reaching out to their supervisors or other leaders, and do they do it quite often for business and non-business-related matters?

_____

_____

_____

What is the degree of trust within the top team? How do you as a team define what it means to trust one another individually and the team collectively? (This is often a very difficult but highly rewarding dialogue for the top team to have.) What would you need to do differently to improve this score for the leadership team?

_____

_____

_____

_____

_____

_____

_____

_____

Looking at the answers you have given above, and the discussions that followed your answers, what are the most important things for your team to note about trust in your organization?

What is working	What is not working	Options for improving in this area

Authenticity

There is growing recognition of the need for people and organizations to be authentic. Conscious cultures are marked by an absence of artifice. Internal and external communications are frank, devoid of the spin that is common in business and the political world.

Authenticity is something we value in building a sense of trust with people. When companies and leaders try to be something they are not, people can see through that. Zappos prints its core values on the first page of the job application. The company takes great pride in being who it says it is going to be, right from the start. This authenticity helps attract people who will make a good cultural fit with the organization and dissuade those who would not.

Is "what you see is what you get" in our culture? What recruiting story do we tell a candidate whom we really want to join us, and do people who work here experience what we relay in the story? What are the gaps between the story and reality? On websites that rate employers, such as Glassdoor and others, what kind of comments does our company receive?

_____

_____

_____

_____

_____

_____

_____

Do we respect diversity of opinions and lifestyles in our organization? To what degree is our culture open to people being the same person both at work and outside work? What potential biases or unspoken norms might exist about the kind of people who fit in here?

_____

_____

_____

Looking at the answers you have given above, and the discussions that followed, what are the most important things for your team to note about trust in your organization? Fill in the chart below to capture the key points of your discussion and observations.

What is working	What is not working	Options for improving in this area

Caring

Feeling cared for and caring for others are core human needs. They are powerful drives. Conscious cultures are marked by genuine caring for all stakeholders. Caring begets caring, and when the company cares for its stakeholders, the stakeholders in turn exhibit caring toward the company. People in conscious cultures behave in a manner that is thoughtful, gentle, considerate, and compassionate.

Caring begins right at the top with the CEO and the executive team. They set the tone and demonstrate what this means.

A few years ago, one of us came across a billboard on a New York City bus shelter. It read, "If your company cared, it would be in the caring business." The ad was for a job site, and the message was clear: the vast majority of companies do *not* care, and your best option is to find another company that also doesn't care, but where you may be somewhat better off.

The core question here is pretty simple: Do frontline employees believe that the leaders of the company care about them? There is a trickle-down effect around caring in a culture, and if the people on the front line don't feel cared for, then there has been a breakdown somewhere in the chain of command. Ultimately, caring should exist at all levels, but the canary in the coal mine is whether the frontline people believe—consistently, across divisions, and across functions—that they're cared for as human beings.

It's hard to imagine how people who feel uncared for can feel the passion and commitment that underpins the volunteer premium we talked about earlier. In our experience working with one company recently, it was evident from an employee climate survey and focus groups that they had a very performance-driven business culture. People in the organization obviously perceived that performance came first and people came second. Despite being involved in an exciting area of biotechnology, the company is beginning to see attrition increase significantly as people burn out. The excitement of the mission on the cutting edge of science has been very inspirational to people. However, the lack of true caring from management and senior leadership has created an environment in which even the passion for the science can't overcome the drawbacks of the company's performance-obsessed atmosphere. The atmosphere is also beginning to affect the company's ability to recruit. Others in the industry describe it as a sweatshop. Think about what that means when you are trying to recruit some of the best minds in the world to contribute to your success.

Many mistakenly believe that a culture can be either caring or performance-driven, but not both. This is a false dichotomy. While it is more challenging for leaders to foster both approaches, people who feel cared for can be held to high standards as well. As parents, we both care about our children and expect them to meet certain expectations of behavior. In many cases, it is *because* we care about them that we set such high standards for them. Paradoxically, people often see a caring attitude and high performance standards as a trade-off rather than recognizing that the way to realize sustained high performance is having people feel cared about.

Too often, people think of caring in isolation. Caring without accountability, caring without empowering people, and caring without an inspiring vision and good execution mean nothing in the end. So the key challenge for leadership is to create a culture that combines caring with other elements that help drive the performance of the business.

When Bill George became CEO of Medtronics, he found that the company had a very nurturing culture and that people seemed to care, but there was a pronounced lack of accountability. People were letting each other and the company down. George sought to increase accountability without diminishing caring in the Medtronic culture.

Bob Chapman, chairman and CEO of Barry-Wehmiller, likens leadership and caring in business to parenting: you care deeply, but you also have high expectations and accountability. Some people can interpret that as a disempowering, paternalistic approach. But it is not. You can empower and care at the same time. We need to empower, trust, care, set limits, and hold people accountable for their behavior and make very clear what is acceptable and what is not. You need to set up guardrails around what's important to the organization and then empower people to manifest the culture within those boundaries—just as on the tennis court, there are lines that you must play within.

On a scale of 1 to 5, where 5 is the highest, to what extent do people on the front line of your organization feel cared for? How do you know whether they do or don't? If your response is 4 or lower, explain why they don't feel more cared for. What does it mean to care about people in your organization? How well defined is this idea, and when was the last time you discussed with your middle managers what it meant and how you aspire to demonstrate caring as an organization?

What might your team see as the dichotomy between caring for people and being a performance-driven culture? What could you do differently to ensure that you are doing both?

_____

_____

_____

_____

_____

_____

_____

_____

Looking at the answers you have given above, and the discussions that followed, what are the most important things for your team to note about authenticity in your organization? Fill in the chart below to capture the key points of your discussion and observations.

What is working	What is not working	Options for improving in this area

Transparency

We live in a transparent world in which much information of any value soon becomes known. Conscious cultures embrace this reality and benefit from it. There are few secrets in a conscious culture because there's little to hide. The question here is, do people throughout the organization understand how you operate and make money in your business?

At Whole Foods Market, salary information is widely shared with all team members. Financial books are unusually open, and strategic plans are widely discussed and disseminated. As a result, the company experiences greater team member involvement, initiative-taking, and leadership.

An approach that manifests transparency well is open-book management. One key to using this form of management successfully is educating people about your business model. They can't help improve the business results if they don't clearly understand how the business makes money. Sharing the information without putting it in the context of "here's how you contribute to it and can make a difference" can create anxiety and confusion. So hand in glove with sharing the information is education on what this information means and empowering people to do something with the knowledge.

One of our major retail clients had translated the business model down to the level of the store construction department tasked with purchasing, installing, and maintaining fixtures in the stores. A member of that team impressively explained to us how saving 5 percent on fixture costs by this department across all the stores amounted to annual savings that would finance the opening of a new store. The team members saw themselves helping support the growth strategy of the company—not just as cost savers.

Another key element of transparency is communication. How clearly and openly does the leadership team explain things to the organization? Transparent communication includes sharing how the organization is doing and explanations when major programs or changes are announced. The more transparent an organization, the more comfortable the leadership feels in being open about its decisions and why they were made. Again there is an interesting paradox here. Leaders often fear that too much communication will distract people and raise concerns or even fear about things that they can't control or need to know. How often is this fear truly warranted? Just as often, a partial announcement or no announcement gets the organizational grapevine working overtime on rumors and builds more worry and concern: "What is management hiding, and why? Are things worse than they say? Is there more bad news to come?"

Being clear from the start that you will tell people what you know when you know it is a key element of transparency and strongly reinforces trust in the leadership team. If you want your people to act like adults, to have ownership of the performance of the business, and to play a full role in trying to help you achieve goals, then you need to treat them like responsible adults who can handle the truth. Importantly, when people in the organization can see reality clearly, they can act effectively to address the issues and challenges you are facing. Otherwise, they are flying partly blind—never a good place to be if you want them to help you land the plane safely!

How well does everyone in your organization understand your business model and how you make money? Can people explain to an outsider how they help the company make money?

_____

_____

_____

_____

_____

_____

_____

How transparent are you in your communication with the organization? The last time you made a major announcement to the organization, how well did you explain why the change was made and what the expected impact was? If you had asked the frontline workers how well they understood your announcement, what would they have said?

_____

_____

_____

_____

_____

_____

_____

In the future, how can you communicate more transparently and guarantee two-way dialogue so you can get feedback on how well understood your message was and how relevant you made it to the frontline people? (How does it impact you? What can you do to help?)

_____

_____

_____

_____

_____

_____

_____

Looking at the answers you have given above, and the discussions that followed, what are the most important things for your team to note about transparency in your organization? Fill in the chart below to capture the key points of your discussion and observations.

What is working	What is not working	Options for improving in this area

Integrity

A conscious culture is marked by strict adherence to truth telling and fair dealing. The commitment to integrity goes far beyond mere adherence to laws and company policies. There is no tolerance for spin or whitewashing. People say what they mean and mean what they say. Their word is their bond.

Important questions to ask are these: What do we refuse to compromise on? What behaviors are we not going to let slip by? These questions force a leadership team to draw a proverbial line in the sand. The idea of integrity was driven home in a professional service firm that had been working on a diversity program. A well-respected senior partner had a reputation of not being on board with this initiative, saying, "What does this have to do with my clients?" Despite his enviable track record in developing business and connecting with some of the firm's biggest clients, his unwillingness to get on board with the program and his not-so-subtle undermining of the program led the executive team to make a tough choice, asking him to retire a few years early.

What are you unwilling to compromise on? Why? When was the last time the top team based a tough decision on company integrity—an unwillingness to compromise on the company's core values? Can you point to any missed opportunities to do this recently?

_____

_____

_____

_____

What issue, if addressed with integrity, will make the biggest difference in building a sense of what is most important in your organization? Are you willing to be uncompromising on this issue? Why or why not?

_____

_____

_____

_____

_____

_____

_____

Looking at the answers you have given above, and the discussions that followed, what are the most important things for your team to note about integrity in your organization? Fill in the chart below to capture the key points of your discussion and observations.

What is working	What is not working	Options for improving in this area

Learning

As living and self-organizing communities, conscious organizations are continually evolving to higher states of collective consciousness. As expressed by Whole Foods Market, "Many of our Team Members are committed to lifelong journeys of growth and development. Continual growth is not only acceptable, it is also expected. As Team Members learn and grow, so too does the organization as a whole."

Learning is sometimes seen as a "motherhood and apple pie" issue; after all, who is against learning? However, there are noticeable gaps between rhetoric and practice in most companies. At organizations that embrace learning, everyone has a personalized learning agenda each year. Companies should identify what each person wants and needs to learn and ensure that they support that learning.

At Johnson's Sausage, a well-known "small giant" in Michigan, there is only one major fireable offense—if employees don't learn anything new in a year. The key question the company asks at the employees' year-end evaluation is "What did you learn this year?"

Conscious companies encourage a clear learning and development plan for employees and hold them accountable for following it. Accountability means that companies evaluate people on, and reward them for, continuous learning. In a conscious culture, there is great weight put on helping people develop and grow in the organization, and leaders and other people who deliver on this get recognized for it.

What are you doing to help the frontline members of your organization learn to get better at what they do? Do you have systems and support in place for this? Are you helping them develop skills that will help them in their work and in their outside lives?

_____

_____

_____

_____

What is your senior team's collective learning journey this year? Do you each have areas you are learning to get better at? Have you shared this with each other? If not, why?

_____

_____

_____

_____

_____

_____

_____

_____

How well linked are your evaluation and development processes? Do your people have individualized learning agendas for the year? Do you include an evaluation of how well people have followed up on their development and learning plan when you do your performance evaluations? Does this get significant weighting in evaluating people?

_____

_____

_____

_____

_____

_____

_____

_____

Looking at the answers you have given above, and the discussions that followed, what are the most important things for your team to note about learning in your organization? Fill in the chart below to capture the key points of your discussion and observations.

What is working	What is not working	Options for improving in this area

Empowerment

If you hire people who are a strong fit with your company's culture, you can readily trust them to act intelligently and thoughtfully in service of the organization and its overarching purpose. Every team member of a conscious business should be a microcosm of the whole business, authorized to act on its behalf for the benefit of the whole company.

Here the key question is, Are frontline employees and managers empowered to act on behalf of the benefit of the whole company? This sense of empowerment is often manifest in terms of what individual employees can do to resolve a customer complaint. How much leeway do they have to spend resources on such things? A leadership team must consider several issues: Have we empowered people in our organization to make decisions that we feel will be responsible to the organization? Do we trust our people, and have we enabled them, to know what doing the right thing means in our organization? Have we as leaders and managers demonstrated with our own actions what doing the right thing means?

The next set of questions relates to how we empower people. For example, expense-reporting systems that require inordinate amounts of time signal a lack of trust and empowerment. What other systems in your organization might disempower people? The best way to found out is to actually ask people. Most companies have too many rules, which have the impact of diminishing freedom. As Dov Seidman says, "A handful of shared values are worth more than a thousand rules."

In our experience, the critical issue in empowerment lies in the mindsets at the top of the organization. Leaders who can find the right balance between setting standards for their teams and empowering them to deliver results embody more of a servant leadership orientation than they do a traditional command-and-control approach. We will come back to this issue in our discussion of conscious leadership.

What key business decisions can your frontline managers make without seeking permission?

_____

_____

_____

_____

_____

_____

_____

On a scale of 1 to 5 (where 5 is the highest), how empowered do people at the front line feel in your organization? Middle management? Why do they feel this way? If your response is below 4, what would it take to move to a 4 or 5 for both groups? How often do you encourage people at the front line to make their own decisions on key business issues that they have a direct influence over? For example, does customer service have the power to make decisions? Does the production line? For example, think of how Toyota enables its people to stop the assembly line if they see problems. What is your practice in this area?

_____

_____

_____

_____

_____

_____

_____

_____

What are the implications for you as a leadership team and as an organization? What must you do so that decisions can be made closer to the front line? What are the implications for your systems and processes of empowering more frontline employees? For hiring? Onboarding? Training and development?

_____

_____

_____

_____

_____

_____

_____

Looking at the answers you have given above, and the discussions that followed, what are the most important things for your team to note about empowerment in your organization? Fill in the chart below to capture the key points of your discussion and observations.

What is working	What is not working	Options for improving in this area

Final Thoughts

In which of the TACTILE areas are we the strongest?

_____

_____

_____

_____

In which of these areas do we feel we have the most room for improvement?

_____

_____

_____

_____

When we reflect on this chapter, what issues keep us awake at night?

_____

_____

_____

_____

If we worked on only one of these areas, which area would have the biggest impact on our business? What would we do to have an impact on it?

_____

_____

_____

_____

In this chapter, you assessed where your culture is today. In the next chapter, we begin the dialogue around your vision of the kind of culture that would make you the proudest and happiest, and we suggest some concrete steps to move your organization toward that.

Chapter 12

Building a Conscious Culture: The Conscious-Culture Playbook

In this chapter, we will ask you to reflect on the questions and self-evaluation you have been conducting and agree on what this means for your organization. You no doubt highlighted many areas that needed improvement. That is normal; change takes time, and few companies excel at all aspects of TACTILE.

Conscious culture begins with clarifying what such a culture might look like for your organization and identifying the values that will drive the behaviors to get you there. These tasks all come together in the development of what we call a *conscious-culture playbook* and the rollout of that playbook to the entire organization. Clearly, the top team must be aligned on this topic, but the leaders' mere desire for a conscious culture is not enough for success. The team then needs to walk the talk; the organization will be watching what you do, not just what you say. Further, the conscious-culture playbook should be in everyone's hands—and in their hearts and minds. You have to make these values and behaviors relevant to people; conscious culture needs to become "the way we do things around here." Through the playbook, you share the whys and hows of the prevalent behaviors you are evolving in your organization. Don't keep these ideas a secret.

Caring at the Core: The Barry-Wehmiller Culture

Extraordinary cultures are built on truly caring for human beings. The hallmarks of virtually every conscious company are high engagement, passion, commitment, creativity, resilience, and caring. Few companies illustrate this dictum better than Barry-Wehmiller, a 130-year-old industrial machinery manufacturing company headquartered in St. Louis, with operations in numerous other locations in the United States and several other countries. The company has grown from $20 million in annual revenues in 1975 to over $2.5 billion through a combination of organic growth and approximately eighty acquisitions.

Barry-Wehmiller acquires small manufacturing companies that are in similar or complementary businesses. Most of the acquired companies were struggling, and some were dying, at the time of the acquisition. The acquired companies faced somewhat similar challenges: no vision, toxic and dysfunctional cultures, and self-serving leadership. The Barry-Wehmiller culture, in contrast, is based on caring for people as human beings, inspiring them through a shared vision, and recognizing and celebrating their goodness. It's a simple template. When Barry-Wehmiller acquires a company, it empowers people to take charge of their own lives and their own work. It gives them lots of assistance and says, "We know how to do this. You're going to do the work; we're just going to help you." It doesn't have a tight deadline under which things have to get done; it practices what it calls "courageous patience." The company doesn't resort to layoffs; it says, "Everybody who wants to gets to participate. We think all of you can be part of this new system, not just the true believers. Eventually everybody will get it, and each of you will get it on your own time." That is a unique approach, one that is powerful and worth emulating but rare. Few companies have that level of patience or such a strong commitment to the well-being of people. This commitment is encapsulated in Barry-Wehmiller's tagline: "We measure success by the way we touch the lives of people."

Barry-Wehmiller also brings in deep expertise around lean manufacturing and how to empower people to improve the business processes that affect them. But it's not Barry-Wehmiller's knowledge of manufacturing that gets extraordinary results; it's the way the company influences the culture. It empowers people with what it refers to as responsible freedom and holds people to be self-accountable for the lives they want to create.

Barry-Wehmiller changes the culture in the companies it acquires by following three critical elements. One is making sure people understand how important it is to care for people. The second is inspiring people around a compelling vision of what can be. The third is recognizing and celebrating the goodness in people.

There is powerful evidence that this approach—blending a sound strategy with an unwavering commitment to the well-being of people—works to create more value of many kinds. Long-term-oriented actions rooted in caring start to eventually show up in sustained superior performance. Barry-Wehmiller's financial performance has been extraordinary; the share price grew at a compounded annual rate of 15.5 percent over sixteen years. The company has never sold a single acquisition. Creating such a track record takes strong leaders who truly have the courage of their convictions, who believe that treating people well is nonnegotiable, and who give them responsible freedom and hold them accountable. When you do that consistently over time, people rise to the challenge and superior performance follows; ordinary people become capable of doing extraordinary things. The people who were the most cynical at the outset often end up being your most passionate advocates. This has happened repeatedly at Barry-Wehmiller; some of its most inspirational leaders today are those who held out for a long time.

Barry-Wehmiller CEO and chairman Bob Chapman offers this call to action:

That we become Truly Human Leaders, leaders who see their role as the stewardship of the lives entrusted to them; that we see these lives entrusted to us not as functions but each as "someone's precious child" . . . to grasp that the way we exercise this leadership privilege will have a profound impact on this person and the way this person will impact the lives of others in their homes, communities and the world.
We do this by:

CARING: *Caring is much more that being nice/gracious/considerate. It is creating a safe environment where people feel valued for who they are and what they do. Our business and organizational vision seeks to ensure that under our care we are taking them to a better place, and we will get there by enabling them to discover, develop and share their gifts towards the realization of that vision.*

INSPIRING: *We transition from "managing" to "inspiring" our teams, which allows for the highest level of expression of their gifts.*

CELEBRATING: *Along this journey, we focus on positive leadership—looking for the goodness in people and shining a light on their goodness for others to see, appreciate and emulate.*

We can change the world through business by embracing the true essence of leadership and creating a culture where each team member goes home safe, healthy and fulfilled, thereby helping to create a more caring world.

For more on Barry-Wehmiller, see the book *Everybody Matters.*[a]

a. Bob Chapman and Raj Sisodia, *Everybody Matters: The Extraordinary Power of Caring for Your People as Family* (New York: Portfolio/Penguin, 2015).

A Values-Based Cultural Transformation

There are several approaches you can take to bring about the culture you would like to create in your organization. The approach we advocate here is built on a *values-based* culture transformation. In changing or evolving a culture, we must be clear on the kinds of behaviors we are seeking to encourage. The values-based approach outlined here begins with clarity on the values that reflect the desired behavior. We recommend an iterative approach and dialogue between the leadership team and the rest of the organization to develop these values and behaviors. This approach ensures a sense of ownership and input from the entire organization. To start, the senior leadership team provides a preliminary framework around the aspirational culture that the organization is aiming toward and then engages the rest of the organization in a discussion about what is needed for the desired future culture to come to life in the organization. To better involve the entire organization, the senior leaders will create a culture committee that will, at the start, help with the development and rollout of a new conscious-culture playbook and, later, help keep the culture alive and evolving. The steps in this process are discussed in detail in this chapter.

Visualizing the Future Aspirational Culture

In this step, the leadership team envisions what the future culture might look like, and then begins to articulate this vision in terms of behaviors that it is seeking to introduce and encourage in the organization.

The first step is a visualization exercise. Have the leadership team form a small circle of chairs facing each other. Start by having everyone take a moment to settle into their seats and relax. After a minute or two of silence, ask the team to imagine the ideal culture for the organization three to five years from now. One way to do this is to lay out a set of picture cards on the floor and ask the team to pick two pictures that represent what that future culture might look like. (These picture cards can be obtained from various sources, for example, Brighter Strategy cards at https://www.brighterstrategies.com/product/jumbo-cards-30-decks/, or School of Babel coaching cards at https://schoolofbabel.com/store/Picture-Coaching-Cards-p53144757.)

Have each individual write down two or three words, below, about what the chosen pictures represent for this future culture. Have people share what they wrote with each other in pairs.

_____

_____

_____

_____

_____

_____

_____

Now, break out into two groups. Have each group compare notes in terms of the desired future values and come up with a list of five or six values that the participants believe represent this ideal future and post these on a flip chart.

_____

_____

_____

_____

_____

_____

Next, bring the two groups together, and create a consolidated list with no more than five to seven future values of the ideal culture. (If you have more than seven values, you usually start to dilute their significance and impact.) Push the team members to be clear on what they believe is most important to the future culture they are seeking to create.

_____

_____

_____

_____

_____

_____

The next step is to expand on each of these values. On a flip chart, create a page with the name of the value on top. Write a brief one- or two-sentence description of the value. Create a table with the first column showing the desired behaviors, the second column showing the undesirable behaviors, and a third column that reads, "What does it mean for a leader to walk the talk on this value?" Do this for each value.

The following example came from a leadership team that was forming after a merger of two organizations of roughly the same size. The team picked being "one global team" as one of its values, and the value was described as follows: "As our two organizations come together we will leave our legacy behind us and form a new global team that role models for the organization that we act as 'one team.'"

BEHAVIORS THAT SUPPORT THIS VALUE	BEHAVIORS THAT DO NOT SUPPORT THIS VALUE	WHAT IT MEANS FOR A LEADER TO WALK THE TALK ON THIS CHARACTERISTIC
Mutual respect	The way we have always done it	We seek to win as a team.
Trusting each other	"I" versus "we"	We reward teamwork.
"We" versus "I"	Empire building	We seek to bridge the gaps—bring people together from the two organizations.
Teamwork	Discrimination	Focus on the potential of the new entity versus the status quo.
Being considerate	Controlling	

By filling in a table like this, you begin to create a concrete set of behaviors that you are looking for around this value. Repeat this exercise for each of the five to seven values the leadership team came up with. After you have finished, transcribe the flip charts, and pull the responses together into a single document—the first draft of your conscious-culture book. We will come back to this document later in this chapter when we further discuss the role of the culture committees.

Engaging the Organization in the Culture Change

The next step involves getting the organization more deeply involved in the process. There are several ways of doing this. You can engage with a number of focus groups in the organization to get feedback on the first draft of the conscious-culture book. Alternatively, you can be more involved and form a culture committee that will develop the feedback process and then roll out, maintain, and evolve the culture in the organization. In this next section, we will focus on the culture committee approach.

Conscious-Culture Committees

A culture committee keeps the culture alive in the organization, becoming the keeper of the culture. The formation of this committees signals to the organization that this effort is important; it is also the first step in engaging the organization more deeply in the process.

The culture committee is a team of well-connected and respected individuals in the organization who can be champions for the aspirational culture. Typically, they are a combination of A-level players and connectors—people whom the organization looks to as role models or influencers. What they say and don't say can make a big difference to the general mood of the organization. If you can capture their enthusiasm and create commitment within this group, the effort stands a much greater likelihood of success. Their role is as follows:

- Help develop a practical definition of the future culture, and make it real, actionable, and relevant to people in the organization.

- Help sustain the change effort and maintain the gains.

  - Ensure that the rollout and launch of the program is successful.

  - Identify and design the reinforcing mechanisms (processes, infrastructure, and policies).

  - Develop forums and tools to keep the new culture alive in the organization.

Although this culture committee will initially be a single handpicked group, over time you should develop such committees at both the corporate and the local levels. Local committees are responsible for maintaining and encouraging the culture at the local level. They have responsible freedom to innovate on how they bring the culture to life locally. There's a twofold benefit to local committees:

1. By having a group of cultural champions at the local level, you maintain energy around the topic.

2. By having the local committee decide what works best in that environment, you apply the cultural values that have the most impact to that location.

Local activities that the culture committee organizes can be as simple as having Cultural Fridays once a month, where the committee picks a value, offers a free lunch, and facilitates a discussion about what that cultural value means and how people can live it in their part of the organization. Zappos has a number of cultural practices like this. For example, each month, it picks a cultural value to celebrate. During the month, people have weekly conversations that are encouraged on topics around the cultural value of the month.

At the corporate level, the culture committee maintains the consistency of the framework of values and behaviors and, as highlighted in chapter 13, looks for ways to institutionalize the culture in the company's procedures, performance management, and people policies. The corporate culture committee also acts as a sounding board to the executive team on how to evolve the culture.

Forming and Engaging the Culture Committee

Identify potential culture committee candidates from across a variety of departments and locations. Once these candidates are identified, you should agree with the management team on the committee leaders, and invite them for a formal introduction to their new role. This will help set expectations. The idea is not to create culture police but to foster a sense of pride in the organization and the opportunity to have an impact on its future.

Candidate name	Location	Reason

The next step is to onboard the committee members with a deep understanding of the values and what it means to act on them as role models. To kick off the culture committee, consider doing the following with the committee at a daylong meeting:

- Meet with members of the senior leadership team (the committee's de facto sponsors) to discuss and define the committee's role.

- Have the committee members work through the initial draft of values by the leadership team—and provide feedback on what resonates with them and what does not. Ask them for any suggestions to make the draft more meaningful to the organization.

- Codesign and implement culture interventions and reinforcements that are practical and have high impact.

- Start modeling the new culture: "embodying the spirit of the future."

- Define what the committee members will do in their first three phases of work and the immediate next steps to move forward in phase 1 (see next section).

The culture committee will be involved in a three-phase approach to kick off and maintain the culture change.

Phase 1: Validation and Engagement with the Organization

The goal of this phase is to help define, activate, and make relevant the aspirational model of the culture. The culture committee will work with the leadership team to create a tangible description of the aspirational culture. First, the committee members review and give feedback on the initial work that the leadership team has done.

Next, they take this initial draft to the organization to validate it, to get the organization's feedback, and to identify issues that may need to be addressed. They also determine if any parts of the organization are already embracing the desired culture.

To obtain organizational feedback, each committee member should interview five to ten fellow employees. This group should include a fair representation of the organization: middle managers as well as frontline employees and frontline leaders. Sample questions for the focus groups include the following:

- Do these values resonate with you? Why or why not?

- What do you see as good behaviors and bad behaviors around each of these values?

- What does it mean for a leader to "walk the talk" around this value?

- What are the biggest barriers around this behavior today?

After interviewing the employees, the committee members should then come back together as a group to debrief on what they have learned, in particular the following:

- Key barriers and any other issues that need to be addressed

- Places in the organization where a conscious culture is already at play

The committee will present its findings and recommendations to the leadership team and finalize them in a conscious culture playbook (see the sidebar "The Conscious-Culture Playbook"). It will also develop a rollout plan that addresses the potential barriers described above and that takes advantage of the places already enculturated in the organization.

The Conscious-Culture Playbook

After the culture committee shares its findings with the executive team, together they develop the culture playbook. For each of the usually five to seven values the group has chosen, the culture playbook describes the behaviors and the leadership challenges that are involved. This working document should be shared with the organization as a first draft for feedback. The executive team creates the final draft of the playbook and publishes it. The final document should include the following important elements:

- Organizational purpose, mission, and vision

- Values (short, quick to remember and to reference)

- Principles (description of the principles underlying the values)

- Desired behaviors (for each value)

- Over time, real-life examples from the recognition and celebration programs

Access the Zappos culture book though the link below.

URL: https://www.ccfieldguide.com/zappos

Search Words: Conscious Capitalism Field Guide Zappos Culture Book Example

Phase 2: Rollout Plan

In phase 2, the culture committee develops and helps execute a plan to educate the organization on what its cultural values are. To do this, the members will first develop a plan to communicate to the organization an initial understanding of the values and why they are important. They might use a traditional communication campaign, conduct town-hall-like meetings, set up local culture committees, and hold lunch-and-learn meetings with themselves or with the leadership team, or with both groups. The plan should use social-media platforms to make clear what the desired behaviors are and to create a two-way dialogue with the organization around what "good" looks like—and what might be the barriers to consistently behaving in this way.

Design a program to make it relevant to everyone: What does this mean for me? This usually involves department/team level discussions with reflection exercises on what they see as the challenges in moving from the current mindsets and behaviors to the new aspirational model. Ask them how this can be relevant to their roles: What does good behavior look like for them and their teams? The more granular this can be made, the more likely it is to be relevant and therefore "owned and understood."

Phase 3: Maintain and Evolve

The goal of phase 3 is to ensure that the values are alive in the organization and that they evolve in their practice.

As one client reflected to us, you know your values are alive in the organization when people have tough discussions over what the values mean and how they should be applied. If your values are not being discussed, then they are not alive in the organization. This lack of certainty arises because you can never cover all the circumstances and behaviors that arise in the day-to-day business. Therefore, people need to continually use the values as a north pole to guide behavior. There will be times when the value may not be clear. Consequently, when people in the organization start talking about what it might mean to live this value in a particular situation, you know they have internalized the importance of the value. For example, at Whole Foods Market, its eight values are used to make critical decisions. When a major issue comes up and various scenarios are discussed, the last step in the decision-making process is to review those scenarios in light of the company's values and to discuss which scenario is most in line with those values.

Begin a campaign of education to design and host events to remind and reinforce the values within the organization. The key emphasis is on continuing to educate people on what it means to live the values. If the values are not being lived and debated each day, they're not alive.

How Southwest Airlines Sustains a Culture of "LUV"

Southwest Airlines has a unique and powerful culture that is rooted in three core values:

- A warrior spirit
- A servant's heart
- A fun-luving attitude (Southwest spells *love* as "LUV," which is also its stock market symbol)

A "warrior spirit" is about being fearless in creating the right customer experience—being willing to do what it takes to please and delight this group. A "servant's heart" is about putting people first and treating them with care and respect. The third value is self-explanatory; Southwest wants people who have a sense of humor, who don't take themselves too seriously. These core values are reflected in the persona of Herb Kelleher, the legendary leader who built the airline and inspired its unique culture.

Southwest uses these values to hire people and evaluate them once they are hired. The company has extensive recognition programs to celebrate employees who exemplify its values—nearly fifty thousand commendations a year from within the company as well as from customers. Only 2 percent of employees voluntarily leave the company each year, compared to the industry average of 10 to 20 percent.[a]

Sustaining a distinctive culture takes effort and focus. According to CEO Gary Kelly, "The Southwest Culture has thrived, but it hasn't been easy." Maintaining the culture "has been both our biggest accomplishment and our most significant challenge."[b] Southwest has done it by following these guidelines:

- Ensure that the culture is seen as everybody's responsibility.

- Create culture committees. Southwest has both local and corporate culture committees.

- Hire and promote leaders who embody the culture.

- Include how well people are living the culture in annual performance appraisals.

Southwest has a unique "Culture Services" department with nearly thirty employees, charged with overseeing the culture committees and other ways in which the company culture is nurtured. The Culture Services department is also in charge of the many celebrations that take place at the company every year. It also includes an "Internal Customer Care" group whose job is to acknowledge significant events in employees' lives, such as having a baby or dealing with a serious health issue.

The national culture committee has over a hundred volunteers, from mail-room workers to company officers. Volunteers serve three-year terms, and the committee meets four times a year for a mandatory full-day meeting. They learn about key challenges facing the company and brainstorm ways to strengthen the culture and show appreciation to employees. Nominees to serve on the culture committee are vetted by Culture Services employees to ensure that the candidates are exemplars of the company's values and have the time to devote to the committee. Each committee member spends three days in the field each year—sometimes on his or her days off. Once the volunteers complete their three-year term, many join the Alumni Team and continue to support the culture in myriad ways.[c]

a. Ken Makovsky, "Behind the Southwest Airlines Culture," *Forbes*, November 21, 2013, www.forbes.com /sites/kenmakovsky/2013/11/21/behind-the-southwest-airlines-culture/#623e2de63798.

b. Ibid.

c. Chris Lauer, *Southwest Airlines* (Santa Barbara, CA: Greenwood Publishing, 2010).

The Role of the Leadership Team

Obviously, the leadership team will need to lead by example on these values and behaviors. There is a twofold role here: leading by example and constantly referring to and explaining examples of these behaviors in action to the organization.

- Make the following step a part of the management process: Spend at least thirty minutes at least once a quarter (every month for the first six months) talking about one of the company's values and how it has affected the team and individuals' decision making. Cite good examples of these effects. Talk about examples that you or others in the company would do over—the missed opportunities to live the values. Discuss what the people could have done instead.

- Make this step a part of annual leadership feedback: Individual leaders should get feedback from team peers on the perception of their walking the talk. The rest of the organization should be surveyed on the question "Does the leadership team walk the talk on values?"

With the Organization

- Begin *every* presentation to the organization with a review of one value. For example, at DuPont, the value of safety was so important that every meeting in the organization, regardless of location, began with a safety briefing. (In an office setting, a presentation of the value of safety included highlighting where the exits were and, to one of the authors, pointing out that we should tape down the slide projector cord to make sure no one tripped over it.)

- Regularly celebrate examples of great behavior with your teams. You cannot overcommunicate and overcelebrate values and behaviors in an organizational journey like this.

How Can You Make Your Culture Conscious?

By RICHARD BARRETT, chairman and founder, Barrett Values Centre

You make your culture conscious by measuring it. This involves carrying out a baseline cultural diagnostic (a cultural values assessment), including data cuts for each business unit, department, and team, as well as data cuts for demographic categories such as gender and age (see appendix C for more on cultural values assessments).

The results of the values assessment will allow you to identify the cultural health of the organization and the cultural health of the subcultures that exist in different business units, locations, departments, and teams. It will also tell you precisely what you need to change to create a high-performance organization.

One of the best ways to assess cultural values is to use the Barrett Values Centre's Cultural Transformation Tools. The details of how the tools work and examples of how companies have used these to support culture transformation are discussed in appendix C.

Once you have defined your organization's cultural values and made them and the accompanying behaviors relevant, the next step is to institutionalize the values in the systems and processes in the organization. This embedding of cultural values and behavior, which ensures that you are reinforcing the recommendations of your conscious-culture playbook, will be the focus of the next chapter.

Chapter 13

Evolving and Deepening Your Culture

In this chapter, we will focus on the elements of the culture that we call cultural practices—the "what we do around here" that reflects on our culture. For example, a cultural practice at Whole Foods Market is the biannual vote on the benefits program. Given the empowerment and transparency in the organization, team members get to select which benefits they value and how much they are willing to pay for them. Rather than making a top-down decision, the leaders ask team members what they most value—and then respond with those benefits that are most popular.

In chapter 12, we spoke about getting everyone in the organization to understand why the chosen values are important and how we expect people to show up and behave. In this chapter we will turn to the "what we do" and how we reinforce and support these values and behaviors in the organization. If our existing systems and processes encourage different kinds of behavior, that will clearly slow down the uptake of the new behaviors and undermine the credibility of the effort. We find this conflict of purpose most clearly in the area of compensation and rewards. Many companies ask people to take a long view of the business and the implementation of purpose and values and yet employ rewards and bonus systems that focus almost exclusively on short-term financial results.

We need to ensure that we are encouraging the right behavior and eliminating systems and policies that encourage conflicting behaviors. These systems, policies, and procedures are part of the cultural practices of the organization. They must align with the conscious-culture playbook for the success of your conscious-culture journey. Examples of cultural practices at Whole Foods are listed in figure 13-1.

Figure 13-1: Cultural practices at Whole Foods Market

Open-door policy	Team leader surveys
Town halls	Team builds
Paid time-off drives	Walking customers to product
Appreciations	Job dialogues
100% satisfaction guarantee	Future search
Tribal gathering	Team member emergency fund
Panel interviews	Team vote
Sampling policy	Morale surveys
Vision day	Team meetings
Team member awareness group	Sabbaticals
Gainsharing	

Hiring

Perhaps the single most important element of maintaining and deepening your culture is the hiring process. At Southwest Airlines, the motto is, "Hire for culture fit, train for skills." Whole Foods Market uses a panel approach to making hiring decisions, with team members as part of the process.

Some companies highlight their culture and values on the first page of their employment form. People applying to work need to sign a statement that they have read and understood the culture and values before filling out the employment application. As a result, there is no second-guessing that they didn't understand the importance of culture and culture fit in that organization.

On the flip side of hiring is the question of when to let someone go. It can be an act of compassion to allow someone to move to a different organization where there's a better fit. The executive team members should agree on what they will not compromise on, on which values and cultural characteristics are non-negotiable. For one professional services firm, this discussion of what they will not compromise on led to the early retirement of one of their senior-most partners who was not walking the talk on a particular set of values. Everyone knew this; it surprised no one and sent a very strong message to the organization when the senior leadership team finally decided to ask that person to leave.

Zappos has a unique policy of paying people $2,000 to $4,000 (depending on the person's level at hiring) to quit after the first two weeks of onboarding. The idea is to encourage those who realize that the company's culture is not a good fit for them to leave right away. The damage a hire with poor cultural fit can do magnifies over time. The sooner you can assess whether there's a strong culture fit, the better.

What hiring practices do you have in place to ensure a good fit with the values you have in place? Can you recall a time when you made a tough decision and turned down a highly qualified job candidate because of a lack of fit in culture or values? If not, why not? If yes, what was the basis for determining this lack of fit?

_____

_____

_____

_____

_____

_____

_____

What new hiring practices can you implement to support better candidate fit with the culture?

_____

_____

_____

_____

Onboarding

You only get to make a first impression once. As you think about hiring the right people for values and culture fit, the next important interaction with them is their onboarding. This is a great opportunity to share with people what your values are and why and how these translate into behaviors. As Lars Björk, the CEO of software services company Qlik, put it, "We fly every new employee to Lund, Sweden—where it all started—for two weeks so they can understand the corporate culture firsthand; they can learn to build the product and learn to sell the product together with other employees. It doesn't matter if you are an administrative assistant or a CFO; all employees need this common experience."[1]

At onboarding, you have the opportunity to train people on your purpose, values, and expected behaviors and norms and how you expect them to live these. Further, you can introduce them to your business model (how you make money) and help them connect their role to the success of the organization. At this time, new hires can learn the history of the organization and where you are heading. It is a compelling experience when the CEO spends three or four hours reviewing the firm's values with new hires. It sends a message from the start on what is valued in the organization and why.

In addition to the formal onboarding program (which can last from three days to two weeks), conscious companies need to pay attention to what happens in the first ninety days in the employee's new role. The ninety-day mark is a time to check in and see how things are going. It is an opportunity to course-correct and seek feedback on how well someone is perceived to be settling in. Ideally this check-in begins with the employee's self-reflection and then is augmented by a formal or informal collection of input from those who have worked with this person. This is a key teaching moment for this person.

Some organizations go a step further and make the first ninety days a probationary period to make sure that the person does fit in with the culture of the firm. For example, at Whole Foods Market, store-based employees are hired onto teams in the store. The team has significant input through the interviewing process into that person's hiring. Then after a ninety-day trial period, the new hire needs a two-thirds vote by his or her team to move to a full-time spot. This arrangement ensures that the team has responsibility for both the hiring and the fit with the team after the initial trial period.

Managing Rewards, Recognition, and Performance

If a company says that values and behaviors matter and then ignores these elements in evaluating people or giving them annual feedback, a profound disconnect is created. A critical part of maintaining and deepening the culture is therefore recognizing and rewarding people for being exemplars of living the culture. This can take the form of a formal review in which the person is given feedback on how his or her personal performance compares with expectations, or in a mix of formal and informal reward and recognition programs. At its simplest, in a 360-degree annual review, you can ask whether this person walks the talk on values. Ask people to set goals around how they will live the values in the next year.

Your organization must let people know that how they do things matters, not just what they have achieved. This focus should not be seen as a trade-off; doing the right thing *and* achieving results should be the goal. Ensure that anyone promoted into a leadership position, and, most importantly, into a highly visible leadership role, passes the values and behaviors "sniff test" with the organization. Nothing will undermine your success more than people seeing the advancement of leaders who are obviously not exemplars of the culture.

The collection of feedback and the assessment of whether a person is working in alignment with the company values also feed into the compensation approach. Check that what you are formally rewarding with bonuses and salary increases aligns with the values and behaviors you are seeking. As described in chapter 2, for example, beverage company FIFCO adjusted its compensation policies as it became a more conscious company.

Outside of the formal evaluation processes, conscious cultures have both formal and informal reward and recognition programs that reinforce values and the right behaviors. Companies such as Zappos and Life is Good produce annual culture books. At Life is Good, the book is a compilation of letters or stories that the company has received either from employees or from customers or clients about how the company has lived its culture and values. One company we know has an annual Academy Awards of Culture. The event energizes the organization; a grassroots nomination process is followed by companywide voting.

Barry-Wehmiller has a fleet of flashy sports cars that are awarded for a week to a person who best exemplifies the cultural and leadership characteristics that the company holds dear. Many people have reflected on how important this symbolic gesture is. This highly successful practice underscores that financial rewards are not usually the best way to recognize people in the organization. Recognition and authentic appreciation from peers can be far more meaningful.

A Brazilian retailer Reserva, which was cited by *Fast Company* magazine as one of the most innovative retailers in Latin America in 2015, has a very simple practice to recognize behaviors aligned with its values. Every employee, when joining Reserva, is asked to write down three achievable wishes. These wishes should be things the employees would do on their own if they had some extra free time and some extra money to pay for it. The responses are added to the employee's personal file in the HR department.

As Reserva has grown, the distance between people has grown too, physically (operations in different locations) and socially (the number of employees has increased tenfold from the company's inception). So every time someone from one department does something that reflects Reserva's values and helps make the workplace better, the company posts that story on a board where everyone can see it. Once a month, the story that best represents the company's values is selected. A prank is played on the person who lived that value, and in the process, one of his or her three wishes is fulfilled. This experience has a strong impact on company morale. It generates stories, conversations, and excitement for much longer, and with much deeper impact, than any financial reward could ever do.

Tracking Culture in a Meaningful Way

Just as we started the cultural journey by assessing where we were, it is equally important to continue to track the progress that we're making. This step can take a couple of different forms.

You need a tool that creates both a baseline and a means of assessing whether and where we're improving or deteriorating in our living of the culture. The tool can be supplemented with periodic surveys on particular elements of the culture. These surveys can be as simple as ten questions you regularly ask the organization or a handful of questions around each value. You should do an annual deep dive and supplement it with a quarterly pulse check, which we highly recommend in the early rollout of a culture initiative. You need to see small wins and get a sense of traction. Typically, these survey tools also allow you to break the results down by area of the business—business units or departments and geographic locations. The breakdown can help you understand which parts of the organization are responding better than others, learn what they are doing, and spread their practices to other parts of the organization. Conversely, when you see where leaders are not getting traction with their teams, senior leaders and your culture committees can initiate a timely intervention.

The leadership team members should also devote sufficient time to discussing the results and what commitments they're willing to make to address any issues raised. They should develop a follow-up plan and communicate this to the organization. We recommend you do this within thirty days of the survey. Timely communication lets the organization know that you take the survey results seriously and are doing something to respond.

Finally, the level of participation in the survey indicates how much credibility the organization give the survey. Initial response rates at the 50 to 60 percent level should rise over time toward 80 to 90 percent. Critical to participation is the perception that these surveys matter.

While we have discussed a customized approach to surveys, there are also well-developed organizational and culture surveys available to assist with this. These include the Barrett Values Centre's Cultural Transformation Tools (detailed in chapter 12 and appendix C), the Great Places to Work survey, and the

Gallup Engagement surveys. Several emerging new tools are also available for this task: Culture IQ, Culture Amp, and Peakon are recent examples. These instruments can give you benchmarks with peer organizations on your scores. These benchmarks can lead to important discussion about what you aspire to and where you are now on the journey.

State-of-the-Culture Updates

Every one or two years, you should step back and assess how well the overall culture is serving the business. When you are just beginning to change your culture, you should assess your progress every year. Once you are further along, do this every two years. The assessment can involve an off-site where the senior team takes surveys and gathers other feedback from employees, focus groups, and other stakeholders about what's working and what's not working within the culture. A simple way of doing this is for you and your executive team to fill in the following chart:

Do more	Stop doing	Start doing

Mind the Gap

Now the key questions for you and your leadership team are these:

- **What are the biggest gaps between what you aspire to and where you stand today?**

- **What issues, if addressed, are likely to have the biggest impact on the business?**

- **What three areas of your culture could have the biggest impact in the next twelve to eighteen months? List them below.**

    1. _____

        _____

    2. _____

        _____

    3. _____

        _____

At this point, you have a good road map to establish a conscious culture and processes to help maintain and evolve it over time. In part 4, we will explore conscious leadership: how to develop conscious leaders within your organization.

Part Four

CONSCIOUS LEADERSHIP

*L*eadership matters. It matters today more than ever. But the old way has run its course. Leadership today must be based on purpose, inspiration, caring, and compassion. Conscious leadership is fully human leadership; it integrates the masculine and feminine, the heart and the mind, the spirit and the soul. It blends Western systems and efficiency with Eastern wisdom and effectiveness.

For millennia, most people who became leaders were driven to attain these roles because of their thirst for power or lust for riches. They used fear, intimidation, and even brutality to achieve their goals. But their successes were inevitably partial and short-lived, because their actions continually sowed the seeds of the next upheaval, the next rebellion, the emergence of the next ruthless leader.

When businesses are led by individuals who are driven by service to people and the firm's higher purpose—individuals who lead through developing and inspiring others—it creates, in author Fred Kofman's resonant words, "peace and happiness in the individual, respect and solidarity in the community, and mission accomplishment in the organization."[1]

The four chapters in this part of the book will help you evolve as a conscious leader and develop leaders for the organization going forward (see figure P4-1 for a summary of the chapters). We will explore why conscious leadership matters for the future of your organization, dive into the attributes of a selfless leader, offer a wide array of practices to help you develop personal mastery, and finally suggest how this leadership approach can extend to the entire organization. We will share some real-life examples to help you develop leadership in your organization.

Figure P4-1: Overview of part 4

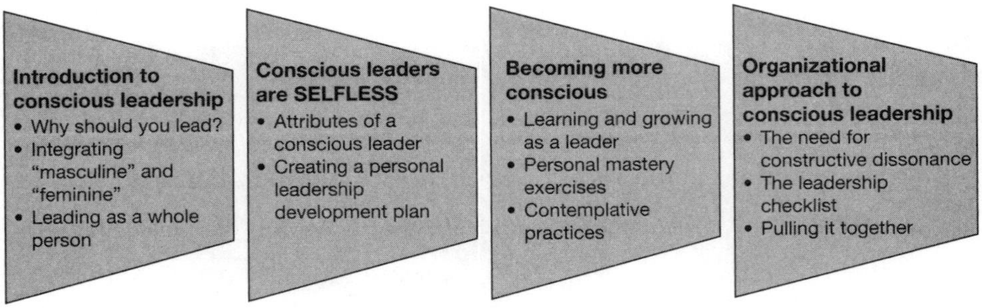

Introduction to conscious leadership
- Why should you lead?
- Integrating "masculine" and "feminine"
- Leading as a whole person

Conscious leaders are SELFLESS
- Attributes of a conscious leader
- Creating a personal leadership development plan

Becoming more conscious
- Learning and growing as a leader
- Personal mastery exercises
- Contemplative practices

Organizational approach to conscious leadership
- The need for constructive dissonance
- The leadership checklist
- Pulling it together

Summary Leadership Assessment

PARTICIPANTS: C-level executives and members of the board of directors

DESIRED NUMBER OF RESPONSES: 10

QUESTION	SCORE
1. Our leaders are deeply self-aware individuals who are in their roles because they passionately believe in the purpose of our organization and in service to our people.	
2. There is a culture of transparent communications between rank-and-file employees and senior leaders of the company.	
3. Our leaders are intuitive systems thinkers and systems feelers. In other words, not only do they think in systems terms, but they also feel the connectedness that exists across stakeholders.	
4. In our company, power and virtue go together. We consciously seek to promote individuals with the greatest integrity and capacity for caring and compassion.	
5. When we hire or promote senior leaders, we try to assess their emotional and spiritual intelligence.	
6. Most senior positions in our company are filled by promotions from within.	
7. Our leaders are passionate about mentoring and inspiring future leaders.	
8. In our company, the accountability between employees and managers runs both ways; employees are accountable to managers for their performance, and managers are accountable for making sure employees have the resources necessary to do their jobs well.	
9. Our senior leaders operate as a close-knit team.	
10. Most strategic decisions in our company emerge through consensus building.	
11. In our company, employees at every level can contribute to the strategic direction of the company.	
12. When a new leader is appointed at our company, other leaders who were considered for the position usually do *not* leave the company.	
TOTAL	

SCORES

5: We are exceptionally good at this, to the point that others should learn from us.

4: We demonstrate this most of the time, but there is room for improvement.

3: This is true for us sometimes, but our record overall is mixed.

2: This is rarely true for us.

0: We seem to embody the opposite of this, or it is missing entirely.

Add up your scores to identify the overall gap between your company and best practice (60 points). How did you score? What surprised you? What did not? Why? What are the implications?

_____

_____

_____

_____

_____

_____

_____

Chapter 14

Introduction to Conscious Leadership

The book *Conscious Capitalism* describes what conscious leadership is and how you can cultivate some of the attributes of conscious leaders. Now, however, we will highlight three additional points. The first is the vital question "Why should you be a leader?" Second, good leadership remains as essential as, if not more than, ever before, even though people have become far more capable at an individual level. Finally, we have a deeper understanding of the need to blend what have been traditionally called masculine and feminine qualities so that each of us—men and women alike—can lead as a whole person rather than as fragmented beings.

Why Should You Lead?

Why should you be entrusted with leadership? For too many people, the primary motivations for seeking to be a leader are about position and power—moving up in the world and gaining all the material rewards that usually come with that. But if those are your motivations for becoming a leader, you are highly unlikely to become a *conscious* leader. You will succumb to the temptation of using people to achieve your objectives—getting them to do things that serve you and your personal goals. These may occasionally align with what is best for all the organization's stakeholders, but usually the goals do not. If you coerce other people into doing what you perceive as good for you personally, you are not a true leader; that is the behavior of a tyrant.[1]

Why we do something matters a great deal; true leaders aspire to leadership so they can help shape an inspiring vision of the future and help people get there together. They bring out the strengths in other people and build a culture in which more people aspire to become such leaders. In his book *Leaders Eat Last*, Simon Sinek cites a tradition in the US military: at mealtimes, everybody lines up in reverse order of seniority; the soldiers are fed before the generals. That's the core idea; leaders must make sure that the people they lead are taken care of first. It is similar to a servant leadership mindset.

Leadership Matters More Than Ever

As we have said, leadership is essential today. In today's world, ordinary people are highly educated, informed, awakened, and rapidly becoming more intelligent. But the population's increased awareness does not undermine the importance of leadership.

Peter Drucker points to how critical leadership remains: "Only three things happen naturally in organizations: friction, confusion and underperformance. Everything else requires leadership."[2] In a group of any size beyond two people, you'll start to see those negative things happen. People will operate at cross-purposes and there will be friction, confusion, and underperformance—unless somebody is willing to take on the awesome responsibility of leadership.

People individually today have more inherent power and potential than in the past. The absence of conscious leadership can lead to larger negative consequences than ever before. Good leadership can enable "ordinary" people to achieve extraordinary things; poor or absent leadership can make those same people accomplish little of value or actually cause great harm.

Integrating "Masculine" and "Feminine"

Consider how leadership has been thought about and practiced for almost all of human history. In most civilizations, virtually every institution has been led by men under a limited set of traditionally regarded "hypermasculine" values. These qualities, such as domination, aggression, ambition, ruthlessness, brutality, winning at all costs, short-term thinking, and a dog-eat-dog mentality, have coexisted with but prevailed over "mature" masculine virtues such as strength, discernment, focus, discipline, and courage. So-called feminine qualities, such as a nurturing nature, compassion, the tendency to think about win-win outcomes, a longer-term perspective, and a life-affirming approach, have been suppressed and largely kept out of leadership.

We are now seeing a far greater appreciation of so-called feminine values in society. This shift is largely because we are living in a transformational time when women around the world have far greater access to education, employment, and opportunities than they did. Women now outnumber men in the workforce in the United States. The increase in women's access to higher education has been dramatic. A century ago, fewer than 20 percent of college students were women. Today, women account for nearly 60 percent of college students in the United States. The numbers are similar in other industrialized countries; in fact, women outnumber men in college everywhere except for South Asia and sub-Saharan Africa. On average, women also perform better academically. As a result, most white-collar professions will soon be numerically dominated by women, especially in fields such as law, medicine, and education.

We know that so-called masculine and feminine qualities exist in both men and women. These are all human qualities, though some are generally more pronounced in men than in women, and vice versa, but all of us have them. What has been lacking for almost all of history is an appreciation and recognition of the so-called feminine qualities or relational qualities.

John Gerzema and Michael D'Antonio, in *The Athena Doctrine: How Women (and the Men Who Think Like Them) Will Rule the Future*, surveyed sixty-four thousand people in thirteen countries and found that feminine attributes are strongly correlated with more-effective leadership, greater happiness, and higher

TEDx Talk on the Athena Doctrine

By John Gerzema

In a global survey, John Gerzema found that feminine attributes are strongly correlated with more effective leadership, happiness, and other positive impacts.

URL: https://www.ccfieldguide.com/athena

Search Words: Conscious Capitalism Field Guide the Athena Doctrine

levels of ethics and morality.[3] Two-thirds of the respondents believed the world would be a better place if men thought more like women.

Leading as a Whole Person

Carl Jung observed that every woman has an inner man, and every man an inner woman. How do we get in touch with that other side of our own personas and learn how to harness it so that we can become integrated whole humans? It's dangerous to lead from a place of not being whole. When you're not whole, you're fragmented and filled with fear and insecurity. Leading as a whole person requires men and women alike to tap into and integrate our innate "masculine" and "feminine" qualities.

We also must learn to flex as needed. Certain situations clearly call for more "mature masculine" energy; you have to step in and make something happen. Doing so might cause short-term pain, but you cannot let that deter you. There are other situations that call for a nurturing, compassionate response. Leaders need to cultivate the ability to gauge the situation and respond appropriately. But we must first learn how to cultivate all those qualities within us.

You can start by understanding your own leadership style, looking at which side of the masculine-feminine continuum you tend to fall on. You can then learn how to cultivate the other side. Figure 14-1 helps you identify your default state and areas to focus on.

Look at the figure, and total your score (where +3 is the most "masculine," −3 means the most "feminine," and 0 is neutral) for all five domains depicted in the figure. The higher your number, the more "masculine" your leadership style.

Now think of a dilemma you are facing. Which of the five domains in the figure is related to your dilemma? Which style—stereotypically masculine or feminine—should you dial up or down to help with the dilemma?

Figure 14-1: Masculine and feminine assessment map

Masculine ←——————————————————→ Feminine

1. Structure
(How you structure your team and work)

Hierarchy	___ ___ ___ ___ ___ ___	Network
Level and status matter	___ ___ ___ ___ ___ ___	Relationships matter
Clear, separate roles	___ ___ ___ ___ ___ ___	Overlapping roles
Top-down power/info	___ ___ ___ ___ ___ ___	Power/info shared

2. Orientation
(What you focus on to get the job done)

| Goal/result | ___ ___ ___ ___ ___ ___ | Process |
| Push aside distracting ideas | ___ ___ ___ ___ ___ ___ | Gather multiple inputs, weigh related issues |

3. Influence
(How you get others to do what is important to you)

Command	___ ___ ___ ___ ___ ___	Persuade
Give orders/tell	___ ___ ___ ___ ___ ___	Make requests/ask
Direct/clear	___ ___ ___ ___ ___ ___	Indirect/polite
Appeal to logic/prove	___ ___ ___ ___ ___ ___	Appeal to emotion/inspire

4. Motivation
(What energizes or drives you when working with others)

Competition	___ ___ ___ ___ ___ ___	Collaboration
Work is a game to be won	___ ___ ___ ___ ___ ___	Opportunity to cocreate/belong
Coming out on top is key	___ ___ ___ ___ ___ ___	Involving team and sharing power is key

5. Conflict
(How you resolve disagreements)

Confront directly	___ ___ ___ ___ ___ ___	Approach indirectly
Facts have priority	___ ___ ___ ___ ___ ___	Feelings and facts are important
Seek closure	___ ___ ___ ___ ___ ___	Seek healing
Transactional (don't take personally)	___ ___ ___ ___ ___ ___	Emotional (go through hurt/pain)

+3 +2 +1 0 −1 −2 −3

Source: Adapted from Caroline Turner, "A Balance of Both Masculine and Feminine Strengths: The Bottom-Line Benefit," *Forbes.com*, May 7, 2012, www.forbes.com/sites/womensmedia/2012/05/07/a-balance-of-both-masculine-and-feminine-strengths-the-bottom-line-benefit.

Chapter 15

Becoming a SELFLESS Leader

Humanitarian and Nobel Peace Prize winner Albert Schweitzer once said, "I don't know what your destiny will be, but one thing I do know: the only ones among you who will be really happy are those who have sought and found how to serve." Conscious leaders are acutely aware of the importance of service in helping their organizations realize their highest potential. They also know that helping others leads to greater personal fulfillment and happiness.

Such leaders have learned the secret of the *helpers' high*: we feel good when we make other people happy. Servant leaders embrace transpersonal values—goodness, justice, truth, love, the alleviation of suffering, the salvation or enlightenment of others, and so on—that lift them to higher levels of consciousness.[1]

Muhammad Yunus on Selflessness

The profit orientation is only one orientation of a person. The same people who are interested in profit making are also selfless. I am not saying that capitalist theory is wrong. I am saying that it has not been interpreted and practiced fully. The selfless part of human beings has not been allowed to play out. As a result, we created a concept of business based on money-centric, one-dimensional human beings. But real human beings are multidimensional.

People climb to the top of Mount Everest. What's their incentive? Making money is an incentive. But making other people happy is a super incentive. We haven't explored that part of it. I'm inviting you to have a taste of it. If you like it you'll make your own decision. I tasted it and I found it an exciting thing to do—more exciting than making money.

We've used our creative power to focus on making money—and we've done it like it's the only game in town. It's not. There's a more exciting game in town.[2]

The essential elements of what it means to be a conscious leader can be captured in a single word, which also serves as an acronym: SELFLESS. A leader who operates with a primary emphasis on his or her self-interest naturally views other people as a means to that end. You cannot be a true leader if you operate at that level of consciousness.

The great Austrian psychiatrist Viktor Frankl wrote of "self-transcendence" as a state beyond self-actualization, which is the highest level in Maslow's hierarchy of needs. For a self-actualized person who becomes a leader, the sensibility can all become about "the grandness of you": you see others as bit players in *your* journey of self-actualization. The organization comes to reflect your personal priorities and goals.

Self-transcendence is not about losing the self; it is about not getting *stuck* there. You could say it's about thinking of the *larger* self—recognizing that we are all interconnected and interdependent and are serving the collective self. By thinking of this larger self, you become a much more powerful leader in service of something bigger than yourself—the well-being of all the people whose lives are affected by your actions. *Selfless* is the perfect word to encapsulate that sense of awareness. The eight qualities that SELFLESS connotes are strength, energy and enthusiasm, long-term orientation, flexibility, love and care, emotional intelligence, systems intelligence, and spiritual intelligence (figure 15-1).

Figure 15-1: Qualities of a SELFLESS leader

S	Strength
E	Energy and enthusiasm
L	Long-term orientation
F	Flexibility
L	Love and care
E	Emotional intelligence
S	Systems intelligence
S	Spiritual intelligence

Strength

We start with strength, because leaders must be strong and resolute. They have to have moral fiber, confidence, and the courage of their convictions. They have to be unshakable, able to stand up to doubters or to opposition that is motivated by baser instincts. They are confident without being arrogant. The key is that their strength is deployed in the service of noble ends: the flourishing of all the lives they lead and touch. That strength is sourced both from within and from outside. They draw on the strength of their teams (without depleting the power of those teams), and they tap into the moral power of the universe, which is available to anyone engaged in genuinely right action. As Martin Luther King Jr. famously said, "The arc of the moral universe is long, but it bends toward justice." Leaders who are trying to bend that arc away from justice will find their efforts ultimately stymied, while those who engage in right actions and pursue noble goals will find the wind at their backs.

Conscious leaders are not limited by their personal strengths. They recognize that their areas of weakness can be supplemented and complemented by others in their leadership team. You should lead from your strengths, but recognize that your strengths and what is needed in a particular situation may not be the same. Therefore, you'll want to assemble a team that collectively has the necessary qualities to move the organization forward.

In the first column in the following exercise, explore your strengths as a leader. In the second column, list your weaknesses, and in the third column, list the names of individuals on your leadership team who can supplement your strengths and complement your weaknesses.

Strengths	Weaknesses	Leadership complement

Energy and Enthusiasm

Conscious leaders can tap into an infinite source of power because of their commitment to a higher purpose and a righteous path that is in harmony with their innate nature. This power gives them great energy and enthusiasm. This doesn't mean that all leaders have to be extroverts. Introverts can make exceptional leaders, as many studies have found. When you're aligned with your purpose, you can't help but be enthusiastic. Passion is hard to fake if you don't have it.

In the space below, describe the last time you were very enthusiastic with your team about your business. What made you enthusiastic? What can you do to experience this more often?

_____

_____

_____

_____

_____

_____

_____

There is also the practical aspect of taking care of yourself so that you have the energy to accomplish the things you care most about (figure 15-2). Tony Schwartz at the consulting firm The Energy Project talks about energy as the new time management for the twenty-first century. Our ability to manage our energy and to deepen our capacity for it is critical if we want to show up every day and accomplish with enthusiasm our purpose. Sleep is also increasingly understood to be *the* key component of energy. It is hard for us to be at our best as conscious leaders when we are exhausted from a lack of sleep.

Figure 15-2: Energy for the journey to Conscious Capitalism

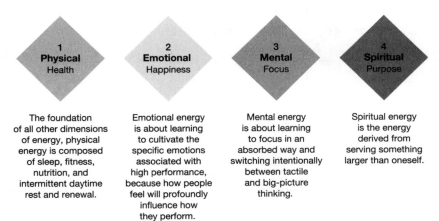

1 Physical Health	2 Emotional Happiness	3 Mental Focus	4 Spiritual Purpose
The foundation of all other dimensions of energy, physical energy is composed of sleep, fitness, nutrition, and intermittent daytime rest and renewal.	Emotional energy is about learning to cultivate the specific emotions associated with high performance, because how people feel will profoundly influence how they perform.	Mental energy is about learning to focus in an absorbed way and switching intentionally between tactile and big-picture thinking.	Spiritual energy is the energy derived from serving something larger than oneself.

Source: Tony Schwartz, The Energy Project.

Long-Term Orientation

Conscious leaders operate on a time horizon that extends beyond their tenure as leaders, even beyond their own lifetime. They are trying to accomplish something significant. Leaders such as George Washington and Franklin Roosevelt took far-sighted actions that had lasting consequences. The founders of the United States led with an eye toward eternity, putting in place ideas and principles that would endure for centuries and, hopefully, millennia.

The success of a leader is best gauged by what happens once he or she is gone. Does the organization continue to operate at the level the leader established? If it does, then the leader has put the essential elements into place, made them part of the DNA of the organization, and made sure that the right kind of leader takes over. Jerry Porras and Jim Collins in their book *Built to Last* compare these "clock builder" leaders with those who are "time tellers." Clock builders create organizations that will endure once the leaders are gone, not organizations that rely on the leaders to "tell the time." Good leaders build clocks so that everyone who comes after them can tell the time, too.

As a personal reflection of your own long-term orientation to the business you lead, list three long-term initiatives that only you could undertake to ensure that your organization will stand the test of time.

_____

_____

_____

_____

_____

_____

_____

_____

What could threaten these initiatives? How could you alleviate the threat? What is your next step?

_____

_____

_____

_____

_____

_____

_____

_____

Flexibility

We define flexibility, an essential leadership capacity, as "the capacity to switch modes seamlessly and to bend without breaking, as the situation or the context requires." The bamboo tree is a great symbol of flexibility. It has become central to various sacred traditions for good reason, as it embodies uprightness, tenacity, elegance, and simplicity. The bamboo bends and sways as conditions warrant, but does not break, no matter how harsh the wind. Leaders also need to be able to bend but not break, adapting to circumstances in a principled way, without sacrificing their core values.

Every leader needs to develop a toolkit, like a golfer with many clubs. You have to identify the right approach in each situation and know how to implement it. In particular, conscious leaders have to know how to flex between "masculine" and "feminine" energy as the situation or context requires. Most of us tend to get stuck in one mode and don't know how to cycle to the other. That's the habitual nature of the mind. Yoga and Chinese martial arts and techniques such as Tai Chi and Qigong can be quite beneficial to help us overcome this inflexibility; when you make the body flexible, the mind becomes flexible as well.

Our friend (and *Shakti Leadership* coauthor) Nilima Bhat uses the phrase "wise fool of tough love" to describe a truly conscious leader. Such leaders can embody seemingly opposite qualities such as wisdom and lightheartedness, and toughness and love, simultaneously. They can draw on any of these qualities as needed in a given situation. Leaders have to be fully present in each moment to discern which approach is called for. The presence practice (which we describe in chapter 16) helps leaders cultivate deep presence and discernment.

Being flexible when you are not operating from a state of full presence can be disempowering and can come across as weakness, indecision, or a lack of personal conviction as a leader. But if, as will be described later, you are in presence and holding your center, you can exercise the needed flexibility without any loss of power.

Love and Care

A fundamental leadership quality is the ability to operate from love and care. Throughout human history, the great leaders (such as Ashoka, Lincoln, Gandhi, King, and Mandela) who transformed society in a lasting and positive way all possessed tremendous strength along with a powerful capacity for caring. They expanded their circle of caring to encompass more and more of humanity, even including their own perceived enemies. They truly, deeply cared about human beings and had a clear sense of right versus wrong. Leaders like Alexander the Great or Akbar the Great built vast empires and conquered many territories. These leaders built geographically huge and militarily formidable empires, but to what end? Did they fundamentally transform the world into a better place? In most cases, they didn't, and their empires fell apart soon after they died. Those empires lacked a noble purpose rooted in human flourishing; they were driven by the insatiable egos and hunger for power of the leaders.

Truly great leaders take the world to a better place. They manifest love, rooted in a foundation of caring. When you come from a place of genuine caring and possess great strength, you operate as a peaceful warrior—a warrior battling all odds for a just and righteous cause.

The opposite of love is fear. Conscious leaders recognize the crucial importance of driving fear out of their organizations. An organization suffused with fear is inherently incapable of genuine creativity and innovation. Its people are condemned to lives of intense dysfunctional stress, unhappiness, and ill health.

When leaders combine great strength with a profound disposition of caring for people, they wield extraordinary power to do good. As King said, "Power properly understood is nothing but the ability to achieve purpose. It is the strength required to bring about social, political, and economic change. There is nothing wrong with power if power is used correctly . . . Power at its best is love implementing the demands of justice, and justice at its best is power correcting everything that stands against love."[3]

The identification of love in an organization is not always easy. On the other hand, fear is much easier to identify. Look at your current practices, and ask if any of them are creating fear in your organization. Write them down, and think of what you could do to eliminate them.

Practice that could cause fear	Actions to eliminate or replace the practice

Acting from Love versus Fear

By Casey Sheahan, CEO of Patagonia

There was a critical moment about two years after I became CEO of Patagonia, when we had just gone into the global economic crisis. All business leaders at that time were looking with great fear to the future that business might really slow down, that we might go into a depression, that sales and orders and every other aspect of the business would be hurt. I was having meetings with my executive team and the owners of the company, trying to figure out what to do next.

The first inclination in traditional businesses is to cut costs. The biggest area of cost for most companies is payroll and overhead. So, I thought, business is going to be tough; we may have to lay off some people. I didn't want to

do that, because Patagonia is my family and I think of every individual there having children in school and mortgages and car payments. I was really anguished about it. I came home that night after having these discussions at work and talked to Tara, my wife at the time. She asked, "Well, are you making these decisions out of love or fear?" I said, "Fear, of course. Business could get bad, and I don't know what's going to happen, but we need to batten down the hatches and tighten our belt and get ready for a really rough ride." Then she asked, "What would happen if you looked at this from a place of love?" I thought about it and said, "I would never let anybody go. I would find other ways to save money; I would have the workers and sales associates in the stores do the window washing and the cleaning, and I'd try to find creative ways to save the money that we would save if we laid off a bunch of people."

Well, that's the course I took. I could have taken the traditional fear-based path of saving money, trying to do the best thing for the profit and loss statement, and the balance sheet, or think of a more creative way to save the jobs of people who are part of this family. They were very appreciative, and knowing they might have lost their jobs, they worked much harder. And the company pulled together very collaboratively in a creative way to get through the economic crisis. Simultaneously, we were introducing our beautiful, new product line for a snowy winter, and sales went through the roof. Patagonia came out gaining market share for the next five years and becoming a much more powerful company than it was before.

When I took the love decision, I could actually sense a shift in my consciousness, a shift in my energy. I felt in myself a sense of calm and relief around making that kind of a decision. But I also was quite excited to be able to use my mind and work with my team to develop solutions that were creative and we knew hadn't been done before. So it became actually a very exciting time. The company definitely galvanized around that.

There's a collective consciousness at work in any company. They all knew listening to the news or reading the newspaper that things were very tough in the business world and in the United States especially. Some real transgressions had taken place in the banking industry on Wall Street, but we would be a company that could stand apart from that in the way we approached this crisis. There was a lot of excitement in me, especially when it started to work out and the company started to enjoy success. Everyone was moving along with that, including our customers, who saw that we were a good company.

Was there a time at work when you could have cared more but didn't? Describe that time.

_____

_____

_____

_____

If you could replay this time, what would you do differently?

_____

_____

_____

_____

_____

_____

_____

Emotional Intelligence

For leaders, high analytical intelligence is a given; by the time you get to be anywhere near the leader's role, you have had to demonstrate that you are smart. In the past, most companies only valued that kind of intelligence. Today, we're recognizing that other forms of intelligence are even more important, in particular emotional intelligence, spiritual intelligence, and systems intelligence. The great news here is that while our analytical intelligence (or IQ) is fixed at birth and can only decline, these other kinds of intelligence can all be cultivated. Emotional intelligence can be developed through greater self-awareness, and spiritual intelligence can grow from having good teachers and being exposed to questions of meaning and purpose. You can learn systems intelligence by studying natural systems and becoming familiar with the tools of system dynamics.

Emotional intelligence combines intrapersonal intelligence (understanding oneself) and interpersonal intelligence (understanding others) (figure 15-3). Self-awareness is the first pillar of emotional intelligence. Empathy—the ability to feel and understand what others are feeling—is the second pillar. High emotional intelligence is increasingly being recognized as important in all organizations because of the growing complexity of society and the multiplicity of stakeholders who must be understood and communicated with effectively.[4]

Figure 15-3: Components of emotional intelligence

A time-tested way to learn and grow, as Socrates said, is to "know thyself." Self-awareness is one of the key qualities that Daniel Goleman identified in his influential book *Emotional Intelligence.*[5] Growing our self-awareness is a continuous process that lasts a lifetime, since there is an entire universe within us waiting to be discovered. We can learn about ourselves by becoming aware of our emotions and by understanding why we're experiencing them. It's useful to ask yourself, "Why does this make me angry?" "Why am I excited about that?" "Why am I envious of that person?" "Why do I feel joyful about this?" "Why am I experiencing love?" Each of our emotions is a window into who we are and what we care about, often at a subconscious level. As Jung said, "until you make the unconscious conscious, it will direct your life and you will call it fate."

If we lack awareness and understanding of our own feelings and aspirations, we go through life following our own impulses and giving in to every desire without being conscious of why we're doing what we are doing. Emotions arise from the interpretations we make about situations and events. But most of us don't realize that we are free to interpret situations and events in different ways. For example, the emotion of anger is based on the interpretation that we have been somehow wronged and that some type of punishment is appropriate for whoever has wronged us. However, if we change our interpretation about what has made us angry, we are likely to find that our anger diminishes as well. We may not be able to fully control our emotions, but we can certainly be more conscious of them, take responsibility for them, learn from them, and transcend them when appropriate.[6]

In which area could you improve the most? Why?

_____

_____

_____

_____

Describe how you could improve.

_____

_____

_____

_____

_____

_____

_____

_____

As we become more aware of our emotions, we begin to realize that many of them, such as envy, resentment, greed, bitterness, malice, anger, and hatred, do not further our well-being; they are life-stultifying. They are all natural human emotions, but getting caught up in them seldom makes our lives better. On the other hand, emotions such as love, generosity, gratitude, compassion, and forgiveness are life-enhancing. We need to consciously cultivate life-enhancing emotions and learn to neutralize life-stultifying ones. This is the essence of personal mastery and emotional intelligence.

Conscious leaders transcend self-centeredness and cultivate empathy.[7] The potential for expansive love is virtually limitless, but it starts with empathy. As children, we are naturally very egocentric, but as we grow emotionally, we develop the ability to empathize and sympathize with others. We begin to care about more than just ourselves, first with our love for family and friends and then toward our larger community. Beyond that, virtually every human being alive is someone we could care about, empathize with, understand, even love. And even beyond that, we can love animals and potentially all life and all existence.

Think now about the last time someone in your organization came to you for help. What kind of listening did you do? Were you ready to answer, or were you trying to step in the other person's shoes?

The Four Levels of Listening

By Otto Scharmer, Senior Lecturer, Massachusetts Institute of Technology

Watch this video from Otto Scharmer about listening.

URL: https://www.ccfieldguide.com/otto

Search Words: Conscious Capitalism Field Guide Four Levels of Listening

After listening to Scharmer's explanation of the levels of listening, fill in the following chart.

LISTENING LEVEL	GIVE A RECENT PERSONAL EXPERIENCE
Downloading	
Factual listening (open mind)	
Empathic listening (open heart)	
Generative listening (open will)	

Systems Intelligence

Systems thinking or intelligence, another important type of intelligence for leaders, is "a holistic approach to analysis that focuses on the way that a system's constituent parts interrelate and how systems work over time and within the context of larger systems. The systems thinking approach contrasts with traditional analysis, which studies systems by breaking them down into their separate elements."[8]

Many conscious leaders are natural systems thinkers. They can see the bigger picture and understand how the different components of the system interconnect and behave over time. They can anticipate the immediate as well as long-term consequences of actions. Given their intuitive understanding of systems, conscious leaders are excellent organizational architects. They understand the roots of problems and how the problems relate to organizational design and culture, and they devise fundamental solutions instead of applying symptomatic quick fixes.

Many leaders in business and in politics lurch from problem to problem, repeatedly allowing situations to deteriorate until the problems reach a crisis point. They then take drastic actions to solve the crisis, but the responses often don't work. The best leaders prevent problems from arising in the first place. Their genius may go unrecognized and even unrewarded, but they are the most effective leaders, with keenly developed systems minds and sensibilities.

Systems intelligence is a talent that most societies haven't recognized, understood, encouraged, or rewarded. Yet in the twenty-first century, as our organizations become more complex and the world becomes increasingly interdependent, it's hard to overstate how valuable this type of intelligence is.

How can we develop our systems intelligence? First, recognize that it is different from analytical intelligence but also complementary to it. Our analytical intelligence shows up in our ability to compare things and to break them down into parts so we can analyze them. As the basis for logic, it is a useful tool that our educational systems have developed reasonably well. But it isn't enough.

One way to develop our systems intelligence is to study disciplines that clearly embody systems principles, such as ecology, which is the science of living organisms and the relationships between them and the environment. This type of intelligence enables us to see how things connect. Another good way to develop our systems intelligence in the business context is to practice thinking in terms of the stakeholder system. The stakeholders of a business all exist in relationship with the business and with each other. Conscious leaders know that every strategic business decision must be made after considering how it will affect and create value for each of the major stakeholders. Will the decision harm one or more of the major stakeholders in some way? How can we get around the trade-offs? Can we devise strategies that create more total value for the entire interdependent business system?

The exercises that develop emotional intelligence and spiritual intelligence can also help develop our systems intelligence. Slowing our minds down is essential; the speedy, skittish mind breaks things down, while the less speedy but attentive mind is more capable of being in the here and now, noticing the relationships between things, and seeing the larger system.

Spiritual Intelligence

Conscious leaders frequently have high spiritual intelligence, which has been well defined in *Spiritual Capital*, a wonderful book by Danah Zohar and Ian Marshall: "Spiritual intelligence is the intelligence with which we access our deepest meanings, values, purposes, and higher motivations. It is . . . our moral intelligence, giving us an innate ability to distinguish right from wrong. It is the intelligence with which we exercise goodness, truth, beauty, and compassion in our lives."[9] Spiritual intelligence helps us discover our higher purpose in our work and our lives. Leaders with high spiritual intelligence have a remarkable ability to align their organizations with their organizations' higher purposes. They also have uncanny discernment to sense when things are beginning to go off track.

Living Your Spiritual Vision

By Casey Sheahan

Many leaders I work with are suffering for various reasons because they are beholden to this paradigm of ambitious male energy. This model is brutal because you can never be good enough. You can create a goal and you can work toward it, but it always seems to recede into the distance. Failure feels really bad. You're separated from other human beings; it's us against them and make money at all costs. That is really, really tough on people, and it burns them out.

On the other hand, you can bring your own spiritual vision into your business. It should integrate with what you do; there should be no difference between how you are, what you do, and what you like to do if you're at the right job. It all happens naturally. I loved my job as CEO of Patagonia because I would leap up the stairs two at a time every morning to see what new business adventure awaited me. If you have the right vision for your life and for your work and stay true to yourself, then you know what you're doing every day when you wake up. It has nothing to do with the twenty things on your to-do list; it's how you show up and how you're going to impact others. It is real work, but if it is in accordance with conscious leadership, it's how you're going to help others realize their full potential and be the most incredible happy human beings that they can be. That's really what it's all about. You have that opportunity; the role can be all about you as the hero, or it can be about supporting every other character, every other human being on the planet. It made me enjoy life even more and I had great success with my business, as well.

Cindy Wigglesworth, author of *SQ21: The Twenty-One Skills of Spiritual Intelligence*, defines spiritual intelligence as "the ability to behave with wisdom and compassion while maintaining inner and outer peace regardless of the situation." The attribute is most simply stated as living less from the "ego self" and more from your "higher self." You might call this higher self by another term: authentic self, spirit, soul, Buddha, nature, or Atman. Wigglesworth describes the twenty-one skills of spiritual intelligence:[10]

The Twenty-One Skills of Spiritual Intelligence

AWARENESS OF HIGHER SELF VERSUS AWARENESS OF EGO SELF

Awareness of own worldview

Awareness of life purpose (mission)

Awareness of values hierarchy

Complexity of thought and holding multiple perspectives

Awareness of ego self and higher self

UNIVERSAL AWARENESS

Awareness of interconnectedness of all life

Awareness of worldviews of others

Breadth of time and space perception

Awareness of limitations and power of human perception

Awareness of spiritual and universal laws

Experience of transcendent oneness

HIGHER-SELF VERSUS EGO-SELF MASTERY

Commitment to spiritual growth

Keeping higher self in charge

Living your purpose and values

Sustaining your faith during difficult times

Seeking guidance from a higher power, a spirit, or your higher self

SOCIAL MASTERY AND SPIRITUAL PRESENCE

Having a wise and effective spiritual teacher or mentor

Being a wise and effective change agent

Making wise and compassionate decisions

Being a calming, healing presence

Being aligned with the ebb and flow of life

Source: Conscious Pursuits Inc., all rights reserved/cindy@deepchange.com.

Assess yourself on each of these twenty-one skills, and identify those that you are most deficient in. Develop a plan to improve these weaker skills.

Spiritual skill	Plan to cultivate

Creating a Personal Leadership Development Plan

A personal leadership development plan starts with taking an inventory of yourself and understanding your own strengths and weaknesses: the areas in which you are especially good, extraordinary, decidedly mediocre, and simply terrible. Consider these in light of the qualities needed to be great leaders (e.g., SELFLESS). Some qualities could be considered good to have, but others are absolutely essential. You can recognize your blind spots and significant weaknesses, things that you really need to change because without them, you cannot be an effective leader (or a successful human being, for that matter). Some weaknesses might be okay; they have little impact on other people, and you can get your team members to compensate for these gaps. Once you recognize what you need to cultivate, you can use the toolkits designed for helping people make those shifts.

Psychologist and author Gay Hendricks has developed a framework called the *zone of genius*.[11] He suggests that we occupy four zones for various aspects of our lives: incompetence, competence, excellence, and genius.

The zone of *incompetence* includes things that you are not at all good at. These just don't come naturally to you, and even if you try very hard, you don't seem to get very far with them. The general advice is not to worry about the activities that fall into this zone, unless they are really critical; you do need to discern what is critical and what is not. If it is not critical, you should just hire other people to do the activity that falls into the incompetence zone—or just do without it in your life.

The zone of *competence* includes things you can do quite well, but so can countless other people. Is it the best use of your time to do those things? Generally speaking, you're better off outsourcing these activities to others who can do them better, faster, or cheaper. Sure, you can mow your lawn or set up a new wireless network, but somebody else could do in minutes what might take you half a day.

The zone of *excellence* includes things that you do very well and get paid well to do. Once upon a time, these activities challenged you and required that you function at your peak. But if you just keep doing those things, you're not stretching yourself or growing. It just gets too easy, almost automatic. If you get stuck here, you hit a plateau.

Finally, there is the zone of *genius*: this is where you're most alive, fully in flow and engaged. These activities stretch you and challenge you and force you to create rather than just replicate. The key is to understand what this zone is for you and then to spend as much of your time as you can toward that end of the spectrum, striving for a healthy and sustainable blend of excellence and genius. Let go of as much as you can at the other end. The zone of genius is where you will make your unique and most lasting contribution and find your deepest fulfillment.

Exercise: Self-Assessment on SELFLESS

On a scale of 1 to 5, where 5 is the highest score, evaluate yourself on each of the elements of SELFLESS. For the elements on which you scored yourself a 3 or less, identify how you can improve.

ELEMENT	CURRENT ASSESSMENT	ACTIONS TO IMPROVE IF NEEDED
Strength		
Enthusiasm		
Long-term		
Flexible		
Loving		
Emotional intelligence		
Spiritual intelligence		
Systems intelligence		

Becoming More Conscious

You cannot have a conscious business without conscious leaders. You cannot be a conscious leader unless you are a conscious human being. This chapter is about embarking on becoming a more conscious human being and leader. This change will be lifelong—there is no limit to how conscious we can become.

In this chapter, you will take several steps toward becoming a conscious leader:

- Deal with your fears.

- Develop a mindfulness practice.

- Move into a place of presence, empathy, and love.

- Bring this together in the notion of self-mastery.

- Integrate contemplative practices to help develop a deeper level of consciousness.

Learning and Growing as a Leader

A business cannot truly evolve, learn, and grow if its leaders—particularly the CEO—are not learning and growing as well. Companies become blocked from vital organizational evolution if their leaders are psychologically and spiritually stuck. For example, the Ford Motor Company reached great heights and had a huge impact on the world under Henry Ford's leadership. But eventually, his obstinate refusal to adapt his thinking to changed market circumstances (e.g., the practice of buying cars on credit, which Ford strongly opposed on moral grounds) started to hurt the company.

Poor leadership prevents the company from reaching its highest potential. Thus, the best motivation for leaders to learn and grow is that their personal growth will benefit not just their own lives, but also the lives of all those with whom they interact, including the company and all the people whose lives it touches.

To become a conscious leader, you have to aspire to be one. Without high intentionality, it just doesn't happen. Personal growth is not easy; it takes great effort and perseverance as we make mistakes and learn from them.

Continuous Learning

By Casey Sheahan

I made many trips to India and met with many beautiful teachers in my quest to become a better leader and human being. I was looking at how I was showing up in the world personally, and I knew that any personal suffering connected to my self-centricity would have an effect on others. So, I did this work to diminish my ego and become a different kind of leader, one who would be a powerful fit for the culture at Patagonia. It's not as if I didn't fit into it before, but I started to show up as a different kind of business leader and really benefited from the lessons from my personal spiritual journey. I created a higher vision for myself, starting with myself and my family and then my employees and my company, to try to give back to our communities and the rest of the world and to help make it a better place. It started with looking at my own emotions, ideas, actions, and conditioning and being aware of when I was doing things for ambition or other self-interest. The sense of self-directed ambition is very common with leaders of companies, where you fall into a pattern of thinking that if you have a big job or you're becoming successful, it's all about you. Once I changed that pattern, I felt far more effective. It is just a better way to show up.

People need to carefully address where they are coming from and understand what state they exist in. We are human, and to be human is to be less than perfect. Humans live on a spectrum between altruistic caring and being in the shadow, the dark and fearful side of ourselves. We need to reconcile our darker motivations, since we are complex beings.

A person who mostly resides in a state of insecurity and fear should not be in a leadership role. If we are in such a state, we need to work on fixing it before we step back into a leadership role. Leaders operating out of fear and insecurity can do extraordinary damage to other human beings and to society at large.

Aspiring leaders first have to work toward growing as conscious human beings and cultivating practices that will enable them to get back to that state when they do fall into the other states. Cindy Wigglesworth, author of *SQ21*, has created "the SQ Shortcut" as a simple way for us to respond to situations in a more empathetic and loving way (figure 16-1).

Practices like those recommended by Wigglesworth are essential for us as leaders, because we must be coming from a place of calm, caring, and expansiveness before making any decisions that have an impact on other people. Another example is the presence practice, featured in the book *Shakti Leadership*.[1] It includes a set of affirmations that are designed to bring you into the moment and get you away from negative energy states. The practice helps you get back into a state of presence, without which you simply cannot be an effective leader.

Figure 16-1: The SQ [spiritual intelligence] Shortcut: four steps to a SOULful™ Response

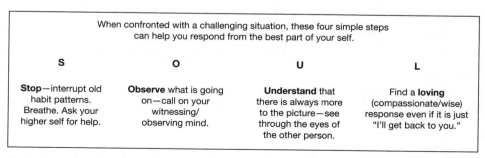

Source: Reprinted from Cindy Wigglesworth, *SQ21: The Twenty-One Skills of Spiritual Intelligence* (New York: SelectBooks, 2012), www.SQ21book.com/cindy@deepchange.com.

Presence, a profound sense of present-moment awareness, is the source of true power from which we experience balance, completeness, connection, and contentment. Most of the time, we are not fully present; our minds are distracted. We are either rehashing the past, worrying about the future, or simply daydreaming.

Being fully present is a wonderful gift you can give yourself and others. Imagine how many energy fields are interacting in a workplace. Most of them are operating from a state of absence rather than presence. By being fully present, you can induct others into their presence instead of getting sucked into their drama.

Try the following exercise in a quiet room where you know you won't be interrupted. You can do this alone or with a group.

Be comfortably seated in your chair with your eyes closed; feet uncrossed and firmly planted on the floor; spine straight; and head, neck, and shoulders relaxed. Keep your palms relaxed, facing upward or downward on your thighs.

Begin with the foundation of presence, which is a relaxed body. Start by squeezing the face muscles, the scalp, everything in the head and neck area very tight. Squeeze, squeeze, squeeze, and release. Completely release those muscles until they are deeply relaxed.

Now squeeze the shoulders and arms and make fists with the hands, and squeeze everything very tight—and release. Relax. Next, move into the torso. Squeeze the rib cage, the abs, the torso, the belly, all the internal organs, everything tight—and release.

Squeeze the hips, thighs, knees, calves, ankles, feet, and toes. Curl the toes in tight, tight, tight—and release. Take a deep breath from the top of your head all the way to the tips of your toes, and flush out any remaining tension as you scan your body. Let it all relax.

From that relaxed body, you're ready now to move into the next signal of presence, which is an even breath. Become acutely aware of your breathing. Note whether your breathing is even or uneven. Your shoulders are squared back, and your belly is soft. Your entire rib cage is available for full-lung breathing. Inhale, expand the chest, balloon the belly, and as you exhale, empty the lungs completely and drop the chest. Again inhale, expand the chest, balloon the belly, and exhale. Continue at your own pace until your inhalation and your exhalation feel even.

Once the breath is even, go one level deeper. The next signal of presence is a clear, calm mind. Become aware of your thoughts. Imagine that your brain is dissolving into a liquid, crystal-clear lake high up on a mountain, with the perfect breeze and temperature. You see no moss on the surface, no ripples in the water, and no turbidity. This is your mind: crystal clear and calm. Step forward to the edge of this lake, look down, and see your face reflected back at you: calm, quiet, relaxed. Your whole body is calm and relaxed.

Start moving into this lake now, stepping into these waters of a clear mind, feeling completely refreshed and regenerated in it until it reaches all the way to your heart. As those cool waters touch your heart, allow your heart now to relax open. Feel this physical organ inside your rib cage. Feel a sense of love and gratitude toward this organ that has been a faithful companion to you from the time you were just a cluster of cells in your mother's womb. It is thumping away for you, powering you, beating for you, keeping the rhythm of life for you. Feel gratitude and open that heart out. When you open your heart, it's as if you can step in through it and enter a state of pure presence that lies on the other side. You've shifted your state from the ordinary outside surface consciousness to a state of pure being.

This is your state of presence. You know this when you affirm these truths, starting with "The reality of this moment . . . is that . . . I have nothing to defend." Imbue it with deep meaning and connection. Take a deep breath, and allow your gut to know this truth now; let it relax. Next say, "The reality of this moment . . . is that . . . I have nothing to promote." Breathe into your heart, and know the truth of this statement. Now say, "The reality of this moment . . . is that . . . I have nothing to fear." Breathe into your head, and know the truth of this statement.

Step back from your head, your heart, and your gut into your pure presence deep within you, and affirm with deep conviction: "The only reality of this moment . . . is that . . . I am here now." Breathe deeply, from the top of your head to the tips of your toes, anchoring yourself in the column of your being in your spine.

From here, become aware of a powerful light as if a river of light were flowing from above, flowing through you. It is powerful and energizing, with the power to completely rejuvenate you. It moves through your spine into all your internal organs, irrigating your whole body-mind, refreshing you, fertilizing you, energizing you. All excess discharges down through your feet as you become a channel of this power. Irrigating Mother Earth with this river of power. Affirm: "I am empowered now. All I need is within me, all I need comes to me, all I need flows through me."

Holding this empowered presence, cultivate the next signal of presence, which is a state of *sensitive sonar*. Become context-aware. Sharpen all your senses. Move into your sense of sight, sound, smell, taste, and touch. Empower all these senses to become the most sensitive sonar that can pick up all the critical information outside and inside you that you need to be effective and to be of service.

From this state of a sensitive sonar, become an *energetic inductor* so that you can influence others with your calming presence. Feel your energy field expanding from you in all directions. In your mind, embrace the persons to your right and left and all the people in this space and in your life. Everything is getting inducted, as if in a warm embrace, into your presence.

You are now fully anchored and empowered as a fully present and powerful leader. Holding this state, bring your awareness back to this moment in time and space. Wriggle your fingers and toes, rotate and relax your shoulders. Move your head and neck from side to side. Continue to be present. Flow with the power of your being. Rub your hands together to warm them, and cup your eyes with them. Slowly blink open your eyes and gradually remove your hands. Look around you and feel the energy fields interacting. Notice how you're feeling inside, and feel a deep, visceral sense of gratitude.

Excerpted from Nilima Bhat and Raj Sisodia, *Shakti Leadership: Embracing Feminine and Masculine Power in Business* (Oakland, CA: Berrett-Koehler Publishers, 2016).

Being fully present is key to our development as leaders. If you can embody full presence for five minutes on day one, ten minutes the next, fifteen minutes on the third, and so on, presence will gradually become an integral part of you and will eventually become your natural state. The more you cultivate presence, the more impact you can have on the people who need it. You can help them instead of getting sucked into their drama.

Self-Mastery

Self-mastery, or personal mastery, is an essential quality to cultivate as conscious human beings, especially for those in positions of leadership. Attaining self-mastery means that you're not at the whims of your own "monkey mind," which can jump all over the place with all kinds of seemingly random thoughts. We can use our higher self (our intellect) to observe our day-to-day, minute-by-minute self and recognize when we're falling into certain patterns.

Mental chatter is the inner talk, or as some people call it, the "committee" that's always in session inside our minds. It is generally critical and anxious; few people have positive mental chatter! It's normal and natural, but the constant sniping voice inside people's heads can be debilitating. The first exercise around self-mastery is to start to become aware of our mental chatter and learn to recognize it for what it is. You start to recognize this duality between the one who's observing your own mind in action and your other self, the one who is being observed. The idea is to be the one who's observing rather than the one being observed. As you practice this over time, you can greatly reduce the amount of mental chatter and be less affected by it.

Ultimately, we can cultivate a more positive inner dialogue, as revealed in Martin Seligman's work. Before Seligman created the field of positive psychology, his work centered on learned optimism, which has to do with our default explanatory style: how we explain events to ourselves, how we make sense of things. People can learn to have a positive way of explaining things to themselves. The idea is captured in three *p*'s: personal, pervasive, and permanent. When people with a negative or pessimistic view of themselves make a mistake of any kind, they may immediately think something like "I'm such an idiot; I can never do anything right." That's personal, pervasive, and permanent. It applies to everything: "I can never do *anything* right." It's permanent: "I can *never*." And it's personal; it's all about *me*. That view naturally fosters a feeling of pessimism and feeds a negative self-view. Once you become aware of this tendency, you can, when something bad happens to you, try to make it not personal. You can say, "That was certainly a mistake, but it could have happened to anybody." You can make it not permanent: "It was something I did, and now I'm going to learn from it and I will try to make sure it doesn't happen again." And you can make it not pervasive, by realizing that it only applies to particular domains. There's lots of empirical research showing that people can change their explanatory style and that, by doing so, they can rise significantly on the optimism scale.[2]

By the same token, when something positive happens, most people go the opposite route: they tend to downplay it. They'll say, "Oh, I was just lucky." You got an award? "Oh, it's nothing." In that situation, unless you're a narcissist or an egomaniac, the advice for most people is to acknowledge that you really do have strengths in this area and are blessed and fortunate to have them. You can also acknowledge the effort that went into making that positive outcome a reality. In other words, acknowledge to yourself that the drivers of your success *are* personal, permanent, and pervasive!

Personal Mastery Exercises

Srikumar Rao, of the Rao Institute, teaches Creativity and Personal Mastery, a popular course for current and aspiring leaders. With his permission, we are pleased to offer some of the personal-mastery exercises from his course here in abridged form:

- Quieting mental chatter

- Becoming more mindful

- Cultivating gratitude and appreciation

- Living is another centered universe

- Good thing, bad thing, who knows?

During this experience, you should practice keeping a journal. Write down your insights, outcomes, feelings, and answers to the questions provided for each of the proposed exercises.

Quieting Mental Chatter

Become aware of your mental chatter, of the random thoughts that spring to mind when you are not focused on things you have to do and sometimes even when you are. Especially become aware of what is flashing through your mind the first thing in the morning, when you wake up. Is there a single powerful thought coursing through your mind like water from a fire hose, or do numerous disjointed thoughts spring up unbidden and vanish just as fast as they arise?

Carry around a notebook. Categorize the types of mind chatter that assault—or beguile—you during the day.

First be aware of two broad categories: Is your mental chatter taking you to a place where you are upbeat, energized, optimistic about the future, and full of beans? Or, is it taking you to a dark place of fear and insecurity about what will happen to you? Become aware of how much of the time your mental chatter is taking you to a place of hope, serenity, and joy and where you want to be. Become aware of how much of the time it is taking you to a place of stress, anxiety, and fear and where you do not want to be. Report on how much time you spend in each of these places.

It is possible, of course, for your mental chatter to be neutral, but this is rare. Even supposedly neutral mental chatter like making a to-do list will take you to one or the other of the two places mentioned above. Either you feel great because you are getting organized and feel your life is under control, or you feel overwhelmed and demoralized at the thought of how much you have to do and how you will never get to it all.

Then become aware of how often you do each of the following:

- How often do you criticize yourself and run yourself down about things you did that were daft, about things you didn't do that you should have, about characteristics that you should have and don't, about characteristics that you shouldn't have but do? How often and how unmercifully do you beat yourself up?

- How often do you criticize others about everything from dress to mannerisms to physical characteristics?

- How often do you compare yourself with others? Do you generally find yourself insecure as you contemplate their accomplishments, or do you find yourself gloating at the thought of how much better you are than everyone else?

- When introduced to a new person or when thinking about persons you know, do you tend to notice their strengths and good qualities? Or do you dwell on their faults and foibles? Perhaps you do both, but which of these is predominant?

- How much time do you spend blaming others for unpleasant situations in your life? Your parents for not doing stuff they should have? Your significant other for not being supportive in some way? Your boss, your work colleagues, your friends, your children, your teachers, and countless others for doing something or not doing something that has had this negative impact on you?

Become aware of your emotional undertones. Is there a dominant one throughout the day, are there two or three such undertones, or are there many equally strong—or weak—undertones that hold sway at different times? Do these change from day to day, or are they reasonably constant? Are they generally negative (anger, self-doubt, anxiety, worry, etc.), or are they generally positive (hope, love, confidence, etc.)? Feel free to challenge whether the undertones characterized here as negative are in fact so, and vice versa. How do these undertones affect your behavior? Are you a better performer at some task when a particular undertone is in charge? Do you tend to flare up when another one holds sway?

Do these undertones tend to disappear when you start noticing them? What does this tell you? In particular, note the effect of strong emotions such as anger, hate, and fear. Does the intensity of the emotion decrease simply because you become consciously aware of it?

Become aware of where you instinctively go. If your friend gets a great job offer, are you genuinely glad for him or her or do you immediately feel a twinge of envy, or do you feel both ways? If you meet a highly accomplished individual, is your pleasure at the person's achievements tempered by your inability to reach the same place? Are you inclined to go to a place of calm and peace or to a place of insecurity and angst?

It will help if you can set a reminder on your mobile phone to beep every hour or half hour. Each time you hear the beep, become aware of your mind chatter. Persist. Practice will make you better.

How easy was it for you to become aware of your internal mind state? What did you learn about yourself, and what implications does this have for the rest of your life?

Becoming More Mindful

For the next week, do *all* your activities deliberately and unhurriedly. Focus intently on whatever you are doing. Note that unhurriedly does *not* mean slowly. It means doing it without a frantic feeling in your head and at whatever pace is appropriate. Many have reported that doing a task unhurriedly, in this fashion, actually gets the task done *faster* in chronological time.

No multitasking is allowed. No talking on the cell phone while you scan the *Wall Street Journal* and check your email. For most of us, life has become one huge frantic rush. Slow it down. Firmly and deliberately.

Concentrate on the task at hand, and be methodical. Again, do it unhurriedly, not slowly. Your mental chatter will cut in with thoughts of how much you have to do, the consequences riding on what you are doing, how the world is going to hell in a hand basket, and much, much more.

Let it go. Let it all go. Each time your mental chatter carries you away, just gently detach yourself and come back to the task at hand. Breathe slowly, deeply, and evenly. Try to get to twelve breaths a minute or slower. Just being aware of your slow breathing will largely stymie the chatter.

Being mindful is especially important when you are speaking with someone. Do not get involved in your mental chatter, with the wonderful reply you are going to make, with the image of yourself you are trying to project, and so on. Focus on the other person and what he or she is saying. Observe the expression on the person's face. Really notice the other person. Really listen to what he or she is saying. Remove yourself from the picture.

If you are talking on the phone, shut your eyes and focus on what you are hearing. Think of it as a blindfold conversation experience. Do not check your email or scan the headlines on CNN or try to be otherwise "productive." Just concentrate on the conversation and, within that, on what the other person may be communicating nonverbally and what he or she wants. What can you do to help this person?

Imagine, vividly, that your life is like an hourglass. The sand above represents all the things you have to do, all the things that are pressing on you and clamoring for your attention. No matter how much you shake and agitate the hourglass, only one grain of sand at a time goes through the narrow neck.

That grain is the task at hand. Focus on it.

Here is another visualization that you may find helpful: Imagine yourself pouring oil from a jug into a container. See how the oil streams down smoothly with no turbulence or bubbles. Imagine that the oil represents your attention and energy. Pour it, and the essence of yourself, into the task at hand. Mental chatter of all kinds is turbulence; banish it completely.

At the end of a week doing this, reflect on the following: What were your reactions to the exercise? Did you find that you were more productive and effective? What was your emotional tenor during the entire week?

Cultivating Gratitude and Appreciation

Consider gratitude and appreciation. Most of us are blessed in so many ways, which we don't even see. We just take all of that for granted and focus on whatever is lacking or not working, and we do that constantly. If all our attention is only on what we're lacking, then that's all we will see, and this perspective then informs our frame of mind and our ability to relate to others. This exercise is about simply understanding and recognizing all the good things in our lives, meditating on them, and learning to never take them for granted. It cultivates a humble and positive frame of mind, which then affects us in our lives and certainly affects others through our leadership.

Try this for a week, for five to ten minutes every night, just before you retire. Give this important exercise your utmost effort.

Let a deep feeling of appreciation and gratitude well up in you. Allow this feeling to surface. Permit it to take hold of you, to envelop you. Broadcast it as a silent statement of who you are. It is okay if you feel you are play-acting. Do it with the greatest sincerity and emotional commitment of which you are capable.

Doubtless you can find many reasons to be grateful: your health, your family, your career, the opportunity to experience travel and the finer things in life. All the above are valid reasons for gratitude, but go beyond these things if you can. Be appreciative and deeply grateful for the opportunity to be appreciative and deeply grateful, for the feeling such gratitude evokes in you. *Remember:* whatever you give thanks to and appreciate will increase in your life.

The timing is important. *This should be the last thing you do at night.* Pay special attention to your first-thing-in-the-morning mental chatter the next day. Report on whether you notice any changes from observations in previous weeks.

Let this feeling of gratitude take hold of you many times during the day. Don't force it. Introduce it gently, and let it seize you if it can. If it does not, there's no harm done, but keep trying at irregular intervals. What does this practice do to the mental tenor of your day?

You will find that it is easier to hold on to the feeling of gratitude if you use your body and physical actions. Walk with a spring in your step. Walk with this spring even if you are merely rushing to hit the restroom during a break. Smile, smile, smile. Don't smile with just your face; smile from your heart. Let laughter begin in the pit of your stomach, engulf you, and overflow through your face.

Every time you interact with a person, even if it is a casual interaction such as paying a convenience store cashier for gum, earnestly wish that person every happiness possible. Do this silently; we do not want to make people uncomfortable with such a strong outpouring of emotion from a stranger. Mentally wishing everyone happiness may be a challenge for some of you if you have toxic people in your life. Do it anyway.

We live in a frenetic society and rush all the time. You are hurrying somewhere and an acquaintance says, "Hi, how are you?" and you say, "Fine, how are you?" over your shoulder as you carry on. Slow down whenever you can. Really look at the person you are speaking to. Observe the face, the expression, the body language. Wish him or her well silently and sincerely.

It is perfectly okay for the interaction to be brief. Just be conscious and beam out peace and well-being as if your life depended on it. In a funny way, it does.

Specifically notice the following:

Do your feelings about people and the nature of your interactions change?

Do you perceive that others' feelings and interaction patterns have changed?

Finally, what has your emotional tenor been during the week, and how does it compare with the week when you were doing the mental-chatter exercise? Did you fall asleep more easily, and was your sleep deeper and more refreshing? What was your mental chatter the first thing in the morning? Was it less insistent and more peaceful? Did you find yourself greeting the new day with more joy than before? Did you observe changes in other persons' reactions? What were they?

Living in an Other-Centered Universe

Great leaders become leaders to serve, to help other people evolve and grow. By serving, they attain deep satisfaction and a sense of accomplishment. How can we cultivate this other-oriented take on life?

In the book *Give and Take*, Adam Grant classifies people as givers and takers and matchers.[3] On a spectrum of happiness and impact, takers are at the bottom and matchers in the middle. Givers are distributed between the top and bottom. The happiest and most influential givers focus on giving to other givers. They avoid giving to takers, as that type of giving can thoroughly deplete a person.

We live in a me-centered universe. We evaluate events, near and distant, in terms of their impact on "me." Our spouse got a great job offer, and we think about how this will affect our relationship. Our daughter got a tattoo and piercing, and we think about how our friends will react and what they will think of our parenting. More violence in the Middle East, and we worry about what this will do to oil prices and how much more we will have to pay for gas and heating oil.

Even our altruistic inclinations are frequently tainted. We want to do good for the world and to give back, but it is important to us to be recognized as doing so. We want our jokes to be laughed at, our contributions to be acknowledged— loudly and repeatedly—and our advice solicited and acted on.

Go back to your mental chatter, and examine how often the word *I* comes in. *I* should have done that, said that, felt that. *I* am an idiot for doing that or not doing something else. What will someone else think of *me* for doing or saying something? How wonderful am *I* for pulling off that brilliant conversational riposte, that wonderful suggestion that others were too dumb to recognize the value of, that significant help *I* provided? Why can't *I* be as gorgeous as, or as witty as, or as brilliant, successful, or rich as X?

It is an unbroken and unending string of *I*, *me*, and *my*. All the stress in our lives is because the universe has an unfortunate tendency of not paying any attention to what *I* want, and we will not accept this.

Even when we are genuinely moved by compassion or love or sympathy, it does not take long for the *I* and *me* to creep back in. Tragedy in some part of the world? Let me call up the toll-free number in the news article and make a contribution followed by How Dare That Person Put *Me* on Hold for So Long?

Pause for five minutes, and think about this. Think about how *everything* we do is, in some way, a monument to *I* and *me*.

Don't beat yourself up about this. Just recognize and acknowledge it.

For two weeks, practice living in an other-centered universe. At every instance, look for opportunities to serve: you give up your place in line, you buy something for the person behind you, you clean their room, and so on. It's similar to random acts of kindness, but goes beyond acts to a way of being: self-transcendence. The impact can be startling. It changes the energy around you, and—though you don't do it for this reason—it usually comes back to you manyfold.

An other-centered outlook is incredibly hard to maintain for lengthy periods, so I suggest that you pick a few one-hour time slots each day. During your selected times, you will do all things for the sole benefit of the person with whom you interact. In conversation, you will *not* think about the brilliant reply you will make. You will focus on what the person is saying and feeling and think *only* of how you can be of service to that person. If possible, be of service anonymously, or to strangers, thus taking the *I* and *me* out of the picture entirely. Think of how you can be of service to people you know, to people you barely know, to society at large.

Use good judgment! Do not give the contents of your bank account to a panhandler. It is not clear that this is a helpful thing to do anyway.

Be creative! One person left gifts of candy for office mates along with handwritten, anonymous notes expressing appreciation for some positive trait that person expressed. Another paid for tolls for the person behind him and gave the toll collector a page of uplifting quotes to give the person. Another person would—after she had finished with it—leave an unlimited day pass for the New York subway taped to the turnstile along with a note saying "This is an unlimited-ride Metro Card for today. It is meant for someone in need. If you think you qualify, please take it and use it. If there is still time after you have done with it, please tape it to the turnstile from which you exit with this note." Another would tape coupons for products she didn't need to the supermarket shelf where that product was stocked.

Each day, deliberately and consciously, do more than one thing to make the world a little better. Do you get irritated when you see a shopping cart ruining a supermarket parking spot? Get into the habit of taking one and returning it to the nest of carts at the entrance. Do you see a clearly misplaced sweater in a department store? Restore it to its rightful place.

The possibilities are endless. Spread sweetness and light. These are similar to random acts of kindness, but wherever possible, give specific help to specific people who need that help. Is someone you know having a hard time in a particular area of his or her life? Think of one thing you can do to make it a little easier for the person. Even a card with a thoughtful quote in it may help.

Be practical and empathetic. A woman wanted to help a friend whose husband died suddenly, leaving her with small children. Her "What can I do to help?" was met with polite thanks. So she thought for a while and organized a group of friends. One went and gathered everyone's shoes and polished them for the funeral. Three arranged, between them, to bring in breakfast, lunch, and dinner for a week. Another contributed several hours of babysitting for the youngest child. None of this would have happened if the first friend had not set it up.

Your attitude as you do this is important. If you help someone, do *not* expect gratitude from that person. Instead, *you* should be grateful to that person for providing you the opportunity to be of service. Try it. This is a very different paradigm from the one we normally use. Don't get mad at people for not acknowledging how much you have helped them. Focus on being grateful for having had the opportunity to help.

Finally, each day, *make someone's day!*

Have you ever had a random interaction with someone and it left you feeling so good that it uplifted your mood for an entire day? Perhaps it was a sales clerk who sincerely assured you that you looked really lovely in the dress you were trying out. And you somehow sensed that she cared about you and was not just out to clinch the sale. Perhaps it was the jovial guy in the line next to you—the man who cracked jokes that left you doubled up. Perhaps an unexpected and thoughtful gesture from a friend really touched you.

You will go out and deliberately, each day, make someone's day. Just the thought of having to do this will get your creative juices flowing. For some, it will also arouse fears. Shy people will feel particularly pressured. Use making someone else's day as a lever to overcome your shyness. Or else figure out how to do it anonymously. But do it at least once every day.

Eventually you want to make this a part of your life, not an exercise to be completed. This is true of all these exercises!

Good Thing, Bad Thing, Who Knows?

Look back on your life. Have there been events that you immediately classified as disasters, as totally terrible things, that you now recognize as true blessings? Pick something that you are still grappling with. Can you see how the bad thing may actually be a good thing? Perhaps even a wonderful thing? In *Are You Ready to Succeed?* Srikumar Rao quotes the following old Sufi tale to demonstrate how the way we categorize events in our lives does not always reflect what they ultimately mean to us.

> An old man lived in a verdant valley with his son, a handsome and dutiful youth. They lived an idyllic life despite a lack of material possessions and were very happy. So much so that feelings of envy arose in their neighbors.
>
> The old man used practically all his savings to buy a young wild stallion. It was a beautiful creature and he planned to use it for breeding. The same night he bought it, it jumped over the paddock and disappeared into the wild. The neighbors came over the next morning and commiserated. "How terrible," they said.
>
> "Good thing? Bad thing? Who knows?" said the old man.
>
> Ten days later the stallion was back, bringing with it a herd of about a dozen wild horses. The old man was able to lure all of them into his paddock, which he had fixed so escape was no longer possible. "What good fortune!" said the neighbors as they clustered around.
>
> "Good thing? Bad thing? Who knows?" said the old man.
>
> His son started to train the horses. One of them knocked him down and stomped on his leg. It healed crooked and left him with a permanent limp. "Such misfortune," said the neighbors.
>
> "Good thing? Bad thing? Who knows?" said the old man.
>
> The next summer, the king declared war. Soldiers came to the village and rounded up all the young men to serve in the army. The old man's son was

spared because of his game leg. "Truly are you lucky," exclaimed his neighbors
as they bemoaned their own losses.

"Good thing? Bad thing? Who knows?" said the old man.

That very winter . . .[4]

"Good thing, bad thing, who knows?" is about the idea that when things happen to us, we instantly label them as good or bad and respond accordingly. But in reality, when most people look back on their lives and connect the dots, they may discover that the label was inaccurate. "When I failed and got fired, it felt horrible at the time, but in retrospect, it was the best thing that could have happened to me. I got out of that terrible job, and I had to find something new that I really loved." "The promotion that I thought was the best thing in the world turned out to be terrible, because now I was in a role that I wasn't really suited for." This disconnect between our initial label of an event and what it ultimately means to us can occur with many other life experiences—not all of them, of course. We need to avoid being quick to label, instead recognizing that although one door may have closed, another one has opened, and the "adjacent possible" has now shifted into something new.

A top student at an Ivy League university had his heart set on a summer job in investment banking. A serious illness put him in the hospital for four weeks, and when he got out, the opportunities for summer work in a bank had come and gone. Not only did he not get his dream job, but he had no job. The summer dragged on, and he comforted himself by wallowing in a deep depression. When a family friend introduced him to a doctor who was leaving for Africa to work in a clinic, the doctor asked him to tag along. Having nothing better to do, he went.

There was filth and grime and ignorance and stark deprivation. But as he worked in the most menial of jobs, something came alive in him. The next summer, he turned down the investment banking job he was offered and returned to Africa. After college, he did two years in the Peace Corps. "That illness was the best thing that ever happened to me," he states flatly.

There are strong elements of "If you get a lemon, make lemonade" in this exercise, but it actually goes much deeper. Consider the possibility that you are *never* given a lemon. You are given the opportunity to make lemonade. Even better, you are given the opportunity to make a double-dip sundae that tastes delicious and actually causes you to lose weight!

Some life experiences are so painful that you cannot handle thinking of them as good things. Examples are death of loved ones, troubled relations with close relatives, and serious injury. Don't force yourself to work with such situations; pick something that you are comfortable working with.

Do not do this exercise in reverse. Accept the good things in your life at present as they are. Don't try to see how they could be bad things.

Achieving personal mastery is critical to becoming more a conscious human being—to become peaceful, happier, and more powerful. When you become a leader, all this matters a great deal. All these exercises do ultimately make us more effective as leaders, because they deliver us to a better place as human beings, and we see the world with greater clarity with a more positive outlook.

Contemplative Practices

Contemplative practices such as meditation, yoga, Tai Chi, breathing exercises, chanting, affirmations, visualizations, and prayer are all very valuable in helping an individual develop into a more conscious leader. Setting aside time to be by ourselves is critical for self-awareness, as well as for helping us center ourselves, become aware of our feelings, and slow down the mind.

Most great religions have cultivated classical meditative traditions in one form or another. The most important thing we can do is practice regularly. We can't just have a theoretical understanding of meditation—it's the practice that makes the difference. Almost any type of meditation will work, provided we do it regularly. A type of Buddhist meditation called *insight meditation* can be done as part of our normal working lives.[5] Insight meditation doesn't require us to be alone, do breathing exercises, chant, or concentrate on a mantra. It is a discipline for being fully present and aware in each moment instead of becoming lost in our own mental chatter. The practices is challenging; as we go through our workday, we can easily get caught up in things and forget to stay in the moment. But as soon as we become aware that we've slipped, we can learn to immediately nudge ourselves back to the present moment.

Chapter 17

Organizational Approach to Conscious Leadership

A conscious company needs to have conscious leaders, not only at the top but also throughout the organization. To infuse your organization with conscious leadership, you need to change the way you hire, identify, develop, and promote leaders throughout the organization. In hiring leaders, a conscious organization identifies people who score high on the SELFLESS screen, in addition to possessing the technical skills that a position requires.

When a company is identifying future leaders from within its ranks or promoting leaders to higher levels of responsibility, it should use similar criteria. In addition, the company needs to ensure that individuals are seeking to become leaders not for the salary, prestige, or power gained through leadership, but rather because they are driven to serve the organization's people and its purpose. Are they willing to embrace the "awesome responsibility of leadership" (as expressed at Barry-Wehmiller)? It is important to have people who are intrinsically motivated for the right reasons. It should not be a top-down approach wherein certain people are anointed as the "chosen ones" to be leaders. You can certainly recognize talent, and you know who's doing what in the organization, but you should look at it through a lens of "Who are the people who have a big positive impact on those around them and on the business?" rather than "Who is delivering the numbers at any cost?"

Leadership development needs to be aligned with the values and guiding principles of the organization as well as with the elements of SELFLESS. One practical way to accomplish this is to create a leadership checklist and orient leadership development programs around that. We will describe this approach in this chapter.

Many people try to climb the corporate ladder by doing whatever it takes; they tend to be the ones who get promoted in traditional profit-centered companies. A study presented at the Australian Psychological Society Congress suggested that psychopaths are as prevalent in the corporate sector as they are in prisons. In the general population, according to forensic psychologist Nathan Brooks, studies have shown that one in one hundred people displayed psychopathic traits. In a study of 261 corporate professionals in supply-chain management, 21 percent of the participants were found to have clinically significant levels of psychopathic traits—a figure comparable to prison populations. These leaders are described as "successful psychopaths." The highfliers with a psychopathic nature have traits such as an egocentric, charming, or superficial nature and a lack of empathy or remorse.[1]

A Conscious Approach to Leadership Development

We recommend starting by defining the kind of leaders you want and identifying people who are innately aligned with this definition. However, becoming a leader should never be mandated; people need to have an intrinsic desire to become leaders. Once potential leaders are identified and have expressed their desire to take on the responsibility of leadership for the right reasons, we have to help them on the journey by creating learning experiences geared to developing the requisite qualities in them. Ideally, the teaching in such courses should be done by other exemplary leaders in the organization: leader-to-leader teaching and coaching can be very effective. Outside experts offering standardized leadership training are not nearly as effective; this training often doesn't align with the organization's purpose, values, and culture. Potential leaders must understand what it means to be a leader in *your* organization; what are the core values, competencies, and behaviors expected of leaders? All of that has to be related to actual experiences and how leaders have dealt with challenging situations in the past.

Consider the leadership development programs you have in your organization. What is your most effective program? Why?

_____

_____

_____

_____

Which leadership development program has had the least impact? Why?

_____

_____

_____

_____

_____

_____

The Need for Constructive Dissonance

Many people are uncomfortable with dissonance. But dissonance can have a higher purpose, which is to help us grow and evolve. For those of us who are conflict-averse, we need to recognize this tendency in ourselves, to appreciate that sometimes, friction can be good. The absence of friction means too much consensus, which means too much status quo and groupthink. It is about seeing reality clearly. As individuals, we don't always see reality clearly; it's only collectively that we can get a read on reality, provided we can guard against groupthink.

Whole Foods Market CEO John Mackey describes the need for dissonance in organizations:

If we become too cookie-cutter about leadership development, we might create conditions where there's too much stability and we're perpetuating already-existing ways. We need to not only tolerate but also encourage dissonance and challenging ideas. If you stop growing and evolving, then you start dying. Conscious leaders don't always agree; they should also challenge one another. They must have the will and the courage to see and call for change when it is needed. The organization will die if the leaders do not constantly think about what they should be doing differently or how they could be evolving from where they are. It's not about becoming conscious and then staying there; it's a never-ending journey of becoming more *conscious, seeing reality as it truly exists as opposed to what you think it is, and having a deeper sense of right and wrong.*

Many virtues come from alignment. We get alignment in an organization when there is broad agreement on purpose and values. Organizations that have high alignment also have a very high degree of trust. People collaborate. Purpose, trust, and collaboration lead to higher morale. The energy in the organization increases, resulting in greater creativity and innovation. Every conscious business should strive for alignment, because of all the wonderful things that flow from that.

But alignment is not a risk-free proposition. One outcome that can result from a high degree of alignment is groupthink: everybody starts to think alike. Yet the world never stops changing. Competition is continually evolving. If you're locked into your own dialogue internally and everyone in the organization agrees, you may not tune into what's going on with your customers or competitors. That can result in stagnation: continuing to do the same thing, with the philosophy of "If it ain't broke, don't fix it." A "kumbaya" mentality develops: "We're all aligned, part of this happy tribe, celebrating and doing great things." If only it could be that way all the time. Remember: anytime the rate of change outside an organization exceeds the rate of change inside that organization, irrelevance becomes inevitable.

Organizations create cultures, and cultures develop immune systems. Like all immune systems, cultures resist change. But change is essential. An organization that is not changing and growing continually is slowly dying.

If we aspire to be truly conscious, we need to be transparent and bring unpleasant truths to light. We can't shrink from difficult questions. Dissonance can be irritating but in a stimulating way, like a grain of sand that irritates the oyster but can lead it to produce a pearl.

Dissonance involves new ways of seeing—ways that enable us to think critically about our business and its worldview. With a critical eye, we can challenge the organizational paradigm and the organizational immune system—an immune system that wants alignment and resists dissonance. Dissonance disrupts the comfort zone, which is why it can feel threatening and dangerous to many.

Dissonance comes naturally to some leaders, but not to most. Leaders who embrace dissonance are often seen as mavericks and troublemakers, but effective leaders need to see how the company is falling short and how it must evolve.

Here is a paradox: alignment stimulates invention because when people feel safe, when they're not afraid, creativity flows and flourishes. But paradoxically, dissonance also creates innovation, because it gets people out of their comfort zones. In fact, when people disagree, this is when you are likely to find truly radical innovation. You only truly stretch when you are challenged.

Alignment in an organization is always temporary. Dissonance, which becomes necessary and inevitable, is a kind of healthy paranoia, similar to healthy stress. It depends on how we use it. We can use it to help the organization evolve, or we can allow it to destroy the organization.

CEOs should be mavericks who simultaneously foster alignment while not letting the organization stagnate with too much of it and actively work toward dissonance. Organizations need both alignment and dissonance, and if the two conditions are mixed in the right proportions, the result is organizational evolution. Alignment plus dissonance equals evolution.

What is the capacity for dissonance in your leadership team? On a scale of 1 to 5 (with 5 meaning the highest level), how would you score the team?

_____

_____

_____

_____

How do you think others on the team would score it? Why?

_____

_____

_____

_____

_____

_____

_____

What do you think you can do to encourage more constructive dissonance on your team? In your organization? What kinds of things can the leadership team do to encourage this in their teams? At the next level below that?

_____

_____

_____

_____

_____

_____

_____

The Barry-Wehmiller Approach to Leadership Development

When it comes to creating an environment in which there are conscious leaders at every level of the organization and in every form of leadership, Barry-Wehmiller takes an instructive approach. This diversified machinery manufacturing company based in St. Louis has created a detailed template for what a great leader in its system looks like.

Barry-Wehmiller has identified its key pillars of leadership as a caring attitude, inspiration, and celebration. The approach starts with caring for people as human beings first, not as functions or people doing certain things, and seeing that the essential responsibility of leaders is to inspire people. In many cases, leaders don't do that; they tell people what to do. True leadership is about inspiring people to creatively help move the company in a direction that makes strategic sense. The third element is recognition and celebration. At Barry-Wehmiller, there's a tremendous emphasis on catching people doing good things, holding up that goodness to the organization, and celebrating those things meaningfully. Everybody feels valued and listened to. People enjoy a great deal of responsible freedom to act according to their unique perspective: they are encouraged to take ownership of their work and come up with new ideas and initiatives and so forth, as long as these are consistent with the values and priorities of the business.

This journey started in 2000, when the company assembled a group of leaders from across the organization to think through what they had collectively learned about leadership and cultural transformation. This led to the creation of a document titled "Guiding Principles of Leadership," which describes the values and the kind of culture the company is trying to create and sustain.

Over the years, Barry-Wehmiller has developed a tradition of what it calls "truly human leadership," which is leadership practiced in a way that leadership is seen as the "stewardship of the lives that are entrusted to us." Because Barry-Wehmiller recognizes the huge impact that the quality of leadership has on the quality of people's lives, the company takes leadership extremely seriously (figure 17-1).

Figure 17-1: Guiding principles of leadership at Barry-Wehmiller

Guiding Principles of Leadership

We measure success by the way we touch the lives of people.

A clear and compelling *vision*, embodied within a sustainable business model, which fosters personal growth

Leadership creates a dynamic environment that:

- Is based on *trust*
- Brings out and *celebrates* the best in each individual
- Allows for teams and individuals to have a *meaningful* role
- Inspires a sense of *pride*
- *Challenges* individuals and teams
- *Liberates* everyone to realize "true success"

Positive, insightful communication empowers individuals and teams along the journey.

Measurables allow individuals and teams to relate their contribution to the realization of the vision.

Treat people *superbly* and compensate them fairly.

Leaders are called to be visionaries, coaches, mentors, teachers, and students.

As your sphere of influence grows, so grows your responsibility for *stewardship* of the Guiding Principles.

We are committed to our employees' personal growth.

barrywehmiller
BUILDING A **BETTER WORLD** THROUGH BUSINESS

In light of Barry-Wehmiller's guiding principles of leadership, what five to ten principles would you like your company to embrace? Consider using a process similar to Barry-Wehmiller's: on off-site with twenty or so participants drawn from different levels of the organization.

_____

_____

_____

_____

_____

_____

_____

Eventually, the company created a *leadership checklist*, which identified the leadership behaviors consistent with its values and culture (figure 17-2). Barry-Wehmiller likens it to checklists used by pilots and surgeons, because leaders too have the lives and well-being of people in their hands. The company expects its leaders to adhere to everything on the checklist *every day* they are in their role. The leadership checklist became the foundation for Barry-Wehmiller's thorough and rigorous Leadership Fundamentals course.

Figure 17-2: Leadership checklist created by Barry-Wehmiller

Leadership Checklist

I accept the awesome responsibility of leadership.
The following describe my essential actions as a leader.

- ☐ I practice stewardship of the Guiding Principles of Leadership through my time, conversations and personal development.
- ☐ I advocate safety and wellness through my actions and words.
- ☐ I reflect to lead my team in Achieving Principled Results on Purpose.
- ☐ I inspire passion, optimism and purpose.
- ☐ My personal communication cultivates fulfilling relationships.
- ☐ I foster a team community in which we are committed to each other and to the pursuit of a common goal.
- ☐ I exercise responsible freedom, empowering each of us to achieve our potential.
- ☐ I proactively engage in the personal growth of individuals on my team.
- ☐ I facilitate meaningful group interactions.
- ☐ I set, coach to and measure goals that define winning.
- ☐ I recognize and celebrate the greatness in others.
- ☐ I commit to daily continuous improvement.

When we engage our heads, hearts and hands around these habits, extraordinary levels of trust and fulfillment will result.

BARRY-WEHMILLER
UNIVERSITY

If you had to create your own leadership checklist, what ten things would each leader have to review at the beginning of the day and at the end of the day to ensure that your leadership team is on track with your organization's culture and principles?

_____

_____

_____

_____

_____

_____

_____

_____

_____

_____

_____

_____

_____

_____

_____

_____

Barry-Wehmiller pays a great deal of attention to the issue of motivation, of why people become leaders.[2] At most companies, the practice is to identify so-called high potentials as future leaders, who are then pulled out and given special opportunities to grow and develop. We are reminded of the expression, "Some people are born leaders, some people become leaders, and others have leadership thrust upon them." In most companies, people have leadership thrust on them. While that may work in some instances, in many cases it does not, because it's seen as an entitlement for "superior" people to become leaders. Those are cultures in which leaders typically get lots of material rewards, so it reinforces the mercenary mindset of why people want to become leaders. At BW, leadership is about service and stewardship; they constantly use the phrase "the awesome responsibility of leadership."

Becoming a leader at Barry-Wehmiller is voluntary, not mandated; people who aspire to be leaders under this definition of leadership put up their hands and say, "I want to be a leader. I'm an assembly shop floor worker now but I really want to lead." There are opportunities for leadership at every level of the organizations, not simply at the executive ranks. People have to apply to be admitted into the Leadership Fundamentals course; they have to write a detailed essay about themselves and why they want to lead. Those selected after a thorough process have the opportunity to deeply learn the Barry-Wehmiller approach to leadership. They then go back to their jobs and apply what they have learned and come back and learn further and get feedback on what happened and what worked. The courses mix people with different backgrounds; you could have somebody from software development and a chief financial officer in the same course sitting next to each other not even knowing what the other person actually does. It is about developing the human being as a leader, not about their current title and position.

––––––––––––

Developing great leaders is not an accident. The best organizations do it with a clear intent and approach. Like the leaders at Barry-Wehmiller, you must ask the key question "What kind of leaders do we want in our organization?" You began that process above by articulating your philosophy or point of view on what kind of leadership traits you want in your organization. You now need to think about four other key elements that go into your leadership development programs:

1. Decide on how you select and promote leaders.

2. Develop a learning and development program to grow and develop leaders.

3. Develop a mentoring and career-tracking program.

4. Pull all this together into a personal leadership development plan for each leader in your organization.

Selection and Promotion

The organization will watch what you do more than what you say. Therefore, whenever you promote someone onto or up the leadership track, you send a message to the people in the organization about what you value. Often, there can be a perceived tension between rewarding someone for high performance and ensuring that he or she is setting an example or growing as the type of leader you want to have in the organization. Who you select to come into the organization and how much weight you put on the person's past leadership behavior also signal to the organization what you value in leaders. Consistency in promotions and hiring will reinforce the value you are placing on leadership quality and behavior.

Learning and Development

While you can't teach leadership per se, you can develop leaders. You need to think through what you want in your leaders and then work with people who are knowledgeable in this area to design a series of programs that can help you develop these kinds of leaders. Beyond developing people's skills and capabilities, a conscious company can support their development as human beings—their emotional, spiritual, and systems intelligence.

Mentoring and Career Tracking

Leaders learn best about how to become better leaders by leading. Leadership is an on-the-job training adventure at its core. So you want to place people in the right kinds of positions where they can be both stretched and supported to gain new experiences and grow as leaders. All leaders should have a plan that includes where they are today in their career and what their next two steps in the organization might be, with more focus on what the immediate next step might be. This career tracking should integrate with their development plan, above, to ensure that they are also developing in their current role and are preparing for this next step. In addition, you should develop a mentoring program where they are paired with a more experienced leader who can offer them informal advice on how to learn on the job. This mentorship should be done outside the normal reporting chain. A mentor is someone with whom you can talk through the challenges and key decisions you need to make. A mentorship is a safe place to be vulnerable about what is hard and where your growth edge is. It is invaluable as a support on the leadership learning path.

Pulling It All Together: The Leadership Development Plan

Take the plans for leader selection, promotion, and development, and integrate them to create a leadership development plan for the organization as a whole. Use this overall plan to create individualized plans for key leaders. This is not something that is done *to* or *for* people. The best plans are cocreated between the individual leader and the senior leadership and HR people overseeing leadership development. Ideally, individuals self-curate a process with the support of the organization; they take the lead in developing their plan and advocating for the development opportunities that they feel will help them the most. This requires an iterative process of development between the organization and the individual and usually also involves the incorporation of some form of 360-degree feedback to help anchor the development process in reality. Hence when we say that leaders are developed, we are implying that an organization has made a serious commitment to creating an environment where the model of great leadership is clear, reinforced with promotions and supported by an integrated development plan and process. This is the conscious development of conscious leaders.

Kids Talk about Leadership

This video shares the thoughts of kids on leadership, what qualities they expect, and how they think a leader should lead.

URL: https://www.ccfieldguide.com/kids

Search Words: Conscious Capitalism Field Guide Kids Talk about Leadership

Part Five

IMPLEMENTATION

*I*n this final part of the journey, we'll address two themes. The first theme is pulling together the work you have into an action plan—a practical, focused set of initiatives with timelines and project plans. Our goal is to help you and your organization transform the intentions and plans explored in parts 1 through 4 into a clear plan of action that starts today and extends out three years.

The second theme is to address the basics of change management and transformation. This journey is fundamentally about how you change the way people on your team and in your organization think. Lasting behavior changes come from thinking about the business differently. We'll discuss what it takes to make these changes, and we'll give you some guidelines for how to organize and execute your campaign of change. Having a clear, phased approach to transformation helps accelerate the time to impact of the work, and developing this approach with your team builds their commitment to the execution process.

Figure P5-1 presents an overview of this final part of the book. In chapter 18, we will help you focus on the highest-impact initiatives that will make your organization a more conscious business. We will show you how to select your top ten initiatives, prioritize them into three phases over the next six months to three years, and develop the immediate next steps to get moving quickly on the execution. In chapter 19, we will help you transform the DNA of your business to deepen and broaden your organization's journey to Conscious Capitalism.

Figure P5-1: Overview of part 5

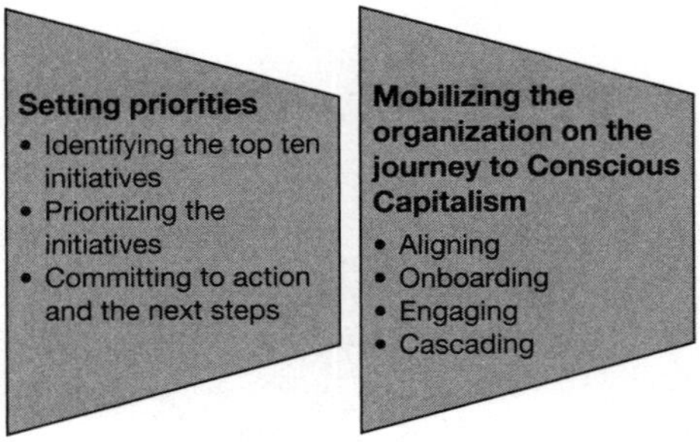

Setting priorities
- Identifying the top ten initiatives
- Prioritizing the initiatives
- Committing to action and the next steps

Mobilizing the organization on the journey to Conscious Capitalism
- Aligning
- Onboarding
- Engaging
- Cascading

Chapter 18

Setting Organizational Priorities

Changing behavior and habits is not easy. If it were, people would change the things that they are most dissatisfied with. Consider David Maister's essay "Strategy and the Fat Smoker."[1] Fat smokers know they need to stop smoking, go on a diet, and begin to exercise. But the gap between knowing what you need to do and doing it can be large. For example, sadly, three years after having a heart attack, only about 5 to 10 percent of overweight smokers make significant, sustained changes in their lifestyle.

So, change isn't easy. In the previous parts of this book, you have completed many exercises and created potential actions and initiatives around each of the four pillars of Conscious Capitalism. In this chapter, your goal is twofold: to set priorities and to move to action. We believe that it is better to complete a few things well than it is to start many and finish few. Therefore, we will take you on a step-by-step process to prioritize and commit to action plans and your immediate next steps.

Up until this point, you may have completed sections of work in this book on your own, with your team, or in some combination. For this chapter, you need to do this work with your team. To accelerate implementation, the people who will be involved need to have a significant role in creating the action plan. Involvement in this process helps them understand why you are doing things and the order you are doing them in, and ultimately gives them ownership of the plan. Thus, involvement of the whole team speeds up the execution.

What We've Done So Far

Let's start by going back to each pillar of Conscious Capitalism covered earlier and recall what you or your team have identified as the highest-priority actions or initiatives with the most impact. If you have been doing the exercises in the book, you should go back and review your work in each chapter. For each pillar, capture the top three or four action items that you have developed. It is our experience that this is a very powerful exercise for your team, both in looking at the areas for development in each pillar and in building alignment on what is the highest priority area for each pillar. Figure 18-1 will help you compile all these ideas and initiatives together on one page.

Figure 18-1: The four pillars of Conscious Capitalism

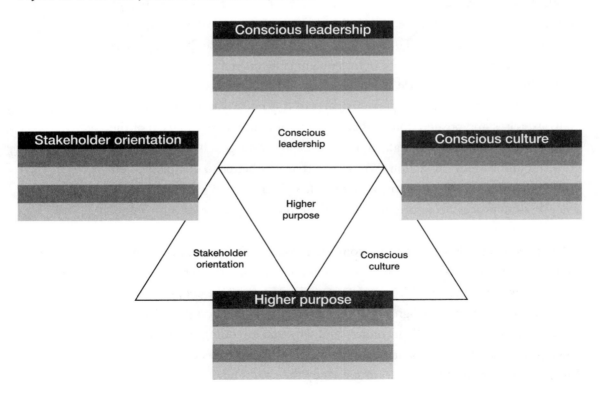

What did you and your team notice as you pulled together these action items together in figure 18-1? Was it easy to do or hard? Why?

_____

_____

_____

_____

_____

_____

_____

How aligned were you on priorities? What are some of the key takeaways for you? For the team?

_____

_____

_____

_____

_____

_____

_____

Your Top-Ten List

Having listed twelve to sixteen potential action items, you can next prioritize these actions according to potential impact—a top-ten list of initiatives that you will address over the next three years—by doing the following exercise.

The following prioritization techniques ensure that everyone has a chance to add his or perspective to the list of priorities. First, use a whiteboard or flip chart to list all the action items identified in figure 18-1, by pillar. You can set up the chart like figure 18-2 (we'll explain the last column later).

Figure 18-2

Worksheet for determining your organization's top ten initiatives

NO.	INITIATIVE AND PILLAR	VOTES
1.		
2.		
3.		
4.		
5.		
6.		
7.		
8.		
9.		
10.		
11.		
12.		
13.		
14.		
15.		
16.		

Next, hand out dot stickers or small sticky notes (four for each participant), which people will use to vote with. Have all the team members go to the flip chart or whiteboard and place their four markers next to the four items that they consider the organization's highest priority. Try to avoid having each individual voting one at a time; it is a group exercise whose goal is to see what the whole team thinks, not how one individual (including the leader) thinks. We suggest that the leader be the last person to vote to avoid unduly influencing the choices of the other team members. At the end of this exercise, the highest vote initiatives will usually be obvious by the number of stickers (votes) each received. Typically, a handful (three to five) initiatives will clearly be agreed to by most; these are the highest priorities and should be added to the top of your top-ten list (figure 18-3). Then there is usually a second group with several votes but no broad support and, finally, a number of initiatives that have one or no votes.

Figure 18-3

Worksheet for your organization's top ten priorities, determined by team voting

NO.	INITIATIVE NAME	DESCRIPTION
1.		
2.		
3.		
4.		
5.		
6.		
7.		
8.		
9.		
10.		

Remove the clearly agreed-to items from the main list (they are on your new top-ten list). Now do a second round of voting with everyone having three votes this time. Everyone chooses three top priorities from the remaining list and places their sticky notes or dots beside these choices. Review the second round of voting, and discuss as a team the remaining priorities. Transfer to the top-ten list the new "prioritized" initiatives from the second round. Do this until you have ten top priorities. If a third round is necessary, give each team member only two votes. The goal here is not to let the perfect be the enemy of the good. Get this list to the 80 percent level of team agreement, and then move on to the next exercise.

What did you learn as a team about how you see the priority areas for the organization? How did your priorities differ? What areas did you clearly all agree on, or agree on easily? Why was this so?

_____

_____

_____

_____

_____

_____

_____

If there are still no clear priorities, or if this was a particularly difficult exercise to do as a team, discuss as a team why this was so. Write down your findings so there is recorded evidence to refer to in the future challenges.

_____

_____

_____

_____

_____

_____

_____

Further Prioritizing Actions: The Vital First Few

We are now going to do a further sorting of priorities by balancing business impact and the effort or resources required to execute the initiative. Inevitably, there will be excitement at this stage about moving forward with several initiatives. However, as stated earlier, finishing a few key initiatives is better than starting many and finishing few. The team should consider the resources that might need to be shifted and should work on these priority initiatives. Because these resources are limited, it is important to get a rough sense of your organization's available resources for change. To do this, you can organize your top-ten list into a two-by-two matrix (figure 18-4).

You'll now compare the estimated resources required to execute this initiative and its potential impact on your business. The vertical axis depicts business impact, and the horizontal axis roughly represents the level of resources or effort required. At this point, you don't need to be precise about estimating the resources. Think in terms of a high, medium, or low level of resources relative to

Figure 18-4: Prioritization matrix

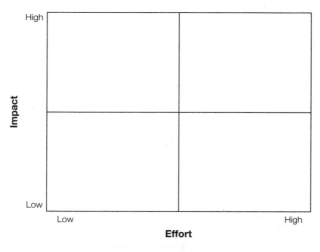

Source: Adapted from Alex Lowy and Phil Hood, *The Power of the 2 x 2 Matrix: Using 2 x 2 Thinking to Solve Business Problems and Make Better Decisions* (San Francisco: Jossey-Bass, 2010).

the size of your organization. What might take three or four people would be a high-resource requirement in a startup but might be a low-resource requirement in a larger organization. Review this prioritization matrix as a team, and decide roughly what you mean by impact and resource level. Now take your top-ten list, and, one initiative at a time, starting at number one, place your initiatives in the matrix. Using the prioritization matrix diagram, you can identify four groups of initiatives (figure 18-5):

High impact and low effort (top left corner): These are the initiatives you and your team should start with and that should be the focus of the short-term plan.

High impact and high effort (top right corner): You should consider these initiatives for the medium term and second wave of your implementation.

Low impact and low effort (bottom left corner): Consider these initiatives for the medium term and second wave of your implementation.

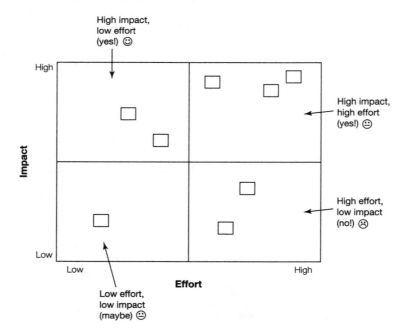

Figure 18-5: Interpretation of prioritization matrix

Low impact and high effort (bottom right corner): There should be very few initiatives in this quadrant, but because of the forced ranking, there may be one or two. These should be tabled for later in your execution planning.

With this priority matrix in hand, we will now develop a phased approach to our execution plan.

Difference Makers and Early Wins

With a set of priorities and a long list of potential action items, executive teams and organizations can get overwhelmed. Consequently, you need to step back and ask, "What are the one or two things that would have the highest impact on our organization?" We refer to these items as the *difference makers*. Typically, an organization can only work on one, or possibly two, of these big items at a time. At the same time, several things will undoubtedly fall into your high-impact, low-effort box. These items, which are more evolutionary, are called *early wins*. These are important for building early momentum and a sense that the organization is making progress. This may be where you pick an area—for instance, the interviewing process—and add questions or criteria to an existing process. For example, add questions about culture fit: "How do you typically react when things don't go as planned within your team?" or "Describe a scenario when you clearly made a bad decision that had an impact on your team, and how you handled it." You should think about the phasing of activity and what you do in phase 1 to make a distinction between the big things that are difference makers and those things that are more evolutionary, or early wins.

Declaring that you will focus on one or two big-impact items for the next six to twelve months and then executing them builds credibility and momentum in the organization. Our advice is to underpromise and overdeliver: it is better to focus on a handful of things that the organization can do well rather than overcommitting.

A Phased Approach

You have created a top-ten list and prioritized it in terms of impact and resources required. In this section, we will create a phased approach to executing these initiatives. We will seek to ensure that you have clear focus in the short term and a road map that reaches out twenty-four to thirty-six months. Although you want to be practical and take one step at a time on this journey, you also need a map of what comes next and why. For this reason, think in terms of what you can accomplish in three phases: within six to twelve months (phase 1), within twelve to twenty-four months (phase 2), and within thirty-six months (phase 3).

Your goal is to make sure that you have focused on one or two high-impact items for the next six to twelve months (phase 1) and perhaps one or two smaller, evolutionary initiatives that can be done with few resources or that can be added to programs already in process.

Go to your priority matrix in figure 18-5, and answer the following questions with your team:

- ❏ Which items can you work on immediately and will have the highest impact on your business—the "one big thing"—over the next six to twelve months?

- ❏ Which items will take longer to get started and may require more advanced planning before you can address them?

- ❏ Which items do you see as being important and having an impact but will take a couple of years for the organization to be ready to address them?

These answers guide your decision on what you'll do in phase 1 (6 to 12 months); phase 2 (12 to 24 months); and phase 3 (36 months and beyond). Use the chart in figure 18-6 to help you see the overall time frame of your transformation to a conscious company, and then answer the questions below.

Figure 18-6: A time frame for implementing conscious initiatives

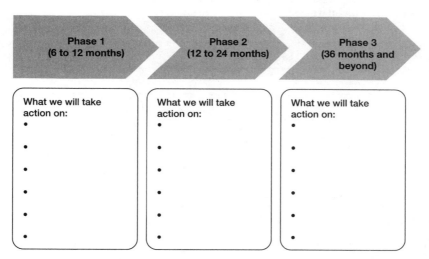

Phase 1 (6 to 12 months)	Phase 2 (12 to 24 months)	Phase 3 (36 months and beyond)
What we will take action on: • • • • • •	What we will take action on: • • • • • •	What we will take action on: • • • • • •

Reflections

How easy or difficult was this exercise for your team to do?

_____

_____

_____

What were the key areas of disagreement? What was hard to let go of? Why?

_____

_____

_____

_____

_____

_____

_____

_____

Will the initiatives you picked to work on first have the biggest possible impact on your business? If not, why not?

_____

_____

_____

_____

_____

_____

_____

The goal in this exercise was about focus and impact. Often people struggle with where to start on the journey to Conscious Capitalism. Hopefully, you and your team now have clearer answers to the question "What are the few things that, if done well, would make the biggest difference to your business?"

Action Plans and Initiative Teams

After deciding on your phase 1 initiatives, focus on moving from high-level intentions to an action plan that is concrete, with actual time commitments, resource requirements, and clear next steps. Figure 18-7 is an illustration of what a good initiative plan includes.

Figure 18-7

Action plan framework

NAME OF INITIATIVE	
Purpose (1–2 sentences)	
Name(s) of executive champion(s)	
Deliverables and dates (what are the end products from this initiative; what will we deliver at the end of it?)	
Major milestones and dates (key steps or checkpoints for the initiative)	
Who is on the team (initial thoughts on who might be on the team, and key roles and types of skills or positions that need to be on the team)?	

This exercise should be done with your team. The goal is to keep it simple, yet at the same time to have enough detail around the action plan that it is clear who is accountable for what and when. Take your first item in phase 1, and fill in the action plan. Repeat this process for your next two items in phase 1. This is basically the team charter or starting point you will use to launch the teams that are responsible for executing on these initiatives.

In our experience, it is best to appoint one or two members of the executive leadership team to be the champions of each of these phase 1 initiatives. Sometimes, having two champions creates the balance needed for credibility and execution across the organization—for instance, the right mix of functional expertise (HR, information technology, etc.) and frontline operating expertise (operational management of the business). The champions create and empower a team to execute the initiative, provide the team members with the resources they need, break down barriers, and are held accountable to the executive team for the impact of the initiative.

The initiative team, the group tasked with the everyday execution of this initiative, can consist of an additional two to four people who either have direct day-to-day responsibility or experience in the appropriate area or have a deep passion for the topic. For example, a field project manager at a construction company stepped into a role that she was passionate about: lean construction. She went on to lead a new organizational function that gained nationwide recognition for the impact it has had on advancing the whole field. The initiative team will ensure that the initiative delivers the impact that is expected. Once the team is formed, its first step is to create a more detailed project plan of how it will execute the initiative, building on the team charter above.

Commitment and Next Steps

It is one thing to develop an action plan; it's another to commit to it. Think of your organization as a sponge; how much water can it hold? As you run your day-to-day business, prioritized initiatives in your journey to Conscious Capitalism will take time and resources from the business. You and your team need to be deeply committed to make sure that this day-to-day pressure does not overwhelm these key initiatives. The trick is to ensure that your top team is committed to the importance of all these initiatives. This commitment goes beyond the individual champions for the initiatives. The leadership team is ultimately responsible for getting regular updates on progress (monthly) and for maintaining focus and keeping resources on these initiatives as needed.

Reflection Exercise

☐ Go around the room, and ask each team member to verbally commit to your key initiatives. The verbal "Yes, I am committed to it" creates a stronger dynamic that just wanting, hoping for, or trying something. There is great power in the words "I commit" (see figure 18-8).

☐ Ask if the team sees any undiscussed barriers to the execution of the action plans. How can the team get in front of these issues now to ensure successful execution? It is far better to have a frank discussion now than to have excuses come up six months from now.

_____

_____

_____

_____

_____

_____

_____

_____

Figure 18-8: Words used on a continuum of commitment

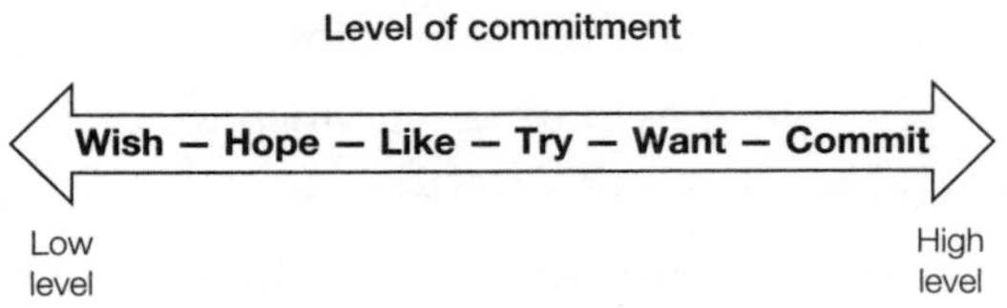

Level of commitment

Wish — Hope — Like — Try — Want — Commit

Low level   High level

At the same time, you need to make sure you have a concrete commitment to the immediate next steps to get started. You can obtain such a commitment by calling a first meeting for an initiative team, proposing a budget, or by having the two executive champions get together within the next two weeks to lay out the plan of action in more detail. The critical element is to identify action steps that you will take in the next thirty days. This kick start builds momentum around this effort. On a chart similar to the one in figure 18-9, you should therefore record the following information: What are the immediate next steps? When are they due? Who will be responsible for ensuring that these steps are taken? Include this chart in your meeting agenda to review progress at your next executive session.

Figure 18-9

Immediate-action framework for steps due in the next thirty days

NAME OF INITIATIVE	IMMEDIATE NEXT STEP	BY WHICH DATE	WHO WILL DO IT

To summarize this chapter, we have asked you to reflect on the things that you have discussed and identified as potential areas to work on, in each pillar, on your journey to Conscious Capitalism. You prioritized this list in terms of impact, resources required, and time frames on which to work on these areas over the next thirty-six months. Armed with these tasks, you are now clear on what has been committed to getting executed over the next six to twelve months and are developing team charters for each initiative and a clear commitment to the immediate next steps in the next thirty days.

In this next chapter, we will discuss how to get the most leverage from these initiatives and how to prepare the organization for what is coming as you evolve your culture toward Conscious Capitalism.

Chapter 19

Mobilizing the Organization

At the core of the Conscious Capitalism journey is a shift in how we think about business—changing the narrative, or story, of business. The change-management agenda thus needs to include both what we will do (chapter 18) and how and why we do it, which will be addressed in this chapter.

Change-management expert John Kotter has noted that successful transformations have both a rational reason for change and an emotional appeal for why it matters. We will guide you in creating a dialogue in the organization about Conscious Capitalism and what your organization is aspiring to. The transformation will entail both a top-down and a bottom-up approach. There are two core elements to these approaches:

- Engaging and aligning the top team

- Engaging and enrolling the whole organization by developing a campaign of influence and creating an ongoing dialogue within the organization

These two elements, over time, will change how people think about your organization. We will discuss each of these in more detail in the following pages.

Aligning the Top Team

A critical step on the journey to Conscious Capitalism is to bring the top team along. If the top team is not aligned and engaged, it is very difficult to build trust and credibility with the rest of the organization. The organization watches what the top team says and does. If the leaders' actions don't reflect what they're saying, the organization recognizes these conflicts and becomes more skeptical about the change effort. For this reason, the top team must understand why you are going on the journey and what the immediate steps to implement this are. Not everybody on the top team will become a true believer, but the leaders must at least understand the basics of what is being proposed and why.

The top team can be defined as needed in your organization. In some organizations, this team is just the executive committee, typically three to five top leaders. Other organizations may expand this team to ten to twelve people. The goal is to involve the people who are viewed as key influencers in leading and managing the day-to-day business. The size of the top team will also be based on how new and different the concept of Conscious Capitalism is to the way the team or organization has been operating to date. If it represents a significant change in cultural direction, you should begin with a smaller team. If the concept is building on a philosophy and business approach that has been in place for several years, you can consider a broader team. The goal is to have the right team that will build credibility and trust in the organization.

Figure 19-1 depicts a typical progression of organizational commitment to a major change initiative. You can expect a similar trajectory for the journey to Conscious Capitalism, if it is successfully executed.

It is our experience that most people find Conscious Capitalism deeply inspiring. The philosophy helps people see business as a means to create greater meaning and personal fulfillment. Realistically, not everyone on your team will get there immediately. Some "reverent skeptics" will want to wait and see what changes you are proposing and what gets accomplished. Be patient. The key is to have on the top team at least two or three members who are onboard and excited about pursing Conscious Capitalism. Then, your initial successes will speak for themselves. If after twelve months, there still are one or two top-team members

Figure 19-1: Stages of organizational commitment over time

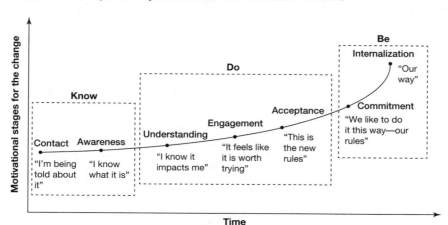

who remain unconvinced about the importance of a conscious culture, then you may have a problem of values alignment. You may need to consider if these team members are a good fit for the type of organization you want to create.

We recommend that you take a two-step process to onboarding the top team. First, you help the top team understand Conscious Capitalism and what it means for the aspirations of the company. We will outline this step in the next section, "Top-Team Onboarding Workshop." You need to onboard the top-team members before you can work with them on the exercises in this book. The members need to understand the why of the journey before they can dig deeply into how it will get done.

The second step is to work through the exercises in this book and to move from aspiration to action. This means taking the team through the tenets step by step and then pulling this all together, as you did in chapter 18. The details of this step are expanded on later in this chapter.

Introducing Conscious Capitalism to the Top Team

The first step you take with your top team should be to introduce them to Conscious Capitalism. Then work through the exercises on the action steps for the next twelve to eighteen months.

To introduce the basic concepts of Conscious Capitalism to the top team, we recommend the following:

- Visit the consciouscapitalism.org website, and look for the video of Raj Sisodia on Conscious Capitalism. Have the team view John Mackey's introduction to Conscious Capitalism as well.

- There are TEDx talks on Conscious Capitalism by Raj Sisodia and Thomas Eckschmidt (in Portuguese). These can be found at www.ccfieldguide.com.

- Distribute the links for these videos to the team, and give each team member a copy of *Conscious Capitalism: Liberating the Heroic Spirit of Business* (Harvard Business Review Press).

- Ask your key team members to participate in the spring event that the Conscious Capitalism organization holds each year. This event will expose your team to examples of conscious leaders and how they operate in their organizations. Some of the leaders who have presented and participated in these events include Raj Sisodia, Daniel Lubetzky, Bob Chapman, Melissa Reiff, and Tony Schwartz. You can find links to these annual conferences on the consciouscapitalism.org website.

- If you are the CEO of your organization, we recommend that you attend the Conscious Capitalism CEO Summit, held annually in October in Austin, Texas.

- Begin a dialogue with individual team members about why Conscious Capitalism is important to you. Do this before you have the off-site.

Going into the off-site, the team members need to understand the core concepts of Conscious Capitalism and be familiar with the four pillars: purpose, stakeholder orientation, conscious culture, and conscious leadership.

Top-Team Onboarding Workshop

The goal of the workshop is to make the journey to Conscious Capitalism practical and meaningful, to help the team understand the what and the why of this philosophy. There is a saying from the *Tao Te Ching* that the longest journey begins with the first step. This workshop is your first step! Your team needs to understand and support what you are trying to accomplish. Begin with the end in mind: What does success look like over the next thirty-six months or beyond? Explore the needed shifts in behavior and beliefs you have about the business. Then, make this personal: "What does this mean for me, and what changes do I need to make in how I think and show up as a leader?" Finally, make sure the team agrees on how you are going to tell the story of the journey you are committed to going on to the rest of the organization.

The top-team workshop is divided into five blocks:

1. Ground the team on understanding what Conscious Capitalism is and why you as a leader are personally committed to this journey.

2. Create an aspiration—a vision of what the organization can become over time.

3. Explore what shifts are required in thinking and in behaviors. Create a "from-to" map that captures the essence of this shift from one type of mindset and behavior to another (see figure 19-2 later in this chapter).

4. Create the story of change that you will bring forward to the rest of the organization—why we as individual leaders, and as a team, believe this is an important journey, an existential imperative.

5. Bring in the action plan that was developed in chapter 18. If your team hasn't already created such a plan, now is a good time to do this exercise with your team. If the team has already created a version of the action plan and phased approach, have them review it.

Table 19-1 presents a sample agenda for this workshop and the five blocks. It assumes that you have worked with the team and done the exercises and other

TABLE 19-1

Agenda for the introductory workshop

Block	Activity	Hours requirement
1	Introduction to Conscious Capitalism and why it is important	1.5
2	Future vision	1.5
3	Shifting how we think and behave	1
4	Making it personal, taking a stand	1
5	Pulling it together	1

work in chapter 18: the work on each of the pillars, the three-phase implementation plan, and the "one big thing" for the next six to twelve months.

If you have not worked with the team on completing the implementation plan in chapter 18, then you should build this step into the workshop. You should allot three to four hours to work through the exercises in chapter 18 together as a team. Do the implementation-plan exercises right after completing block 1—the grounding of why Conscious Capitalism matters. Doing implementation planning here will quickly ground the team on the practical implementation for the next thirty-six months. Then, go further with the team on building the vision and the necessary changes to make this plan stick. Pragmatically, this order helps the team build the case for the deeper changes that come with this journey.

Block 1: Why Conscious Capitalism Matters to Me or Us

Review with your team why, for you as a senior leader in the organization, this journey to Conscious Capitalism matters. This is your opportunity to express what you consider important and why you are excited about the opportunities. It's also a chance to review, briefly, the four pillars of Conscious Capitalism. After you have spoken and introduced the concept, capture the questions that the team would like to address during the day. This is your opportunity to better understand which parts are resonating and are clearly understood by the team and which parts are not.

The *five-why exercise* below helps you better understand why Conscious Capitalism matters to you.

Why are you here? (Respond five times why until you drill down to the core of why you are really here.)

1. Why? _____

2. Why? _____

3. Why? _____

4. Why? _____

5. Why? _____

Block 2: Visualizing a Future Conscious Capitalism Organization

The goal of this exercise is to develop alignment in the team around an aspirational future. You want to move beyond the constraints of today's situation and have the team let loose and dream a bit. Have them play the what-if game in a guided-imagery exercise.

As the leader, you should run this exercise, unless you have a facilitator for the workshop. Have the team members sit quietly in a circle of chairs, and have them close their eyes, get comfortable in their seats, and check their posture. Ask them to imagine what the organization would look like as a Conscious Capitalism company five years from now. Ask them to have fun with this exercise. There are no right or wrong answers. Loosen up and dream a bit. You are trying to access people's imaginations to see what pops up for them when you ask the question. Guide them to imagine this picture fully. Tell them to walk around their image—notice the colors, the texture of its material, its size. These details help make the image more concrete for them.

- Ask them to open their eyes and write down three to five words that best capture their image. Instruct them not to think about this too much. Ask them not to judge what they wrote down. The key here is not to be too practical; the goal is to be aspirational. If we could, what would we want that future to look like? Do this exercise quickly, so the participants don't spend too much time trying to get the words perfect. Capturing first impressions is the goal here.

My Aspiration on the Journey to Conscious Capitalism

- Describe your vision in a few words.

  _____

  _____

  _____

  _____

- "In the next three to five years, my aspiration for becoming a Conscious Capitalist organization is . . . " What would your organization look like? Write one or two sentences—or even just a few words—that would catch the essence of this aspiration.

  _____

  _____

  _____

  _____

- Next, break up the team into smaller groups of three to four people. Create more teams if you have more people. Have each group's members share their words with each other and create, as a group, what they believe are the four or five words that best capture a common vision of this aspiration. Have them write down these words on flip charts. This exercise will force people to have a dialogue, to refine what they originally thought, and to build consensus.

- Now, pull the groups together, and look for a common set of words or phrases that capture this aspirational future. Have the groups share their common aspirational words with the entire team. What do these words have in common?

_____

_____

_____

_____

- What is different? Why?

_____

_____

_____

_____

_____

_____

- Work as a team to combine the lists of the groups, and create a single list of three to five phrases that best capture what this aspiration might look like for your organization. Make this description about 80 percent complete. There will be time later to come back and wordsmith it. As we've advised before, don't let perfection be the enemy of the good.

_____

_____

_____

_____

_____

_____

For a Pharma Merger: Team Aspirations

- Reaching patients and helping create healthy, beautiful lives

- Conquering fear and other adversity

- Innovative work; fearlessly working together with a focused pioneering and aspirational goal

- Positive, fun, high-energy teamwork

- Fostering synergy and collective intelligence across the organization

- Pride in accomplishments

Block 3: Shifting How We Think and Behave: Create a From-To Model

In this set of exercises, we're trying to identify potential barriers to our journey. Given our aspirational vision, which assumptions might prevent us from achieving this vision? We will then describe what the opposite assumption or belief might look like, and armed with these observations, we will create a list of from-to beliefs and behaviors—changes we'll have to make if our journey is to be successful.

- Have the team members list three to five things that they think could get in the way of achieving their aspirational vision.

_____

_____

_____

_____

- Which assumptions or beliefs might stop your organization from realizing this dream?

_____

_____

_____

_____

- Which practical elements of your business's operation might prevent this dream from being realized?

_____

_____

_____

_____

Capture these obstacles on a flip chart, and discuss with the team which are the top three or four factors that might get in the way.

Take your list of the top three or four obstacles, and discuss with the group what the *opposite assumptions or beliefs would be*. For example, if we believe that people are cynical and don't trust us, the opposite belief or assumption would be that we build a credible and trusting environment. Go through this exercise with the team, and then fill in the from-to box below. Figure 19-2 presents an example from another company that we have worked with.

Figure 19-2: Example of "from-to" mindset shifts

From . . .	To . . .
Believing in **command and control** in a hierarchical, top-down manner	**Letting go** and **trusting** employees to act in the best interests of the organization
Believing in **forecast ability** detailed in a rigid plan	Following a **joint dynamic plan** that is open for innovation and change
Believing that most people in the organization need to be **protected from stressors and complexity**	**Enabling all employees to live with uncertainty and stressors** to stay flexible and able to act in a dynamic way
Believing that the **center needs to manage and limit information flow**	**Letting information flow freely** across the organization

From . . .   **To . . .**

_____

_____

_____

_____

_____

_____

_____

Block 4: Making It Personal, Taking a Stand

This next set of exercises focuses on trying to take the aspirational vision from the organizational level and making it relevant to each team member. The exercise asks a series of questions for them to reflect on in small groups. At the end, they should write a personal statement about why this vision matters to them.

Have each team member spend ten to fifteen minutes answering the following questions:

- **What is it about this future vision that I find most important or inspiring? Why?**

_____

_____

_____

_____

- When I look at the from-to model above, what are my personal challenges in shifting from one mindset and behavior to other ones? Why are these my challenges?

  _____

  _____

  _____

  _____

  _____

  _____

  _____

  _____

- Describe why this change matters to me and what my commitment to change will be.

  _____

  _____

  _____

  _____

  _____

  _____

  _____

  _____

- Have each person take out a blank sheet of paper. At the top of the paper, have the participants write the phrase "Conscious Capitalism Business Times." Instruct them to write a paragraph or two as if they were business journalists writing five years from now about what the company looks like and how it has accomplished this transformation. You could also frame this assignment as if your organization had a *Harvard Business Review* cover story about its successful five-year journey to Conscious Capitalism.

Have them write this story from the point of view of a business writer describing the journey: what, why, and how.

_____

_____

_____

_____

_____

_____

_____

_____

_____

_____

_____

_____

_____

_____

_____

_____

Come back together as a team, and have each team member spend two or three minutes describing their personal challenge and their commitment to meet that challenge to move forward on Conscious Capitalism.

Block 5: Pulling It Together

You have now created the following:

- An aspirational vision captured in three or four phrases or sentences

- A from-to model of the shift in thinking and behavior to enable this future

- A list of each leader's potential personal challenges and opportunities associated with the vision

Have two members of the team pull this material together into a *change story* for the team after the meeting is finished. This story should be no more than five or six PowerPoint slides or two or three pages of written notes in a memo format. Ask them to create a first draft within ten days of the workshop, and have them circulate it to all the team members who participated in the workshop for review and edits. You now have your first draft of the journey to Conscious Capitalism change story!

Top-Team Alignment and Relevance: Aspiration to Action Workshop

The next step in getting the top team's support is to move from aspiration to action. You want to make Conscious Capitalism relevant to the top team and to the core of the business and its operations. Relevance increases as you and your team work through the exercises in this book. For each of the pillars, you need to assess where you are, look at the possible ways you can move forward in this area, and discuss and decide on what the highest-impact initiatives might be for your organization. Then, working through chapter 18, you can pull all these possible initiatives together, prioritize them, and commit to action plans for the next twelve to eighteen months.

In our experience, there are two ways for a top team to approach this more detailed work. As highlighted in the preface, they are:

1. Plan for a two- or three-day retreat in which the entire team is taken off-site. We recommend working through each of the five parts of the book

in sequence, spending three or five hours on each of them. For each of the four tenets of Conscious Capitalism (represented by parts 1 through 4), focus on the areas most pertinent to your situation. For example, your team should focus on part 1, "Higher Purpose," if your organization has not yet developed a clear statement of purpose or if the team thinks that the current purpose doesn't fit your current needs and should be updated. If, on the other hand, the team believes that the organization has a well-defined sense of purpose, the next step is to make sure everyone understands the purpose and is living it. A possible two-day top-team agenda is outlined below.

Day 1

8:30–9:35	Introduction and journey review
9:35–9:45	Break
9:45–11:15	Purpose review
11:15–11:25	Break
11:25–12:30	Purpose: bring it to life
12:30–1:15	Lunch
1:15–3:00	Stakeholder mapping
3:00–3:15	Break
3:15–5:15	Stakeholder deep dives
5:15–5:30	Wrap-up and review

Day 2

8:00–8:15	Reflections on day 1
8:15–10:30	Culture and values
10:30–10:45	Break
10:45–12:45	Conscious leadership
12:45–1:15	Lunch
1:15–2:30	Team working sessions
2:30–2:40	Break
2:40–3:15	Action plans and next steps
3:15–4:15	Team presentations
4:15–4:30	Wrap-up and close

2. An alternative approach is to schedule a series of five sessions, one for each part of the book, for three or four hours each, over not more than five or six weeks. The goal here is to ensure that you have enough time both to do the relevant exercises for your team and to discuss the potential impacts on your business and the concrete next steps to move this tenet into action.

Enroll and Empower the Organization

To create lasting change in the organization, you must bring the organization along on the journey. This means introducing your people to Conscious Capitalism, why it matters to you and the top team, what you aspire to, and how you will get there. As people in the organization begin to embrace Conscious Capitalism, they will start to make decisions and take actions that will slowly turn the organization in this direction. Like a giant cruise ship, organizations don't turn on a dime. But like a flywheel, once the company does begin to turn, the change gains momentum and is difficult to stop. This organizational engagement process can take from two to six months to work through. The timing depends on the size of your organization and the intensity with which you engage in the process.

Every day, people in your organization make thousands of decisions and take actions to run, support, and execute on the direction your business is headed. What influences these decisions and their actions? Hopefully, their decisions and actions are based on their role and work experience and their understanding of what is in the best interest of the business. Therefore, the more they understand the importance and power of Conscious Capitalism, the more this philosophy will influence their decisions and actions.

Building this understanding and mobilizing the organization to think and act differently is the place where, frankly, most transformation programs break down. Too often, only the top echelon of the organization understands and has bought into the vision and execution plan. But the further you share your vision in the organization, the more likely you are to get sustainable change and results. We will outline two overlapping streams of activity to ensure that you begin a dialogue to engage with the organization at all levels.

- Create a core SWAT team of change champions from various levels of the organization. These people will act as emissaries and change agents in the organization.

- Launch a campaign of influence and engagement to create a dialogue with the organization about the what and why of Conscious Capitalism. In this way, the journey to Conscious Capitalism becomes relevant to people in their day-to-day roles in the organization.

Create Your Team of Change Champions

At the initial stage of the campaign of change and influence, you should bring together a core group of ten to twenty change champions who will serve as the eyes and ears of the organization and will be the main supporters of Conscious Capitalism. The size of this group depends on how large your organization is. Typically, these champions have the following characteristics:

- They come from multiple levels in the organization.

- They reflect a diversity of experience, ages, and functional and business experience.

- They are generally seen by their colleagues as key influencers or connectors.

- They are excited about Conscious Capitalism and the organization's commitment to it.

- They are good leaders and managers—they can get things done.

Not everyone on the team will have all these characteristics, but most should have a majority of them. Take the following steps to enlist your champions:

- Make your first draft list of potential change champions.

- Circulate the list to members of the top team for feedback. Add and subtract names as appropriate.

- Finalize your list and discuss with the candidates' managers the time commitment that will be required for this program.

- Personally invite the champions to participate in the program.

- Set the expectation that this will require 10 to 20 percent of their time for the next twelve to eighteen months.

Onboarding the Change Champions

The next step is to gather the change champions so that you can begin incorporating the idea of Conscious Capitalism deeper into the organization. You must first bring the change champions onboard, make sure they understand what Conscious Capitalism is all about, and set your expectations for them. A typical onboarding meeting will include the following elements:

- An introduction to Conscious Capitalism

  - Use the same references and materials you used with the top team (chapter 18).

  - Have the CEO or other senior leaders talk about why Conscious Capitalism is important to the organization, and why it's important to them personally.

  - Have members of the senior team share their perspectives and commitments to this conscious approach.

Review and get feedback on the change story. Have members of the top team present the change story to the change champions. Then, have the top team leave the room.

- Review the aspiration statement, and ask the change champions the following questions:

  - What resonates with you?

  - What does not resonate? Why not?

  - What feedback do you have for the top team on this aspiration?

- Review the from-to model, and ask the champions these questions:
  - What additional behaviors and issues need to be addressed because they might get in the way?
  - What changes or other feedback do you have for the top team?
- Review the action plan, and ask the following questions:
  - What do you see as the key success factors to make sure this plan gets executed?
  - What might prevent execution? How can these barriers be addressed in advance?
  - What is missing from this action plan?
  - What could help accelerate the execution of the action plan?
- Collect all this feedback.

Invite the top team to come back into the room. Arrange the seating of the change champions in a U shape in the room. Have the senior team come in and sit in the center of that U shape. Have the champions present their feedback section by section. Let them give their feedback *before* the leadership team is asked to comment and build on what they have heard.

Typically, this onboarding process will take four to eight hours to do, depending on the size of the team and the time allocated for discussion and breakouts around the different sections that they review. Table 19-2 shows a suggested agenda for this onboarding session.

TABLE 19-2

Example agenda for onboarding the champions of change

Block	Activity	Time requirement
1	Introduction to Conscious Capitalism and why it is important	1.5 hours
2	Aspiration	30 minutes
3	From-to model review	1 hour
4	Action plan	1.5 hours
5	Feedback session	1.5 hours

The Campaign of Influence and Engagement

To engage and enroll the organization, the change champions need to quickly gather feedback on how to make the change story relevant to the organization. This is followed by developing and launching a campaign of influence and engagement to be executed over the next twelve to eighteen months. This campaign will touch and engage everyone in the organization, as well as external stakeholders.

Make the Change Story Relevant

The first task of the change champions will be to take the change story deeper into the organization and gather feedback and present that to the executive team. Typically, this is done through focus groups, in which one to two change champions meet with groups of six to eight people in the organization. Plan on ten to twenty focus groups with an average of 7 people in each, for a total of between 70 and 140 people.

In the focus groups, the change champions should review each section of the change story (aspirational vision, from-to model, and execution plan) and gather feedback. They will focus on what resonates or does not resonate and what might accelerate the shift and what might block it. The champions take notes during each focus group and write up a summary afterward.

After completing all the focus groups, the change champions typically gather for a half day or full day to debrief one another. They summarize and synthesize the feedback, make suggestions on how to improve the change story and the execution plan, and prepare to present their observations to the senior team. The senior team should then meet with the change champions for two to four hours to listen to the feedback from the organization. Working together, the senior team and the champions will create a new version of the change story and action plan to make the journey to Conscious Capitalism more effective in its execution.

Developing a Campaign of Influence and Engagement

The next stage of the process is to engage the entire organization in understanding what the journey to Conscious Capitalism is about and why you are doing this. To this end, you should begin a dialogue within the organization both to help address issues and questions and to continue to make a conscious culture relevant to people.

The metaphor of a campaign is used because this is not a one-and-done communication event. It requires staying on message, letting people the organization know that their input has been heard, and using multiple platforms and media to communicate the messages about the meaning and progress of the journey.

The goals of the communication campaign are typically as follows:

- **Get the word out.** Ensure that every employee understands where the journey to Conscious Capitalism is going and can articulate major issues that employees can have an impact on. Move from giving information to engaging and empowering people.

- **Involve each employee in some significant way.** Quickly move employees from spectators to active participants, from the stands to the playing field.

- **Make it actionable.** Develop ways to involve employees in translating strategic direction into changes in the way they work.

- **Make it fun.** Use creative and high-touch events (i.e., events that are more personal and interactive) and methods to invite participation and acceptance among employees.

- **Learn by listening.** Develop effective ways to hear, understand, and acknowledge employee feedback about the Conscious Capitalism story and implementation, as well as about the communication effort.

- **Measure progress.** Develop metrics to monitor progress, and share these regularly within the organization.

A typical communication campaign will include both high- and low-touch elements:

Low touch: less personal, less interactive

- Conference calls

- Voicemails from CEO

- Email

- Posters

- Intranet (news magazine, informational web pages)

- Videos of CEO

High touch: more personal, more interactive

- One-on-one meetings

- Town hall meetings

- Group informational meetings

- Focus groups oriented to gathering input

- Site events with lots of interaction

- Live webcasts with Q&A

Creating an Ongoing Dialogue

After building a deeper understanding of the journey, work with the change champions to create feedback and dialogue forums on a regular, local basis. Examples of how you can do this are:

- Local "Journey to Conscious Capitalism" councils. They meet regularly and discuss what is working and not working to help the organization become a conscious company. With the aid of a change champion, the councils provide suggestions and other feedback to the change champion team and ultimately back to the leadership team.

- Monthly discussion or reading groups. These are set up with a facilitator who may pick a relevant topic or reading and help the group reflect on the topic's relevance to Conscious Capitalism in the group's part of the organization.

- Monthly lunch-and-learn sessions hosted by a senior leader and a small group to discuss the progress of the journey to Conscious Capitalism and to gather feedback on what is working and what is not working.

The key here is to be creative and create local events and forums where Conscious Capitalism and the action plans become more and more relevant to the organization.

One of the powerful benefits of this kind of campaign and dialogue is that people start looking for ways they can contribute in their day-to-day jobs and responsibilities. Thousands of small decisions get made in any organization every day. When there is an organizational vision and framework for understanding what the desired behaviors are and what the action plans are, people come up with hundreds of creative ways of engaging and helping. This increased level of engagement and inspiration around a meaningful goal allows the organization to be innovative and creative and brings Conscious Capitalism to life in many unexpected ways.

Final Thoughts

This chapter set out to help you develop a successful journey to Conscious Capitalism.

If it takes a village to raise a child, it takes an entire organization to execute a successful transformation. The sustainability of the change you are implementing is strongly correlated with the depth of engagement within the organization. It will also be influenced by the quality of the ongoing dialogue you create to keep your efforts relevant to people's day-to-day work.

As we have explained throughout the book, the journey begins with getting your leadership team engaged and aligned with what you're doing and why you are doing it. An engaged leadership is an absolutely necessary but not sufficient step on the journey.

As we've also explained, the critical next step is to bring the entire organization on the journey. With the help of a team of change champions, you can get rapid feedback on the relevance of the change story that the leadership team has created. You can then develop a campaign to bring the entire organization on the journey.

We cannot overstate the important role that you, the leader of the organization, play in making this transformation happen and stick. This process of bringing your team along begins with clarity on why this matters to you, and your consistency with both the top team and the organization in staying on message on why it matters and how we will do it. As stated earlier, leadership matters, perhaps more than all the other pillars, in ensuring that Conscious Capitalism moves from inspiration to impact. You will have ample opportunity to develop your conscious leadership as you lead the transformation to Conscious Capitalism.

Epilogue

Now that you have made it all the way through this book, we invite you to begin your journey without delay. To use Martin Luther King Jr.'s phrase, there is a "fierce urgency of now." We do not have the luxury of time; we must initiate and sustain major transformations in all our companies as soon as possible.

This is a heroic undertaking that will present you with numerous challenges along the way. But the process is also deeply joyful, because it is calling you to be part of something far greater than yourself or your organization. Conscious Capitalism is also an evolutionary imperative. Our rising consciousness and greater mutuality may encounter occasional potholes and detours, even seeming reversals of direction, but it will and must proceed. We can choose to be an instrument of that which seeks to emerge, or we can try to stand in its way. The latter choice is really not a choice at all. We must grow, we must love one another, and we must cooperate, or we will undoubtedly perish.

We are in the midst of a historic discontinuity, a chasm between the way things have been for too long and the way they can and need to be. We need to systematically examine every assumption, every mental model, every belief, every theory about how to organize and lead businesses, how to motivate and reward people, how to align interests, and how to elevate our sights. As playwright Sir Tom Stoppard wrote in *Arcadia,* "the future is disorder. A door like this has cracked open five or six times since we got up on our hind legs. It's the best possible time to be alive, when almost everything you thought you knew is wrong."

The journey is joyful because humanity has been waiting and is thirsting for this kind of change. Work is a critical aspect of what it means to be human. Each of us only has about a hundred thousand hours to devote to work in our lifetimes. Our work can be a deep source of meaning and purpose, joy and fulfillment, healing and growth. But for the vast majority of us, it has become a daily drudgery, something to be endured to make a living and keep body and soul together. As a business leader, you hold within yourself the tremendous power and awesome responsibility to give people the opportunity to realize and experience so many extraordinary gifts that life has to offer. Why would you choose to forgo that extraordinary opportunity?

Moving toward conscious business is a human imperative. Most people never get to share even a fraction of the gifts that they have to offer with the world; they are born, live, and die with their music still trapped inside them. And what extraordinary symphonies we are capable of! The human "seed" has never been more powerful or potent. Our intelligence has been rising rapidly, we have access to all the world's information at our fingertips, we are extraordinarily well connected, we have far better access to higher education, we are living longer, and we are continually awakening to higher consciousness. But even as the human seed has evolved, the organizational soil has remained inhospitable, even toxic. That is where we must place our attention. As leaders, we have the responsibility of improving that soil to create the conditions in which ordinary human beings can achieve extraordinary things. By doing so, we can enable people to live richer, deeper, more fulfilling and joyful lives than they could have imagined.

Conscious Capitalism is also a societal imperative. Businesses need to understand and be stewards of the systems in which they and their people are embedded. We need to play our part, alongside governments and civil society, in bringing about the ideal society—a society in which everybody matters and everybody wins.

And of course, Conscious Capitalism is a planetary imperative. Most of our great advances in the last century were predicated on the use of nonrenewable resources that we are now rapidly running out of. We need to invent new ways of doing everything—ways that are not just sustainable but also generative, ways that restore and replenish ecosystems that have been damaged through neglect or callousness.

David Cooperrider, professor of social entrepreneurship at the Fowler Center for Business as an Agent of World Benefit, Case Western Reserve University, describes an optimistic outlook of conscious business:

Everyone is beginning to imagine the once-in-a-civilization opportunities— it's no longer utopian to speak of our witnessing the end of extreme poverty through profitability; or the emergence of a world of abundant, clean renewable energy; or of the spread of education to 100% of the earth's children; or of business as a pragmatic and dependable force for peace; or of cradle-to-cradle factories and supply chains that turn so called waste to wealth; or of the birth of a full spectrum economy where businesses can excel, people can thrive, and nature can flourish. Moreover, it's a time where the innovations are leaping beyond the tired vocabularies of social responsibility or "sustainability." We believe that sustainability has lost its capacity to inspire the future. Doing less bad is not the most compelling call and simply surviving does not equate to thriving. We see a next episode in capitalism emerging where the task involves a decisive shift: it's the shift from sustainability to full spectrum flourishing and it is being fueled by today's fertile verge between business innovation, exponential technologies, and the rise of whole new human factor capacities, commitments, and consciousness.[1]

Finally, there is a compelling financial imperative for conscious business. Evidence is mounting that this way of doing business not only creates far less harm, but also actually produces far more value of every kind than does the old approach, which was all about profit. The conscious approach to business recognizes that there is no trade-off between purpose, people, planet, and profits; we can simultaneously serve all these.

Knowing what you now know, how can you justify clinging to the old approach, replete as it is with heartbreaking and unnecessary trade-offs between the well-being of people and the corporate bottom line? That would be egregious managerial malpractice. We owe it to all those whose lives we touch to lead our organizations according to our best understanding of what is needed and how we can make everyone flourish.

Every journey starts with the first step, so take that step today! The road ahead is a long one, but do not despair. There will be many moments to cheer and derive encouragement from as you go along this journey. Cultivate what the leaders at Barry-Wehmiller refer to as courageous patience. The old maxim urges us to "go slow to go fast." Just as you cannot cause a plant to grow faster by tugging on it, you cannot short-circuit a transformation by demanding immediate results. In a few short years, your company could be transformed for all time. Allow that process to unfold in a natural and organic manner. Be patient also with the people who do not seem to get it immediately. Focus on those who do get it; the vast majority of others will eventually follow, especially as your actions increasingly start to line up with your words.

Leadership in traditionally hierarchical organizations can be a lonely undertaking. But it doesn't have to be so. Embrace a team-based approach to the transformation. Your entire team needs to be working together with shared purpose and shared responsibility to see this transformation through. Approach the change with a beginner's mind but a leader's disposition. Focus relentlessly on what is possible while recognizing present-day reality.

You and your leadership team are not alone on this journey. A large and growing community of companies and leaders are taking the same path. Find them through your local Conscious Capitalism chapter, at the Conscious Capitalism CEO Summit, or at the organization's annual spring conference. It is very helpful to form a small group with other CEOs who are on the same journey and continually check in with each other to help address challenges and seek solutions.

If you are in a public company, you have to ensure that your board of directors is an integral part of this effort. Make sure that every board member understands the context (why a conscious business is essential today), the concept (the tenets of Conscious Capitalism), and the case (the human, social, planetary, and financial case for Conscious Capitalism).

A Letter to the CEO

By **JOSEPH JAWORSKI**, author of *Synchronicity: The Inner Path of Leadership* and *Source: The Inner Path of Knowledge Creation*, founder and chairman of Global Leadership Initiative, and founder of American Leadership Forum

You are embarking on perhaps the most important and challenging undertaking of your life as a senior leader: the creation of a conscious enterprise.

There are three essential elements that, if followed, will ensure your success:

First, you must make an unequivocal commitment to creating a conscious organization. By far, the most crucial factor is your own unequivocal commitment to this mission of high personal and organizational development. You must ask yourself, "Who am I?" and "What is my work?" That is, "What is my purpose for being on this earth?"

Your commitment to this organizational change must be this powerful. It must align directly with your personal purpose—your personal destiny.

When your personal purpose and your organization's purpose align, you will have taken the first and most essential step toward success.

There is a hidden causality in the universe. It is like gravity. You cannot see it, but you can observe its effect. When you definitely commit yourself, there exists beyond yourself and your conscious will a powerful force that helps you along the way and nurtures your growth and transformation. Your journey is guided by invisible hands with infinitely greater accuracy than is possible through your unaided conscious will.

Second, you must gain the same quality of commitment from your top team. This organizational transformation requires significant human development on your part as the CEO and on the part of your management team. Some call this *vertical development*, and it includes the development of the leaders' way of being—their character and higher selves. Human development includes how we think, feel, and make sense of the world around us, including what we believe is possible.

For many on your team, becoming a more conscious leader can be a powerful and exhilarating opportunity for personal growth and development. For others, it may be too frightening and too difficult.

At the outset, you can succeed with only three or four members of your team making this quality of commitment; but eventually, your entire team must operate this way—as a single intelligence. When the entire team is onboard, the team's behavior and collective way of being exerts an enormous attractiveness, affecting the entire organization. Your people will be attracted to the authentic presence of your team and to the unfolding of a future that is full of possibility.

Third, you must take the first bold step, cross the threshold, and then beat the path as you walk it. At the outset of this journey, it is most likely that you will feel hesitant and, in fact, terrified. This is perfectly normal. Those of us who have been on this same journey have felt precisely this way. It is a perilous journey, a place of both terror and opportunity.

The only solution is to take the first bold step. Cross the threshold. Follow the guidelines laid out in this book. Stay acutely aware, and when you are in doubt, use your instincts to tell you which next steps to take . . .

Beat the path as you walk it.

We end with these inspiring words from *The Purposeful Company*:

Great firms are precious economic and social organizations. They are the originators of wealth generation, offering solutions to human dilemmas and wants at scale, and are thus agents of human betterment. They are enabled by the pursuit of clearly defined visionary corporate purposes, which set out how the company will better people's lives. Those purposes are binding commitments on the whole of an enterprise that generate trust and enable increasingly sophisticated forms of value creation.[2]

Conscious Capitalism and the B Corp Movement

By Jay Coen Gilbert, cofounder of B Lab and the B Corp movement

The Conscious Capitalism movement and the B Corp movement are complementary and supportive of each other. Every B Corp is essentially a conscious company, and every conscious company should seriously consider becoming a B Corp.

Many C-suite leaders in the B Corp movement have spoken at the Conscious Capitalism CEO Summit, led practicums at Conscious Capitalism conferences, or cofounded Conscious Capitalism chapters. The companies they lead include Patagonia, Ben & Jerry's, Unilever, Singularity University, data.world, Plum Organics, Campbell Soup, Method, REBBL, Dansko, Cascade Engineering, Ogden Publications, Mightybytes, New Resource Bank, Big Path Capital, and Hanson Bridgett.

Conscious Capitalism seeks to unleash the heroic spirit of business leaders, and the B Corp movement offers concrete tools and a robust community of practice to do so. Whether your company aspires to become a B Corp or simply wants to take the next step in manifesting your conscious leadership, engaging with the B Corp movement offers three things to help you translate your stakeholder orientation into meaningful action: a stakeholder governance structure, a stakeholder management system, and a community of practice consisting of like-minded, high-performing peers.

Note that "B Corps" and "benefit corps" are different. B Corp is a certification; benefit corp is a legal structure. Table AA-1 provides a more detailed comparison.

All Certified B Corporations must meet a legal requirement to adopt a stakeholder governance structure. Depending upon whether the company is an LLC or a corporation, and in what state or country it is incorporated, the company can meet that legal requirement in a variety of ways. If the company is a Delaware corporation, then the only way to meet that requirement is by adopting the benefit corporation legal structure.

Etsy and Laureate are the two public B Corps on a major US exchange. Laureate is both a B Corp and a benefit corp. Etsy has until December 31, 2017, to adopt the benefit corp legal structure or lose its B Corp certification.

Outside the United States, Natura is both a B Corp and has adopted a benefit corp–like legal structure (there is no benefit corp law in Brazil, so they made

TABLE AA-1

B Corporations versus benefit corporations

Issue	Certified B Corporations	Benefit corporations
Accountability	Directors required to consider impact on all stakeholders	Same
Transparency	Must publish public report of overall social and environmental performance assessed against a third-party standard	Same*
Performance	Must achieve minimum verified score on B Impact Assessment (BIA) Recertification required every two years against evolving standard	Self-reported
Availability	Available to every business regardless of corporate structure, state, or country of incorporation	Available for corporations only in 30 US states and D.C.**
Cost	B Lab certification fees from $500 to $50,000/year, based on revenues	State filing fees from $70–$200

* Delaware benefit corps are not required to report publicly or against a third-party standard.
** Oregon and Maryland offer benefit LLC options.

comparable amendments in their articles of incorporation with the approval of their investors).

In addition, there are a few publicly traded B Corps in Australia (Silver Chef and Australian Ethical) and New Zealand (Snakk Media), but neither of those jurisdictions have benefit corp laws on the books and can't amend their articles because—as in Delaware in the United States—the underlying corporate law does not allow for an enforceable expansion of fiduciary duty to consider stakeholder interests when making decisions.

Stakeholder Governance

A stakeholder governance structure ensures that your stakeholder orientation—and your specific company purpose—can thrive through leadership and ownership changes, especially if you think you might need to bring in private capital or access the public capital markets to help your business scale. The stakeholder governance tool of the B Corp movement is a relatively new legal structure called a *benefit corporation*. The benefit corporation legal structure ensures that the directors on your board will consider stakeholder interests—and your company's purpose—when making decisions.

This is particularly useful if you anticipate a future sale or public offering. In a sale scenario, traditional corporate law dictates that directors' scope of considerations must narrow to maximize short-term shareholder returns, even if doing so runs contrary to maximizing long-term value for all of your stakeholders or to serving your specific company purpose. (See the following sidebar.)

The Dangers of Denial

By LEO E. STRINE JR., Chief Justice of the Supreme Court of Delaware. Extracted from "The Dangers of Denial: The Need for a Clear-Eyed Understanding of the Power and Accountability Structure Established by Delaware General Corporation Law."

There is now a tendency among those who believe that corporations should be more socially responsible to pretend that corporate directors do not have an obligation under Delaware corporate law to make stockholder welfare the sole end of corporate governance within the limits of their legal discretion. These advocates of corporate social responsibility contend that Delaware directors may subordinate stockholder welfare to other interests, such as those of the company's workers or society generally. That is, they do not argue simply that directors may choose to forsake a higher short-term profit if they believe that course of action will best advance the interests of stockholders in the long run, they argue that directors have no legal obligation to make—within the constraints of positive law—the promotion of stockholder welfare their end. But, the problem with that argument is that it is inconsistent with both judge-made common law of corporations in Delaware and the design of the Delaware General Corporation Law ("DGCL").

More important, pretending that the nation's leading corporate law is fundamentally different than it is runs contrary to the goal of ensuring that for-profit corporations behave lawfully, responsibly, and ethically. Lecturing others to do the right thing without acknowledging the rules that apply to their behavior and the power dynamics to which they are subject is not a responsible path to social progress. Rather, it provides an excuse to avoid tougher policy challenges, such as advocating for stronger externality regulation and encouraging institutional investors to exercise their power as stockholders responsibly. Those challenges must be confronted if we are to ensure that for-profit corporations are vehicles for responsible, sustainable, long-term wealth creation.

The benefit corporation legal structure offers some protection to publicly traded companies from the virus of short-termism that has infected the public capital markets. For starters, a publicly traded company that has adopted the benefit corporation legal structure may be less likely to be targeted by short-term-focused activist investors in the first place. The power of these kinds of activist shareholders lies largely in their ability to initiate proxy contests to replace existing directors with others more sympathetic to their desire for short-term value extraction. Most of these contests never reach a formal vote but instead are fought privately in a battle for the hearts and minds of large shareholders and publicly through the use of PR firms. When evaluating potential targets, a short-term-focused activist investor would know that a publicly traded company that has adopted the benefit corporation legal structure has two characteristics that make a successful outcome from their perspective less likely. First, the existing institutional shareholder base has already agreed to a governance structure that explicitly commits to a long-term stakeholder orientation, so presumably they would be less likely to side with the activist whose positions reflect a short-term orientation. Second, unlike directors of traditional corporations, the directors of a company that has adopted a benefit corporation legal structure have a fiduciary duty to consider the interests of stakeholders when making decisions, so they would be under less pressure to bend to the demands of activists they believe might destroy long-term value for shareholders, or even for other stakeholders. Leading companies like Whole Foods Market, Unilever, Procter & Gamble, Nestlé, and Etsy have all come under activist pressure or been the target of unwelcome acquisition offers that have often resulted in leadership, management, and ownership changes. While activist shareholders and mergers and acquisitions can play a vital role in an efficient capital market, adopting the benefit corporation structure can help ensure that board decisions made in these contexts are done so with a long-term stakeholder orientation.

There are already more than 5,000 registered benefit corporations in the United States and approximately 800 in Italy (legislation is moving forward in a half dozen other countries). While many companies have converted to the benefit corporation structure from a traditional corporate structure, it is easiest to incorporate as a benefit corporation as a startup, before things get more complicated with new partners and outside investors. After all, you have to file incorporation papers anyway, so doing so as a benefit corporation incurs no additional legal or filing fees. Adopting the benefit corporation legal structure early ensures that your company will be built on the most solid legal foundation to help you preserve your stakeholder orientation and specific company purpose through all stages of the life cycle of your business. For existing businesses, converting to a benefit corporation structure is relatively straightforward, requiring a shareholder vote to amend your articles of incorporation and a filing with your state (typically $70–$200).

> In ten years' time, people will say it's inconceivable that business was done any other way.
>
> **—Lorna Davis, DanoneWave**

> There's no downside to it. You're just aligning your intention, the philosophy of your business, from the very beginning, around a public good. That's something every company can do.
>
> **—Yancey Strickler, Kickstarter**

You can learn more about the benefit corporation legal structure (and similar tools for LLCs), find a list of corporate attorneys familiar with it, and read case studies about how to convert to and operate as a benefit corporation from companies that are publicly traded, venture-backed, *Fortune* 500 subsidiaries, family- and employee-owned, and independent at www.benefitcorp.net.

Workers

What percentage above living wage did your lowest-paid worker (excluding interns) receive last fiscal year?

Community and Suppliers

Is there a formal written Supplier Code of Conduct that holds the company's suppliers accountable for social and environmental performance?

Environment

Does your company measure its carbon and other greenhouse gas emissions (GHGs)?

Customers

Does your company address a social or environmental problem for or through its customers?

Governance

Does your company use a governance structure that requires consideration of stakeholder interests?

Stakeholder Management

A stakeholder orientation will also benefit from a stakeholder management system to plot your course and to measure your progress in turning these powerful principles into peak performance. The stakeholder management system of the B Corp movement is the B Impact Assessment (BIA). Conscious Capitalism has partnered with B Lab since 2013 to encourage its members and followers to use the B Impact Assessment.

The B Impact Assessment is free and confidential, and it is available to any company in the world whether or not the company ever intends to pursue certification as a B Corporation. The B Impact Assessment helps companies measure and improve their stakeholder performance by offering a comprehensive assessment of a company's positive impact on all of its stakeholders—its workers, customers, community (including suppliers), and the environment. While the B Impact Assessment asks all companies questions about their current practices related to each of these stakeholders, the specific questions, the number of questions, and their weightings vary by company size, industry, and location to ensure that each company receives an assessment most useful to its specific situation.

There are already more than 60,000 businesses around the world that have registered to use the B Impact Assessment. Nearly half have completed the full assessment and have received a free B Impact Report, which benchmarks their company's performance against the tens of thousands of other companies that have completed the assessment, as well as against the performance of Certified B Corporations. A typical small to midsized business is asked between 75 and 200 questions and will take between two and six hours to complete the assessment.

The performance standards in the B Impact Assessment are governed by an independent Standards Advisory Council. As with software, new versions are issued periodically; version 6.0 of the B Impact Assessment will be launched in early 2019.

You can learn more about the B Impact Assessment and read case studies of how companies of all sizes and stages of implementation of their stakeholder orientation have used the assessment as a management tool to affirm their culture, engage their team, and improve their performance at www.bimpact assessment.net.

Community of Practice

The leaders of the B Corp movement are Certified B Corporations. These 2,200 companies are leaders because they have met the most rigorous standards of stakeholder governance and stakeholder management. Certified B Corporations earn a verified minimum score of 80 out of 200 available points on the B Impact Assessment. That may seem low at first, but think of that score as a .400 batting average and a first-ballot induction into the conscious company hall of fame. The average B Corp scores in the mid-90s, and B Corps who make B Lab's annual Best for the World lists typically score between 125 and 175. Certified B Corps also make their B Impact Report, which includes their overall B Score as well as scores for more than fifteen individual impact areas, transparent to the public. Lastly, Certified B Corps adopt a benefit corporation structure or its LLC equivalent to institutionalize stakeholder governance. Certified B Corps are diverse: they come from more than 130 industries and 50 countries and vary in size from sole proprietors to multibillion-dollar multinational companies like KeHE (a US natural foods distributor), Laureate Education (the world's largest provider of for-profit higher education), and Natura (the Brazilian cosmetics company and sustainability icon).

> The B Impact Assessment added a new twist to our initiatives—it helped us understand where we are relative to other companies.
>
> **—Rob Michalak, Ben & Jerry's**

> We already felt great about certain manufacturing and employee practices, but the tool allowed us to realize we were just barely touching the surface.
>
> **—Eric Edelson, Fireclay Tile**

B Corp certification is like organic or LEED, but for the whole business, not just for a gallon of milk or a building. Like organic and LEED, the Certified B Corporation logo is public facing and carries value to customers who increasingly seek out good products from good companies and are increasingly skeptical about what companies say about themselves. The combination of verified performance by a credible third party and unmatched public transparency builds trust, which helps turn transactions into relationships and customers into evangelists. The unifying B Corp trust mark builds a collective voice for companies that seek to distinguish themselves in a cluttered marketplace.

Certified B Corps performance is verified by B Lab standards analysts who have review calls with every company seeking certification; review

The B Corp movement inside and outside the United States

	Definition	Number inside the United States	Number outside the United States
Certified B corps	Businesses that have been certified by the nonprofit B Lab to meet rigorous standards of verified social and environmental performance, public transparency, and legal accountability	1,000	1,200
Registered benefit corporations	Businesses that have registered with their state/country as a benefit corporation, expanding their fiduciary duty to include consideration of stakeholder interests	4,500	800
Completed B Impact Assessment	Businesses that have completed the full B Impact Assessment, a free, confidential, and comprehensive evaluation of a company's overall social and environmental performance	25,000	3,000
B Impact management partners	Financial institutions, impact investment funds, business networks, trade associations, supply chain managers, and government agencies who use the B Impact Assessment and B Analytics to better understand the impact of the companies in whom they invest and with whom they do business	90	60
Academia	Faculty actively engaged with B Lab around curriculum and research	90	30

documentation for answers on the BIA as well as any "negative" answers on the Disclosure Questionnaire; and conduct random on-site audits of 10 percent of all Certified B Corps each year. All Certified B Corps must recertify every two years, which means every Certified B Corp completes a new BIA that reflects its performance at that time.

This earned trust has proven valuable not only in attracting customers but also in attracting and retaining talent. CEOs of every size company and across diverse industries point to their Certified B Corp status as a key tool for reinforcing a values-driven corporate culture, for engaging employees of all generations (especially Millennials) who want to bring their whole selves to work every day, and for attracting talent that seeks purpose, not just a paycheck. For most Certified B Corps, the most valuable asset of certification is the B Corp community itself.

Certification grants access to a community of practice among like-minded, high-performing leaders. This community shares best practices in culture building, employee engagement, marketing and communications, raising purpose-aligned capital, creating values-driven supply chains, waste and carbon reduction, workforce development, and many more ways to create value for all stakeholders. Certified B Corps share knowledge via an online community called the B Hive, and in-person gatherings like B Local chapters, regional B Corp Leadership Development days, and annual Champions Retreats that foster collaboration and collective action to help B Corps achieve their business goals and create the change they want to see in the world.

A Few of the 2,200 Certified B Corps

SOLBERG MANUFACTURING—family-owned Midwestern manufacturer working to reduce carbon footprint and increase equity for workers

REDWOODS GROUP—faith-driven North Carolina commercial property casualty insurer working with YMCAs to save lives and money through data analysis

NEW BELGIUM BREWING—employee-owned wind-powered craft-beer company

ELLEVATE NETWORK—global women's network dedicated to closing the gender achievement gap in business

ALTSCHOOL—venture-funded blended learning K–8 schools in Bay Area

GREYSTON BAKERY—making brownies for your favorite Ben & Jerry's flavors to create economic opportunity for returning citizens through open hiring

PLUM ORGANICS—subsidiary of Campbell Soup and one of the largest and fastest-growing organic baby food companies in the United States

TRIODOS BANK—nearly forty-year-old, triple-bottom-line bank in Europe and founding member of the Global Alliance for Banking on Values

SILVER CHEF—publicly traded Australian financier of equipment for hospitality and commercial equipment markets

NATURA—publicly traded Brazilian company that creates economic opportunity for 1.3 million *consultadoras* through direct selling of sustainably produced cosmetics and personal care products

This last point highlights perhaps the most valuable asset of the certification. Beyond a robust community of practice, Certified B Corps have created a powerful community of purpose. Certified B Corps recognize that the change they seek begins with but is greater than the improved performance of individual companies. Certified B Corps recognize that it will take more than heroic individual leadership to fulfill the promise of capitalism to create a shared and durable prosperity. Not even the most enlightened leadership of the largest *Fortune* 500 company can move the needle alone. Each of us is an important but small part of a much larger social and economic system. The culture shift from an era of shareholder primacy to an era of stakeholder capitalism requires the power of collective action from a community of credible leaders.

The first act of B Corp collective leadership is to subject themselves—even, perhaps especially, if they are already perceived to be leaders by their peers and the public—to a credible third-party standard of performance, transparency, and accountability. This rebuilds trust in an economic system that many feel does not care about them and has left them behind. Healthy businesses cannot exist over the long term in an unhealthy society. Capitalism is one of the most powerful systems devised by humans to improve our quality of life; that system is built on trust. Radical transparency of verified high performance within a legal structure that aligns the interests of business with those of society is an important first step in rebuilding trust and thus strengthening the economic system that has delivered so much and yet has so much further to go to fulfill its promise.

> Nine out of ten interviewees listed Azavea's B Corp status as why they were interested in the job.
>
> **—Rob Cheetham, Azavea**

> The B Corp movement is one of the most important of our lifetime, built on the simple fact that business impacts and serves more than shareholders—it has an equal responsibility to the community and the planet.
>
> **—Rose Marcario, Patagonia**

We know the leadership of this community of purpose is already moving the needle beyond their own improved performance as individual companies.

As a result of the collective action of the community of Certified B Corporations, their stakeholder governance and stakeholder management practices are being adopted by tens of thousands of companies around the world. The stakeholder governance requirement for certification has become law in thirty-three US states and has already been adopted by more than 5,000 companies. And this stakeholder governance model is going global. After its adoption in the purpose-aligned governance recommendations of the G8 Social Impact Investment Taskforce, Italy recently passed a benefit corporation law, and similar legislation is in process in more than a half dozen other countries. This stakeholder management system is not only being used by individual companies but also by corporate supply chain managers, impact investors, fund managers, credit providers, business associations, and government entities who want to know more about—and increase the positive impact of—the businesses with which they work and in which they invest.

Unleashing the heroic spirit of business is a team sport. The community of Certified B Corps is proud to be a part of the Conscious Capitalism team and hopes that more conscious companies will become part of the community of Certified B Corporations.

You can learn more about B Corp certification and hear from B Corp leaders as they describe the value they receive from the certification process and the B Corp community of practice at www.bcorporation.net.

Ugli Oranges Exercise

Objective: to illustrate what it takes to make a situation a win-win situation (although we won't call it a win-win just yet)

The following pages are each to be printed and given to two halves of a group confidentially. This is a really fun exercise for an executive team but works at any level in an organization, including the entry level.[1]

The groups should be separated and given about ten minutes to discuss the questions they hope to have answered by the other team.

As the facilitator, you will observe a meeting between delegates (one person from each of the two groups). The rest of each group should attend, listen to, and help their delegate. The meeting between the two delegates should only take five minutes.

In the end, the groups will hopefully have come up with questions that are respectful of the other team's objectives without asking the team members to give up all their information.

What frequently happens is that team members are so focused on getting all the Ugli oranges that they fail to see that they're each after different parts of the fruit.

If the right questions are asked, they are headed for a win-win situation, which is at the heart of the stakeholder interdependence and orientation model.

Confidential Instructions for Dr. Jones

You are Dr. Jones, a biological research scientist employed by a pharmaceutical company. You have recently developed a synthetic chemical useful for curing and preventing Rudosen, a disease contracted by pregnant women. If not caught in the first four weeks of pregnancy, the disease causes serious brain, eye, and ear damage to the unborn child. Recently, there has been an outbreak of Rudosen in your country, and several thousand women have contracted the disease. You have found that your recently developed synthetic serum cures Rudosen in its early stages. Unfortunately, the serum is made from the Ugli orange, which is a very rare fruit. Only about four thousand of these oranges were grown in the whole world this season. No additional Ugli oranges will be available until next season, which will be too late to cure the present Rudosen victims. You have demonstrated that your synthetic serum does no harm to the pregnant women. There are no side effects. Unfortunately, the present outbreak of Rudosen was unexpected, and your company had not planned on having the serum available for six months. Your company holds the patent on the synthetic serum, which is expected to be a highly profitable product when it is made available to the public. You have recently been told that a Ms. Cardoza, a South American fruit exporter, has three thousand Ugli oranges. If you could obtain all three thousand of these Ugli oranges, you could make enough serum from their juice to both cure all the present victims and provide sufficient inoculation for the remaining pregnant women in your country. No other country currently has a Rudosen threat. You have been told that Dr. Roland is also urgently seeking Ugli oranges and is also aware that Ms. Cardoza has some of these special oranges. Dr. Roland is employed by a competitor pharmaceutical company. He has been working on biological warfare research for the past several years. There is a great deal of industrial espionage in the pharmaceutical industry. Over the past several years, Dr. Roland's company and your company have sued each other for infringement of patent rights and espionage law violations several times. You've been authorized by your company to approach Ms. Cardoza to purchase the three thousand Ugli oranges. You have been told that

Ms. Cardoza will sell them to the highest bidder. Your company has authorized you to bid as high as $250,000 (USD) to obtain the juice of the three thousand available oranges. Before approaching Ms. Cardoza, you have decided to talk with Dr. Roland. Think carefully about what information you are willing to tell the other side, and what information you will not disclose.

Confidential Instructions for Dr. Roland

You are Dr. Roland, a research biologist for a pharmaceutical company. Your company has a government contract to do research on methods to combat enemy uses of biological warfare, but the government has asked your company for assistance with an immediate problem. Recently, several old experimental nerve gas bombs were moved to a small Pacific island. While they were being moved, two of the bombs developed leaks. The leaks are presently controlled, but government scientists believe that within two weeks, the gas will leak out of bomb chambers and escape. There is no known method of preventing the gas from getting into the atmosphere and spreading to the coast. If the leak occurs, several thousand people will die or incur serious brain damage. You have developed a synthetic vapor that will neutralize the nerve gas if it is injected into the bomb chamber before the gas leaks out. The vapor is made with a chemical taken from the Ugli orange, a very rare fruit. You've heard that a Ms. Cardoza, a fruit exporter in South America, has three thousand Ugli oranges. If you get all three thousand Ugli oranges, you could make enough of the chemical from the rind of these oranges to neutralize all the gas if the serum is developed and injected efficiently. Your company has not been able to locate any more of these Ugli oranges. As far as you know, there are only three thousand such oranges in the world crop this year. You have learned that Dr. Jones is also urgently seeking to purchase Ugli oranges and that Dr. Jones is aware that Ms. Cardoza has oranges available. Dr. Jones's company and your company are highly competitive, and there is a great deal of industrial espionage in the pharmaceutical industry. Your company and Dr. Jones's company have sued each other twice for infringement of patent rights. One lawsuit is still going on. You've been authorized by your company to approach Ms. Cardoza to purchase the three thousand Ugli oranges. You have been told that Ms. Cardoza will sell them to the highest bidder. Your company has authorized you to bid as high as $250,000 (USD) to obtain the oranges. Before approaching Ms. Cardoza, you have decided to talk to Dr. Jones. Think carefully about what information you are willing to tell the other doctor.

Appendix C

The Barrett Approach to Measuring and Building a Conscious Culture

By Richard Barrett, chairman and founder, Barrett Values Centre

Cultural capital is the new frontier of competitive advantage. Who you are and what you stand for has become just as important as the quality of the products or services you sell.

The increased recognition of the importance of corporate culture raises an important question: How can you make your culture conscious?

How Can You Make Your Culture Conscious?

You make your culture conscious by measuring it. This involves carrying out a baseline cultural diagnostic (a cultural values assessment), including data cuts for each business unit, department, and team, as well as data cuts for demographic categories such as gender and age. The results of the values assessment will allow you to identify the cultural health of the organization and the cultural health of the subcultures that exist in different business units, locations, departments, and

373

teams. It will also tell you precisely what you need to change to create a high-performance organization.

One of the best ways to assess cultural values is to use the Barrett Values Centre's Cultural Transformation Tools.[1] These tools are based on the seven levels of consciousness model (figure AC-1), which in turn builds on Abraham Maslow's hierarchy of needs. The seven levels model shifts the focus of Maslow's hierarchy from needs to consciousness and gives greater definition to the concept of self-actualization. The model can map the values of individuals, leaders, organizations, communities, and nations (figure AC-1).

Figure AC-1: The seven levels of consciousness model

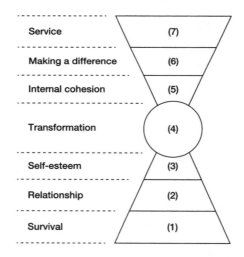

Source: Richard Barrett, "Building a High-Performance Culture," Barrett Values Centre, Manchester, UK, April 2017, www.valuescentre.com/sites/default/files/uploads/article_building_a_highperformance_culture.pdf.

The Seven Levels of Organizational Consciousness

The focus of the first three levels of organizational consciousness is on the basic needs of business—financial stability and profitability, employee and customer satisfaction, and high-performance systems and processes.[2]

The focus of the fourth level of consciousness is on adaptability—continuous renewal and transformation—a shift from fear-based, rigid, authoritarian hierarchies or silos, to more open, inclusive, adaptive, and democratic systems of governance that empower employees to operate with responsible freedom (accountability).

The focus of the upper three levels of consciousness is on organizational cohesion, building mutually beneficial alliances and partnerships, and safeguarding the well-being of human society.

Organizations that focus *exclusively* on the satisfaction of their basic needs are not usually market leaders. They can be successful in their specific niche, but in general, they are too internally focused and self-absorbed, or too rigid and bureaucratic to become innovators in their fields. They are slow to adapt to changes in market conditions and do not empower their employees. There is little enthusiasm among the workforce and innovation and creativity get suppressed. Levels of staff engagement are relatively low. Such organizations are run by authoritarian leaders who operate by creating a culture of fear. They are not emotionally healthy places to work. Employees feel frustrated or disempowered and may complain about stress.

Organizations that focus *exclusively* on the satisfaction of the higher needs lack the basic business skills necessary to operate effectively and profitably. They are ineffectual and impractical when it comes to financial matters, they are not customer oriented, and they lack the systems and processes necessary for high performance. They are simply not grounded in the reality of business. We often find such organizations in the not-for-profit sector.

The most successful organizations are those that develop Full Spectrum Consciousness—the ability to master the needs associated with every level of organizational consciousness: they are able to respond and adapt appropriately to all the challenges that the marketplace throws at them or, in the case of a public

TABLE AC-1

The seven levels of consciousness model

Levels of consciousness	Actions and needs	Developmental tasks
7. Service	Creating a long-term, sustainable future for the organization by aligning with a higher purpose.	*Serving*: Safeguarding the well-being of the planet and society for future generations.
6. Making a difference	Mentoring and coaching staff and aligning with like-minded organizations for mutual benefit as well as supporting local communities in which the organization operates.	*Collaborating*: Building internal cooperation and external partnerships to enhance the long-term resilience of the organization and its partners.
5. Internal cohesion	Enhancing the capacity of the organization for collective action by aligning employee motivations around a shared set of values and an inspiring vision.	*Bonding*: Creating an internally cohesive, high-trust culture that enables the organization to fulfill its purpose and inspires the creativity of employees.
4. Transformation	Increasing innovation by giving employees a voice and making them accountable for the success of the organization and their personal futures.	*Empowering*: Empowering employees to participate in decision making and giving them the freedom to make decisions.
3. Self-esteem	Establishing structures, policies, procedures, and processes that create order, support the performance of the organization, and recognize employees' contributions.	*Performing*: Building high-performance systems and processes that focus on the efficiency, productivity, and agility of the organization.
2. Relationship	Resolving conflicts and building harmonious relationships that create a sense of loyalty among employees and strong connection with customers.	*Harmonizing*: Creating a sense of belonging and mutual respect among employees and caring for customers.
1. Survival	Creating financial stability and profitability, and caring for the health and safety of all employees.	*Surviving*: Becoming financially viable and taking care of employees' survival needs.

sector organization, all the challenges the institutional and political environment throws at them. The actions and developmental tasks associated with each level of consciousness are shown in table AC-1.

Mapping Values

At the core of the Cultural Transformation Tools is the concept that all values and behaviors are motivated by specific needs, and every need is aligned with one of the seven levels of consciousness. Thus by asking employees what their values are, you can find out what levels of consciousness they are operating from. By asking what values employees see in the organization, you can identify what levels of consciousness the organization is operating from (current culture), and by asking employees what values they would like to see in the organization, you can measure the desired culture. Here are some examples of how a cultural values assessment can help us:

- The number of matching personal and current culture values tells the leadership team the extent to which employees can bring their full selves to work—the level of employee commitment and engagement.

- The number of matching current and desired culture values tells the leadership team the extent to which employees think the organization is on the right track—to what extent the organization is meeting its full potential.

- The matching personal and desired culture values that are not part of the current culture tell the leadership team which of the most immediate values it needs to work on. Table AC-2 (in a later section), which shows the gap between what an organization values in its present culture and what it values in the desired culture, also suggests which values should be given a higher priority.

- The level of cultural disharmony, or cultural entropy, in the organization tells the leadership team the extent to which the culture is driven by the fears of the managers, supervisors, and other leaders. Cultural entropy measures the degree of dysfunction in an organization that is generated by the self-serving, fear-based actions of the leaders, managers, and supervisors. As cultural entropy increases, the level of trust, internal cohesion, and well-being decreases. Cultural entropy is inversely correlated with employee engagement. Low entropy leads to high engagement. High entropy leads to low engagement.

- The assessment can also measure the extent to which the espoused values are lived and desired.

Cultural values assessments make intangibles tangible. They enable the leadership team and the rest of the organization to have brand-new conversations on what is important for the growth and development of the organization.

The following provides an example of some of the more important outputs of a cultural values assessment. The values that employees are asked to pick from include positive values and potentially limiting values (values that lead to fear-driven outcomes). For example, commitment is a positive value and blame is a potentially limiting one.

A Typical Organization with Low Cultural Health and High Cultural Entropy

Figure AC-2 plots the values of an eighty-person organization. Each dot on the diagram represents one of the top ten values. An (L) after a value indicates a potentially limiting value. Positive values are shown as shaded dots, and potentially limiting values are shown as white dots. Notice the significant misalignment in consciousness between the personal values (a focus at level 5), the current culture (a focus at levels 1 and 2), and the desired culture (a focus at levels 4 and 2). There are no matching personal and current culture values, and there is only one matching current and desired culture value: accountability. In a culturally healthy organization, we would expect to see two or three matching personal and current culture values, and five or six matching current and desired culture values.

In data plots like these, which we frequently find in low-cultural-health or high-cultural-entropy organizations, the desired culture values are typically

Figure AC-2: Values plot of an organization with low cultural health and high cultural entropy

Personal values

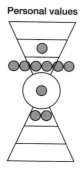

Current culture

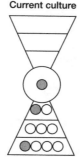

Desired culture

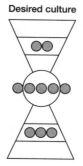

Personal values		Current culture		Desired culture	
1. Commitment	39	1. Cost reduction (L)	64	1. Continuous improvement	40
2. Honesty	33	2. Profit	40	2. Customer satisfaction	36
3. Making a difference	31	3. Results orientation	36	3. Accountability	29
4. Positive attitude	29	4. Blame (L)	34	4. Coaching/mentoring	28
5. Achievement	27	5. Demanding (L)	32	5. Leadership development	26
6. Humor/fun	27	6. Long hours (L)	29	6. Teamwork	23
7. Integrity	27	7. Accountability	27	7. Open communication	22
8. Fairness	26	8. Job insecurity (L)	26	8. Adaptability	21
9. Performance	26	9. Lack of appreciation (L)	25	9. Employee recognition	21
10. Initiative	23	10. Control (L)	25	10. Information sharing	21

concentrated at the transformation level. The values expressed at this level are the remedies to many of the issues (potentially limiting values) at levels 1, 2, and 3 in the current culture. Because of the difficulties the company portrayed in figure AC-2 is having, it has become internally focused—customer satisfaction is absent from the top ten values of the current culture but is the number two value in the desired culture.

Additionally, there are five positive relationship values in the desired culture (accountability, open communication, coaching/mentoring, teamwork, and employee recognition). These values act as a counterbalance to the four potentially limiting relationship values in the current culture (blame, demanding, lack of appreciation, and control).

Figure AC-3 shows the values distribution for the personal, current, and desired culture of this organization. This is the distribution of all the votes for all values. The level of cultural entropy is calculated by adding up the proportion of votes for potentially limiting values (the cultural health score is the inverse

Figure AC-3: Values distribution diagram of an organization with low cultural health and high cultural energy

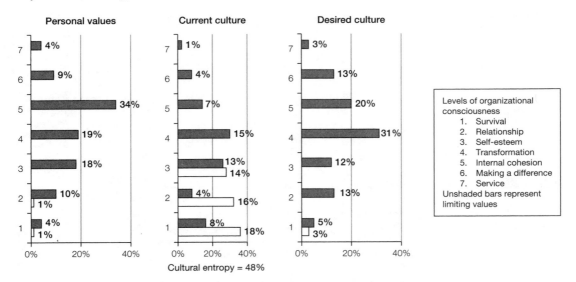

Personal values | Current culture | Desired culture

Levels of organizational consciousness
1. Survival
2. Relationship
3. Self-esteem
4. Transformation
5. Internal cohesion
6. Making a difference
7. Service
Unshaded bars represent limiting values

Cultural entropy = 48%

Source: Modified from Richard Barrett, "Building a High-Performance Culture," Barrett Values Centre, Manchester, UK, April 2017, www.valuescentre.com/sites/default/files/uploads/article_building_a_high-performance_culture.pdf, figure 1.

of the cultural entropy score). The level of cultural health is 52 percent, and the level of cultural entropy 48 percent (in the critical range). The cultural entropy, shown in the middle column by unshaded bars that represent limiting values, is relatively evenly spread across level 1 (18 percent), level 2 (16 percent), and level 3 (14 percent). What is disturbing about this result is the significant cultural entropy at levels 1 and 2 (it is more difficult to reduce entropy at levels 1 and 2 than at level 3).

Table AC-2 shows the top value jumps. A value jump is necessary if an organization needs to value an element much more than the element is currently valued, that is, when the number of votes for a value in the current culture is less than those for the value in the desired culture. You can see from this table that the key issue for this company is the quality of leadership. The greatest differences between what an organization presently values and what its people want the organization to value include the areas of coaching and mentoring, employee recognition, open communication, information sharing, leadership development, and empowerment.

Value "jumps": the differences between where an organization is and where it wants to be

Value	Current-culture votes*	Desired-culture votes*	Value jump
Coaching/mentoring	1	28	27
Customer satisfaction	15	36	21
Employee recognition	0	21	21
Continuous improvement	21	40	19
Open communication	21	40	19
Information sharing	4	22	17
Leadership development	10	21	16
Empowerment	3	26	16

*Columns refer to the number of people in an eighty-person company who voted the value as one of the ten most important values currently practiced in the company or one of the ten most desired for the company's future.

The Way Forward

The high level of cultural entropy in our example company and the seven potentially limiting values that show up in its top ten current culture values are a clear sign of poor performance: the leaders are letting their fears dictate their behaviors. Blame, demands, long hours, cost reduction, and control are all signs that the leadership group has lost its way. The organization is focused on profit, but not on customers. Nor is the company taking care of its people—lack of appreciation and job insecurity are potentially limiting values showing up in the current culture.

The desired culture values point the way to improving the quality of leadership: coaching and mentoring, leadership development, open communication, employee recognition, and information sharing are all desired culture values that do not appear in the top ten current culture values and would require great changes in values for the company. These are the values that the leadership team needs to focus on if it wants to turn this company around. The desired culture focuses strongly on the transformation level of consciousness—empowering employees to participate in decision making and giving them the autonomy to make decisions.

Managing the Organization's Values

If leadership is to improve the culture, the key findings of the cultural values assessment must be shared with employees and acted on. Usually, it is best to focus on two or three important themes. For this organization, the results suggest the need to (a) focus on leadership development, (b) build trust in the leadership team, and (c) empower and appreciate employees. Accountability for progress lies with the leadership team. Twelve months on, the organization should reassess its cultural values to see how successful it has been in shifting the desired values into the current culture. Success will show up as reduced cultural entropy.

Notes

Chapter 1: Why Conscious Capitalism?

1. Decline in poverty: https://openknowledge.worldbank.org/bitstream/handle/10986/25078/9781464809583.pdf; Rise in literacy: https://en.wikipedia.org/wiki/List_of_countries_by_literacy_rate.

2. Raj Sisodia, David B. Wolfe, and Jag Sheth, *Firms of Endearment: How World-Class Companies Profit from Passion and Purpose* (Upper Saddle River, NJ: Wharton School Publishing, 2007; 2nd ed. Upper Saddle River, NJ: Pearson, 2014).

3. These studies are cited in Big Innovation Centre, *The Purposeful Company: Policy Report* (London: Big Innovation Centre, February 2017), www.biginnovationcentre.com/media/uploads/pdf/TPC_Policy%20Report.pdf; and Big Innovation Centre, *The Purposeful Company: Interim Report* (London: Big Innovation Centre, May 2016), www.biginnovationcentre.com/media/uploads/pdf/TPC_Interim%20Report.pdf.

4. J. Derwall, N. Guenster, R. Bauer, and K. Koedijk, "The Eco-Efficiency Premium Puzzle," *Financial Analysts Journal* 61 (2005): 51–63.

5. C. Fornell, S. Mithas, F. Morgeson III, and M. Krishnan, "Customer Satisfaction and Stock Prices: High Returns, Low Risk," *Journal of Marketing* 70 (2006): 3–14.

6. S. El Ghoul, O. Guedhami, C. Kwok, and D. Mishra, "Does Corporate Social Responsibility Affect the Cost of Capital?," *Journal of Banking & Finance* 35 (2011): 2388–2406.

7. A. Edmans, "Does the Stock Market Fully Value Intangibles? Employee Satisfaction and Equity Prices," *Journal of Financial Economics* 101 (2011): 621–640; and A. Edmans, "The Link Between Job Satisfaction and Firm Value, with Implications for Corporate Social Responsibility," *Academy of Management Perspectives* 26 (2012): 1–19.

8. A. Edmans, L. Li, and C. Zhang, "Employee Satisfaction, Labor Market Flexibility, and Stock Returns Around the World," Working Paper 20300, National Bureau of Economic Research, Cambridge, MA, July 2014.

9. N. Bloom, R. Sadun, and J. Van Reenen, "The Organization of Firms Across Countries," *Quarterly Journal of Economics* 127 (2012): 1,663–1,705.

10. G. Serafeim, R. Eccles, and G. Ioannou, "The Impact of a Corporate Sustainability on Organizational Processes and Performance," *Management Science* 60 (2014): 2,835–2,857.

11. L. Guiso, P. Sapienza, and L. Zingales, "The Value of Corporate Culture," *Journal of Financial Economics* 117 (2015): 60–76.

12. G. Friede, T. Busch, and A. Bassen, "ESG and Financial Performance: Aggregated Evidence from More than 2000 Empirical Studies," *Journal of Sustainable Finance & Investment* 5 (2015): 210–233.

13. C. Flammer and A. Kacperczyk, "The Impact of Stakeholder Orientation on Innovation: Evidence from a Natural Experiment," *Management Science* 62, no. 7 (2015): 1982–2001.

14. R. Albuquerque, A. Durnev, and Y. Koskinen, "Corporate Social Responsibility and Firm Risk: Theory and Empirical Evidence," European Corporate Governance Institute, Working Paper no. 359/2013, revised June 1, 2017.

Chapter 3: Introduction to Organizational Purpose

1. Big Innovation Centre, *The Purposeful Company: Policy Report* (London: Big Innovation Centre, February 2017), www.biginnovationcentre.com/media/uploads/pdf/TPC_Policy%20Report.pdf; and Big Innovation Centre, *The Purposeful Company: Interim Report* (London: Big Innovation Centre, May 2016), www.biginnovationcentre.com/media/uploads/pdf/TPC_Interim%20Report.pdf.

Part Two: Stakeholder Orientation

1. Edward Freeman, "What Is Stakeholder Theory?," video presented by Business Roundtable Institute for Corporate Ethics, October 1, 2009, www.youtube.com/watch?v=bIRUaLcvPe8.

2. We are grateful to Conscious Capitalism, Inc. CEO, Alexander McCobin, for his insights on this issue.

Chapter 7: The Stakeholder Model

1. We are grateful to Babson College student Chirag Shah for suggesting this phrase.

2. Whole Foods Market, "Declaration of Interdependence," www.wholefoodsmarket.com/mission-values/core-values/declaration-interdependence.

Chapter 8: Becoming Stakeholder Oriented

1. Raj Sisodia, David B. Wolfe, and Jag Sheth, *Firms of Endearment: How World-Class Companies Profit from Passion and Purpose* (Upper Saddle River, NJ: Wharton School Publishing, 2007; 2nd ed. Upper Saddle River, NJ: Pearson, 2014).

2. Interview with Timothy Henry, December 2016.

Chapter 11: Introduction to Conscious Culture

1. Daniel H. Pink, *Drive: The Surprising Truth About What Motivates Us* (New York: Riverhead Books, 2009).

2. PwC, "Workforce of the Future: The Competing Forces Shaping 2030," www.pwc.com/gx/en/managing-tomorrows-people/future-of-work/assets/reshaping-the-workplace.pdf.

3. Sarah Greesonbach, "Culture Crash Course Lesson 2: The Importance of Corporate Culture," *Culture IQ*, https://cultureiq.com/culture-crash-course-lesson-2-the-importance-of-corporate-culture.

4. David McCann, "Treat Employees Well, See Stock Price Soar," CFO.com, April 21, 2014, ww2.cfo.com/people/2014/04/treat-employees-well-see-stock-price-soar.

Chapter 13: Evolving and Deepening Your Culture

1. Lars Björk, quoted in Raymond V. Gilmartin and Steven E. Prokesch, eds., *How CEOs Can Fix Capitalism* (Boston: Harvard Business Review Press, 2013).

Part Four: Conscious Leadership

1. Fred Kofman, *Conscious Business: How to Build Value Through Values* (Boulder, CO: Sounds True, 2006).

Chapter 14: Introduction to Conscious Leadership

1. Dee Hock, "The Art of Chaordic Leadership," *Leader to Leader* 15 (Winter 2000): 20–26.
2. This quote is cited in numerous locations on the web, including https://journal.accj.or .jp/peter-drucker-on-leadership/.
3. John Gerzema and Michael D'Antonio, *The Athena Doctrine: How Women (and the Men Who Think Like Them) Will Rule the Future* (San Francisco: Jossey-Bass, 2013). The title of the book came from the warrior goddess whose wisdom and civility are celebrated in Greek mythology.

Chapter 15: Becoming a SELFLESS Leader

1. Danah Zohar and Ian Marshall, *Spiritual Capital: Wealth We Can Live By* (San Francisco: Berrett-Koehler, 2004), 55.
2. Excerpted from http://socialbusinesspedia.com/wiki/details/145.
3. Martin Luther King Jr., "Where Do We Go from Here?," speech delivered at the 11th Annual Southern Christian Leadership Convention, Atlanta, August 16, 1967, available at http://mlk-kpp01.stanford.edu/index.php/encyclopedia/documentsentry/where_do_we_go _from_here_delivered_at_the_11th_annual_sclc_convention.
4. Daniel Goleman, *Emotional Intelligence: Why It Can Matter More Than IQ* (New York: Bantam, 1995). Goleman also wrote another excellent book, *Social Intelligence: The New Science of Human Relationships* (New York: Bantam, 2006). We have not separated social intelligence from emotional, spiritual, and systems intelligence into its own category, because we believe it is better seen as a characteristic of the other three categories.
5. Goleman, *Emotional Intelligence*.
6. In addition to ibid., we recommend Robert C. Solomon's numerous books on emotions, particularly *Passions: Emotions and the Meaning of Life* (Indianapolis, IN: Hackett, 1993) and *True to Our Feelings* (New York: Oxford University Press, 2001).
7. Some recommended books on love include Gerald Jampolsky, *Love Is Letting Go of Fear* (Berkeley, CA: Celestial Arts, 2010); Stephen G. Post, *Unlimited Love: Altruism, Compassion, and*

Service (Philadelphia: Templeton Foundation Press, 2003); and Pitirim Sorokin, *The Ways and Power of Love: Types, Factors, and Techniques of Moral Transformation* (Philadelphia: Templeton Foundation Press, 2002).

8. Margaret Rouse, "Definition: Systems Thinking," *TechTarget*, October 2005, http://searchcio.techtarget.com/definition/systems-thinking.

9. Zohar and Marshall, *Spiritual Capital*, 3.

10. Adapted from Cindy Wigglesworth, *SQ21: The Twenty-One Skills of Spiritual Intelligence* (New York: SelectBooks, 2012), page 46.

11. Gay Hendricks, *The Big Leap: Conquer Your Hidden Fear and Take Life to the Next Level* (New York: HarperOne, 2010).

Chapter 16: Becoming More Conscious

1. Nilima Bhat and Raj Sisodia, *Shakti Leadership: Embracing Feminine and Masculine Power in Business* (Oakland, CA: Berrett-Koehler Publishers, 2016).

2. Martin E. P. Seligman, *Learned Optimism: How to Change Your Mind and Your Life* (New York: Vintage, 2006).

3. Adam Grant, *Give and Take: Why Helping Others Drives Our Success* (New York: Penguin Books, 2014).

4. Srikumar S. Rao, *Are You Ready to Succeed? Unconventional Strategies to Achieving Personal Mastery in Business and Life* (New York: Hachette, 2005).

5. There are many books on insight meditation. A good introduction is Joseph Goldstein and Jack Kornfield, *Seeking the Heart of Wisdom: The Path of Insight Meditation* (Boston: Shambhala, 2001).

Chapter 17: Organizational Approach to Conscious Leadership

1. Australian Psychological Society, "Corporate Psychopaths Common and Can Wreak Havoc in Business, Researchers Say," press release, September 13, 2016, www.psychology.org.au/news/media_releases/13September2016/Brooks.

2. This section was reproduced, with permission, from Bob Chapman and Raj Sisodia, *Everybody Matters: The Extraordinary Power of Caring for Your People as Family* (New York: Portfolio/Penguin, 2015).

Chapter 18: Setting Organizational Priorities

1. David Maister, "Strategy and the Fat Smoker," *ChangeThis*, July 4, 2006.

Epilogue

1. David Cooperrider, http://www.davidcooperrider.com/2014/02/12/dean-rob-widing-business-as-an-agent-of-world-benefit-is-an-idea-whose-time-has-come/#more-1328.

2. Big Innovation Centre, *The Purposeful Company: Policy Report* (London: Big Innovation Centre, February 2017), www.biginnovationcentre.com/media/uploads/pdf/TPC_Policy%20Report.pdf.

Appendix B: Ugli Oranges Exercise

1. This Ugli Orange exercise is a role play that simulates a conflict situation. Adapted from George Mason University, Institute for Conflict Analysis and Resolution, Fairfax, Virginia.

Appendix C: The Barrett Approach to Measuring and Building a Conscious Culture

1. For more information on the Cultural Transformation tools, see the Barrett Values Centre home page, www.valuescentre.com.

2. This section, "The Seven Levels of Organizational Consciousness," is reprinted with permission from Richard Barrett, *The Values-Driven Organization*, 2nd ed. (London: Routledge, 2017). The remaining parts of this appendix are adapted from Richard Barrett, "Building a High-Performance Culture," Barrett Values Centre, Manchester, UK, April 2017, www.values centre.com/sites/default/files/uploads/article_building_a_high-performance_culture.pdf.

Index

brands, purpose-driven, 50
Branson, Richard, x
Brighter Strategy, 209
Brooks, Nathan, 288
B Team, x, 120
Built to Last (Porras & Collins), 251
business entrepreneurs, ix
business models, 12

campaigns of influence and engagement,
   343–346
capitalism
   benefits of, 2
   failures of traditional, 3–4
   free-market, history of, 1–2
   investors in, 116–118
   profit maximization as sole purpose
      of, 3–4
   self-interest in, 2–3
   See also Conscious Capitalism
career tracking, 299–300
caring, 181, 188–191
   at Barry-Wehmiller, 206–208
   leadership and, 248, 253–257
car insurance, Brazil, 142–143
Carnegie, Andrew, 124
Case Western Reserve University,
   134, 138
Certified B Corporations, 362–366
champions of change, 340–342
change champions, 340–342
change stories, 337, 343
Chapman, Bob, 113, 190, 206–208
Cheetham, Rob, 367
cohesion, 375, 378
collaboration, 177
Collins, Jim, 251
commitment
   to communities, 130
   employee, 8
   at FIFCO, 25
   to implementation, 318–321
   to learning, 197–199
   stages of organizational, 324–325

to suppliers, 125
to transformation, 353–354
communication
   about win-win thinking, 171
   in campaigns of influence and
      engagement, 343–346
   with investors, 117
   mindfulness in, 277–278
   of purpose, 73–74
   transparency and, 192–193
   of values, 222
communities
   in eco-centric approach, 103–105
   interdependence of stakeholders and,
      101–102
   of practice, 356, 362–366
   as stakeholders, 128–132
compensation systems
   conscious culture and, 229–230
   at FIFCO, 23–25
competence, zone of, 265
Conscious Capitalism
   assessing current state of, 29–32
   barriers to, 332–334
   beginning with, 15–32
   caveats with, 12
   context behind, 1–4
   credo of, 6–7
   definition of, xv
   explanation of, 4–7
   at FIFCO, 18–26
   how to implement, 11–14
   imperatives for, 349–351
   implementation of, 301–347
   introducing to the top team, 326
   performance results from, 7–11
   pillars of, 5–6, 306
   shareholder activism and, xiii–xiv
   support for, xix
   values in, 6
   the "why" of your business and, 15–18
Conscious Capitalism Inc., 120
*Conscious Capitalism: Liberating the Heroic
   Spirit of Business* (Mackey & Sisodia),
   ix, xv–xvi, 326

Acknowledgments

From Raj

I would like to thank my coauthors, Timothy Henry and Thomas Eckschmidt, for a delightful experience working together. I would also like to thank our editor, Melinda Merino, and the wonderful staff at Harvard Business Review Press for helping bring this book to life. I would also like to acknowledge all of our Conscious Capitalism chapter leaders around the world for their tireless volunteer work in advancing the movement; the trustees of Conscious Capitalism, Inc. for the same reason; and all of our friends who have contributed directly to this book: Haley Rushing, Jessica Agneessens, Richard Barrett, Ramon Mandiola, Steve Hall, Joseph Jaworski, and Jay Coen Gilbert. Finally, I would like to acknowledge the immense impact John Mackey and Kip Tindell have had on me personally and on the Conscious Capitalism movement globally.

From Timothy

There are many sources of inspiration and experience from which this book was formed. Many thanks to my fellow members of the board of trustees for Conscious Capitalism, Inc. We have been on quite a journey to help birth this movement. Through our work together over the last ten years, you have inspired and helped shape my fundamental understanding of what is possible on the journey to Conscious Capitalism. Thanks also to my clients and the leaders I have coached and consulted for over the years. Without you none of this practice would have emerged, and with your feedback and guidance we have refined what works—and sometimes discovered what does not. Thank you for the opportunity to be of service and to learn. Thanks to my fellow authors, Thomas and Raj, for their work on crafting and refining this book. Raj, thank you for your friendship and inspiration over the years—it all began with our first meeting and your invitation to come on the journey. To my children, Kaylee and Michael, and my stepchildren, Eliora, Ilan, and Yoran, you are the inspiration for much of my work in trying to make this world a better place for you to live and flourish in. Finally, to Fabienne, for her love, patience, and support throughout this process—thanks!

From Thomas

This has been an amazing journey of writing and living more consciously. I would like to acknowledge my coauthors and the Conscious Capitalism community (chapters, board members, enthusiasts, followers, supporters, and all others) who have asked for this content as a means to help them in their journeys to a more conscious capitalism around the world.

About the Authors

Raj Sisodia is the F. W. Olin Distinguished Professor of Global Business and the Whole Foods Market Research Scholar in Conscious Capitalism at Babson College. He is also cofounder and Chairman emeritus of Conscious Capitalism, Inc. He holds a PhD in marketing from Columbia University. Raj is coauthor of the *New York Times* and *Wall Street Journal* bestseller *Conscious Capitalism: Liberating the Heroic Spirit of Business* (2013) and the *Wall Street Journal* bestseller *Everybody Matters* (2015). He was named one of the Ten Outstanding Trailblazers of 2010 by Good Business International and one of the Top 100 Thought Leaders in Trustworthy Business Behavior by Trust Across America in 2010 and 2011. Raj received an honorary doctorate from Johnson & Wales University in 2016.

Raj has published ten books and over 100 academic articles. His book *Firms of Endearment: How World-Class Companies Profit from Passion and Purpose* was named a top business book of 2007 by Amazon.com. He has consulted with numerous companies, including AT&T, Nokia, LG, DPDHL, POSCO, Kraft Foods, Whole Foods Market, Tata, Siemens, Sprint, Volvo, IBM, Walmart, Rabobank, McDonald's, and Southern California Edison. He is on the board of directors at The Container Store and a trustee of Conscious Capitalism, Inc.

Timothy Henry has more than thirty years of experience working as a trusted business adviser to senior executives and leaders, from *Fortune* 20 to entrepreneurial, owner-managed businesses across the globe. A graduate of Oxford University, he began his career at the consulting firm Booz Allen Hamilton and is currently co-CEO and Managing Partner at Bridge Partnership, a global consultancy that helps leaders and organizations evolve to become extraordinary forces for good in the world. His purpose is to catalyze and coach leaders and organizations to accelerate their journeys to becoming great organizations and conscious capitalists. He is on the board of directors of several private companies and nonprofit organizations.

Thomas Eckschmidt is an engineer who holds an Executive MBA in finance from Business School São Paulo, Brazil. His corporate journey included work in twenty different countries before he launched a successful entrepreneurial career that includes ten business awards, four patents filed, and six books published.

A strong believer that business leaders and organizations can do well by doing good, Thomas has been promoting Conscious Capitalism since 2010. He launched a Conscious Capitalism chapter in Brazil and supported the launch of chapters in other countries. Thomas teaches Conscious Capitalism classes in major business schools and in Corporate Governance programs. He also runs workshops that teach the fundamentals of Conscious Capitalism.

Thomas is a Partner at Integralis Consulting Group, working as a trusted adviser to help organizations implement conscious practices. He cofounded a few conscious businesses along the way, and he also serves on the boards of several different companies.

THE WALL STREET JOURNAL BESTSELLER THAT IGNITED A MOVEMENT

If you enjoyed reading *The Conscious Capitalism Field Guide*, turn to **Conscious Capitalism: Liberating the Heroic Spirit of Business** for provocative insights from Whole Foods Market co-CEO John Mackey and professor and Conscious Capitalism, Inc., cofounder Raj Sisodia.

Featuring some of today's best-known companies—including Southwest Airlines, Google, Patagonia, The Container Store, Whole Foods Market, and more—Mackey and Sisodia argue for the inherent good of both business and capitalism. They illustrate how these two forces can—and do—work most powerfully to create value for all stakeholders: customers, employees, suppliers, investors, society, and the environment. This book provides a new lens for leaders and companies looking to build a more cooperative, human, and positive future.

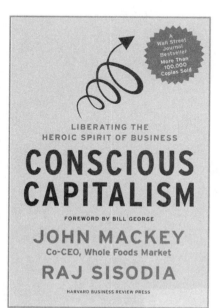

hbr.org/books

ELEVATE HUMANITY THROUGH BUSINESS.

FOUNDED BY LEADERS RANGING FROM WHOLE FOODS MARKET TO THE CONTAINER STORE, **CONSCIOUS CAPITALISM** INTERNATIONAL SUPPORTS BUSINESSES UNDERGOING THE CONSCIOUS JOURNEY IN A NUMBER OF WAYS.

JOIN A COMMUNITY OF LIKE-MINDED BUSINESS LEADERS. ACCESS RESOURCES, WORKSHOPS, AND TRAININGS TO HELP YOUR BUSINESS OPERATE ON CONSCIOUS PRINCIPLES.

SHARE THE STORY OF HOW YOUR BUSINESS IS WORKING TO MAKE THE WORLD A BETTER PLACE. AND HELP OTHERS UNLEASH THE TREMENDOUS POTENTIAL OF BUSINESS AS A FORCE FOR GOOD.

LEARN MORE AND GET INVOLVED AT
www.consciouscapitalism.org

CONSCIOUS CAPITALISM®

31901062627585